The silence of constitutions

The silence of constitutions

Gaps, 'abeyances' and political temperament in the maintenance of government

Michael Foley

Routledge
London and New York

First published 1989 by Routledge
11 New Fetter Lane, London EC4P 4EE
29 West 35th Street, New York, NY 10001

© 1989 Michael Foley

Phototypeset in 10pt Times by
Mews Photosetting, Beckenham, Kent
Printed and bound in Great Britain by
Biddles Ltd, Guildford and King's Lynn

All rights reserved. No part of this book may be reprinted or reproduced or utilized in any form or by any electronic, mechanical, or other means, now known or hereafter invented, including photocopying and recording, or in any information storage or retrieval system, without permission in writing from the publishers.

British Library Cataloguing in Publication Data
Foley, Michael, *1948–*
   The silence of constitutions: gaps, 'abeyances' and political
   temperament in the maintenance of government
   1. Constitutions
   I. Title
   342.2'2
   ISBN 0 415 03068 4

Library of Congress Cataloging-in-Publication Data
Foley, Michael, 1948–
   The silence of constitutions: gaps, 'abeyances' and political temperament
   in the maintenance of government / Michael Foley.
      p. cm.
   Includes index.
   ISBN 0 415 03068 4
      1. United States — Constitutional law — Interpretation and
   construction. 2. Great Britain — Constitutional law — Interpretation
   and construction. I. Title.
   K3165.F65 1989
   342.73'02 — dc 19
   [347.3022]
                                                              89-3458
                                                                  CIP

To Joanna, Nicholas and Louise

'. . . the manner of his prose was the manner of his thinking and that was a dazzling succession of gaps.'

Vladimir Nabokov
on the work of Sebastian Knight

Contents

Preface ix

Part I

1 **The concept and practice of constitutional abeyances** 3

Part II

2 **Constitutional abeyances and crisis conditions: the early Stuart constitution** 15

3 **Constitutional abeyances and crisis conditions: the imperial presidency** 35

4 **Constitutional gaps and the arts of prerogative** 59

Part III

5 **The theory of abeyances and modern constitutional unsettlement in Britain and the United States** 85

Notes 131
Bibliography 157
Index 170

Preface

This book acknowledges that the traditional distinction between written and unwritten constitutions is in many respects analytically redundant. Nevertheless, the customary dismissal of the old typology risks overlooking the possible presence of other dimensions of constitutional study that may be deceptively analogous to the old classification, but which retain an integrity and an interpretive value of their own. This study posits the existence of an unwritten dimension in constitutions that is separate in scale and nature to the standard notion of 'unwritten' conventions. In contrast to conventions which are determinable and amenable to description, 'constitutional abeyances' represent a form of tacit and instinctive agreement to condone, and even cultivate, constitutional ambiguity as an acceptable strategy for resolving conflict. The term 'constitutional abeyance' was chosen because it conveys both the element of dormant suspension implicit in what appear to be quite explicit constitutional arrangements, and the attitudinal habits of wilful neglect, protective obfuscation, and complicity in non-exposure, all of which are required to preserve the effectiveness of abeyances in deferring conflict and containing unresolved points of issue.

Abeyances refer to those constitutional gaps which remain vacuous for positive and constructive purposes. They are not, in any sense, truces between two or more defined positions, but rather a set of implicit agreements to collude in keeping fundamental questions of political authority in a state of irresolution. Abeyances are, in effect, compulsive hedges against the possibility of that which is unresolved being exploited and given meanings almost guaranteed to generate profound division and disillusionment. Abeyances are important, therefore, because of their capacity to deter the formation of conflicting positions in just those areas where the potential for conflict is most acute. So central are these abeyances, together with the social temperament required to sustain them, that when they become the subject of heightened interest and subsequent conflict, they are not merely accompanied by an intense constitutional crisis, they are themselves the essence of that crisis.

The silence of constitutions

In this respect, constitutional crises are of great value as they reveal in dramatic form what before had been concealed in agreeable ambiguity. It is for this reason that Part II of the study is concerned with two constitutional crises of such severity that the internal substructure of the respective constitutions were lain open to corrosive public scrutiny — thereby revealing the reality of those inner contradictions and anomalies that had hitherto been shrouded in protective obscurity. The period leading up to the English civil war in the seventeenth century and the 'imperial presidency' episode of the late 1960s and early 1970s in the United States were the two crises selected to demonstrate the inner properties of such abeyances.

By reputation the Stuart constitution was a moribund arrangement of government containing an unsustainable mixture of royal absolutism, Parliamentary power and common law rights. On closer inspection, however, it is clear that there existed a highly developed and sophisticated constitutional order much of whose extraordinary resilience depended upon its system of abeyances, by which the logically irreconcilable issue of final sovereignty was habitually and effectively evaded by an accustomed acquiescence in the needlessness of constitutional exactitude.

By contrast, the United States constitution appears to be everything the Stuart constitution was not. The latter's disjointed aggregate of apparently competing concepts of power would seem to belong to a premodern era, supplanted since by climactic constitutional settlements like that of the United States where the constitution is characterized by a thorough codification of institutional organization and a clear stipulation of the criteria of legitimate political authority. Yet, as this book shows, such a model of constitutional modernism is just as dependent upon abeyances and upon a constitutional culture to facilitate their perpetuation as the Stuart constitution. From the evidence gathered, it can be argued that the stability of the American constitution has been due not so much to its settled character or to its internal consistency, but to its anomalies and disjunctions being effectively held in abeyance by a constitutional order extraordinarily well equipped, and well disposed, to do so.

Under crisis conditions, it is possible to discern such normally suppressed contradictions rising to the surface and revealing themselves to be of an order of magnitude comparable to those of the Stuart era. In the 'imperial presidency' episode, the exposed anomalies bore a marked resemblance to the very tensions between prerogative and Parliamentary rights which had purportedly been resolved during the course of the seventeenth century. Far from being a sign of decay, therefore, the presence of abeyances can denote the existence of an advanced constitutional culture, adept at assimilating diverse and even conflicting principles of government within a political solidarity geared

Preface

to manageable constitutional ambiguity. If a constitution does not have the means to subdue conflict by these means, moreover, it will be a weaker and less adaptable constitution for that deficiency.

Part III reappraises the nature of recent constitutional development in Britain and the United States in the explanatory light of each system's separate strategies for maintaining their protective abeyances. In many respects, the methods of constitutional management in the 1980s are evocative of the 1620s. Comparisons between Britain and the United States, and between the twentieth and seventeenth centuries, serve to underline the importance of necessarily unexpressed abeyances across both space and time. Giving much emphasis to such inexact and mercurial devices may well disrupt the ordered solidity of our definitions of constitutionalism and liberal democracy. But in coming to understand that a 'tradition of behaviour is a tricky thing to get to know. . . [and] may even appear to be essentially unintelligible',[1] it becomes possible to assimilate the fact that, even though the ethos of constitutionalism is one of declared rules and stipulated powers, the passive virtues surrounding the inconclusivity of abeyances represent a similarly integral property of viable constitutions — irrespective of whether they are written or unwritten.

Part I

Chapter one

The concept and practice of constitutional abeyances

One of the most traditional points of departure in the study of constitutions has been to classify them according to whether they are 'written' or 'unwritten'.[1] This conventional, and even habitual, categorization is employed to denote a generic difference between constitutions. While a written constitution is seen as a formal and codified document embodying the rules and relationships of government, an unwritten constitution is understood to be an informal collection of rules, customs and traditions that pertain to the accepted organization of authority, but which do not possess any collective force that affords them a superior status to either the governing institutions or to their decisions. The degree to which a constitution is written or unwritten has traditionally been accepted as indicative of substantial differences not just in the role and conduct of respective governments, but also in their historical and social origins and even in their whole approach to the principle of the rule of law.

Such differences in the constitutional exercise of authority are almost invariably illustrated by reference to the American and British systems of government. Indeed, it is no exaggeration to say that the distinction between written and unwritten constitutions has become so closely associated with the United States and United Kingdom that their governments have come to epitomize the distinction and to represent the ideal types in what is often taken as an ideal typology. Thus, in the same way that much of the contrast between the American and British systems is portrayed as being attributable to their distinctive constitutional orders, so the distinction itself relies heavily upon the American and British constitutions for its meaning. That each constitution acts as the conventional counterpart to the other on the grounds of their respective positions in the written–unwritten continuum is quite evident from the literature. It is such a well-worn contrast that many commentators cannot help but assume its presence and acknowledge its salience.

The most celebrated point of comparison between the American and

British constitutions is that the American constitution is written while the British is not.[2]

The task of describing the British system of government presents certain peculiar difficulties. There is no one constitutional document, corresponding to the American constitution, which can provide the student with a reliable outline in the form of a central corpus of constitutional rules.[3]

The features of the constitution that help to create this concentration of authority are its antiquity and its unwritten, flexible, and unitary nature, and in each of these respects the British constitution is often contrasted with that of the USA.[4]

The absence of a written constitution is considered a great advantage by many who write about British politics. It is said to permit government to adapt its actions and institutions to changing circumstances and demands, without the procedural difficulties that a written constitution, such as the American, imposes.[5]

Placed in juxtapositon to one another, the written format of the American constitution and the unwritten nature of the British constitution can be pressed to the extremes of differentiation. In contrast to the British constitution, the American constitution possesses not only a definitive point of origin as a purposefully enacted document, but also the appearance of being an exclusively written and, therefore, a systematically ascertainable and comprehensively declared set of legal arrangements. Set against the American constitution, the British constitution looks to be so unwritten — and as a result so dependent upon the nuances of custom and tradition, so mutable in content, so deficient in fixed and precise boundaries, and so mecurial in meaning — that Alexis de Tocqueville's conclusion that England had 'no constitution'[6] becomes both plausible and persuasive.

'If a constitution means a written document, then', Ivor Jennings agrees, 'obviously Great Britain has no constitution'.[7] This prompts K.C. Wheare to ask the question: 'why has Britain no constitution?'[8] In a similar vein, one can almost sense the tone of cultural self-deprecation in the comment of another noted authority on the British constitution: 'in Britain, there is *only* a collection of customs and practices together with some laws'[9] — a common sentiment that provoked the typical response of Anthony Birch: 'what is lacking is a documentary and authoritative statement of the relations between . . . the various institutions of government'.[10]

Assumptions and statements like these betray a certain lack of confidence in the constitutional credentials of the British system. And even though many of these doubts are dispelled by corrective qualifications and by claims that the British constitution's documentary deficiencies are compensated for by different means, the prima facia position still persists. Namely, that there are substantive differences between the American and British constitutions and that these differences are, more than any other single factor, attributable to the American constitution being written and to the British constitution being unwritten.

Just as the 'first classification of constitutions that is usually proposed is that of "written" and "unwritten"',[11] so it is customary to follow this assertion with an immediate, and often peremptory, dismissal of its usefulness as a typology. In many cases, it appears that the written-unwritten classification is introduced for the sole purpose of establishing the empirical rigour of an investigation, in that the distinction is often no sooner acknowledged than it is declared to be analytically redundant. Whatever the reason, it is conventional to portray the division of constitutions into either written or unwritten entities as a misguided, simplistic, deceptive and thoroughly 'old-fashioned distinction'.[12] Somewhat ironically, it is the British and American constitutions which are once again used to substantiate the point.

Normally, the classification is shown to break down on three counts. First, should the British constitution be accepted as an unwritten constitution, it would become (with the possible addition of Israel) the only one of its kind in the world. By virtue of this fact alone, the typology's usefulness is undermined; in effect, the typology serves to distinguish all but one of the constitutions in the world from the British constitution.

Secondly, and more importantly, the British constitution's reputedly unique criterion of distinction is itself challenged. It is claimed that to characterize the constitution as unwritten amounts to a serious misrepresentation of its nature. The confusion is said to be derived from the absence of a central and singular document of codified constitutional rules. It is all too often concluded from this condition that the constitution is unwritten and that constitutional practice, therefore, rests to an overwhelming extent upon informal conventions, codes of behaviour and sets of binding usages.[13]

Such traditionalist views are criticized for being too dependent upon a simple negative (i.e., the absence of a written constitution in documentary form) and for being unduly obscurantist in their accounts of the constitution's nature. The modernist reply is to draw attention to the fact that most of what is regarded as comprising the British constitution is ascertainable, definable, and written. The constitution may well have been the result of an inscrutable historical process and may consist of a disorderly accumulation of principles and practices. Nevertheless, its identity and meaning are discoverable by reference to statutes, judicial decisions, conventions, and constitutional commentaries, and by authoritative opinions, letters, and works of scholarship. In Herman Finer's view 'these, taken together, are as explicit as, and usually more explicit than, the "written constitutions" of other countries'.[14]

Consequently, the British constitution's mark of distinction is not that it is unwritten, but that it is 'unassembled' or 'uncodified'. It exists in written fragments that may or may not have any collective identity, but which in theory do admit to being collected together in written form. 'If the constitution were put down in writing, as the constitution of the United States was put down', then, according to Ivor Jennings, even the reputedly mercurial constitutional conventions not only could be, but 'would be put in as well'.[15] It is merely the element of disaggregation, therefore, that sets the British constitution off from the others and even then it is regarded as being only a difference of degree and not of kind — a feature that leads K.C. Wheare to offer the following corrective formula: 'The truth about Britain can be stated not by saying that she has an unwritten constitution but by saying that she has no written constitution.'[16]

The third way in which the written-unwritten classification is challenged is by drawing attention to the unwritten elements of written constitutions. It is known that even in the apparently explicit and comprehensive framework of the US constitution, accepted codes of practice and norms of behaviour can impinge upon constitutional arrangements to the extent of becoming constituent parts of them. Far from being devoid of the sort of unwritten components known to characterize the British constitution, the American constitution is recognized as being similarly dependent upon conventions for its adaptability. 'It may be asserted without much exaggeration that the conventional element in the constitution of the United States is as large as in the English constitution.'[17]

If this was the position as A.V. Dicey saw it in the nineteenth century, then how much more must the conventional element have come to account for the rapid rise of the modern American state in the twentieth century. Whether it is the changed position of the electoral college, or the rise of the White House staff, or the onset of legislative veto, the American constitution has acquired a reputation for being a living constitution, whose evolutionary character is marked as much by unwritten changes in the guise of generalized custom and informal practice as it is by formal amendments or judicial declaration. This places even further strain upon the written-unwritten criterion in the classification of constitutions because it implies that a written constitution is not all that it documents and that 'the "written" part of the constitution may be its least important part'.[18]

It is clear from the debate that for the most part the written-unwritten classification is challenged on the grounds that it rests upon a false dichotomy. According to Leslie Wolf-Phillips, 'no constitution will be completely "written" or completely "unwritten", completely "codified" or completely "uncodified" '.[19] This being so, a constitution like that of Britain is, to Carl Friedrich, 'just as much "written" as the American or French constitutions, that is to say embodied in written documents of all kinds even though not codified and assembled in a single document'.[20] In like manner, written constitutions have to be interpreted in the light of their unavoidable reliance upon supplementary and supportive conventions without which any constitution would remain incomplete, inflexible, and deficient in motive power.[21]

The general disposition amongst constitutional scholars, therefore, is to refer to the traditional distinction between written and unwritten constitutions as being antiquarian and analytically flawed. As a result, they tend to approach the old typology, which to Herman Finer 'has been paraded until the mind is tired of contemplating it',[22] with every sign of being resolved to dispense with it as an instrument of analysis. It is not simply that the idea of an unwritten constitution is seen as being false, or that 'the concept of a constitution as a formal written document ought', in Friedrich's opinion, 'to be discarded'.[23] It is that the whole basis of the distinction is so widely regarded as being redundant that few, if any, would object to K.C. Wheare's admonition that 'the classification of constitutions into written and unwritten should . . . be discarded.'[24]

Constitutional scholars are no doubt right to dismiss the old written-unwritten classification in their search for more productive categories of analysis. But in moving on to such descriptive and evaluative criteria as rigidity-flexibility, federal-unitary, presidential-parliamentary, monarchical-republican, stability-fragility, programmatic-confirmatory and ideological-legal,[25] they do so at some risk. It is the sheer alacrity with which they depart from the apparently prosaic distinction between what is written and what is unwritten that gives rise to concern. However well-intentioned such a conversion in strategy may be, it runs the risk of overlooking the possibility of other dimensions to constitutional study that may be deceptively similar to the old classification, but which may retain an integrity all of their own. These unexamined dimensions may be substantively significant, but because they are eclipsed by what has become a discredited classification, their value remains unrecognized and their analytical potential unfulfilled. Because the written-unwritten distinction is so commonly portrayed as being irrefutably and conclusively redundant, there is now insufficient protection against losing the contribution of alternative perspectives which may be analogous to, and therefore obscured by, the old classification.

There may well be a number of concealed perspectives, but in this essay it is proposed to show that there is one barely discernible, yet profoundly fundamental, dimension which is all too easily threatened by the tendency to dispense with the unwritten character of constitutions. This dimension rests upon the recognition that in both written and unwritten constitutions there remains an undisclosed component upon which the stability of a constitution's meaning and authority depends. Such a component remains obscure and compulsively unwritten — no matter how written and well-documented the rest of the constitution may be. Its significance lies not just in the fact of its being unwritten, but in its need to remain unexpressed and unfathomable, in order for it to maintain its essential character.

To assert the existence of such an attribute might be construed as an attempt to revive the British constitution's mystique of uncodified rules and informal conventions. While it is true that the traditional portrait of the British constitution at least used to alert the observer to the possible presence of hidden dimensions, any attempt to reinstate the centrality of the unwritten nature of the constitution would inevitably be doomed to failure. Whether by way of levelling up conventions to the status of *de facto* laws, or by way of levelling laws down to generally accepted social practices and customs, the British constitution has been relieved of much of its shadowy and cryptic character. What used to be regarded as unwritten now stands revealed in a substantial literature to be written, recorded, expressed, and therefore 'known'.

It is not the intention of this study to reinvest the British constitution with its earlier enigma. Neither is it intended to concern itself with the other great source of silence traditionally incorporated into constitutionalism, namely the innermost influences and meanings attached to the existence and development of a constitution. Such factors can range from the abstract and metaphysical to the social and historical; from the moral and spiritual to the instinctive and traditional; from Coleridge's observation that the idea of a constitution is more important than the constitution itself[26] to Montesquieu's conception of laws as being determinable in social origin and nature through such factors as climate, soil, economy, religion and manners.[27] All such perspectives remain ultimately rooted in the Aristotelian idea of a constitution being the equivalent of the polity as a whole and, therefore, indistinguishable not only from the general order of society, but also from the totality of physical and moral influences that have woven together that society's collective form.

A constitution in this guise is not amenable to precise knowledge or exact description. The nature of its characteristic essence and formative processes remain highly problematical, indeterminable, and subject to personal belief and philosophical dispute. A constitution's unwritten nature in this respect, therefore, is derived from its resistance to being reliably understood in so far as there can be no agreed criteria for establishing the meaning of a constitution. In other words, much of a constitution's unwritten element is a function of its being unknowable.

What is being proposed in this context is the existence of an intermediate layer of obscurity sequestered between the micro-dimensional world of uncodified rules and customs and the macro-dimensional world of constitutions as abstract manifestations of cultural and historical conditions. This layer represents not just a difference in scale to the other two layers, but a difference in kind. The layer in question accommodates those implicit understandings and tacit agreements that could never survive the journey into print without compromising their capacious meanings and ruining their effect as a functional form of genuine and valued ambiguity. It is not just that such understandings are incapable of exact definition; rather their utility depends upon them not being subjected to definition, or even to the prospect of being definable.

Unwritten conventions are 'unwritten' largely because it is unnecessary to define what is already known and accepted as a convention. The metaphysical and moral adjuncts to constitutions are portrayed as 'unwritten' because they have no observable or tangibly immediate existence and are, therefore, unknowable in any verifiable sense. The 'understandings' present in the twilight zone between these two layers are 'unwritten' because it is recognized that any attempt to define them would be not merely unnecessary or impossible, but positively misguided and even potentially threatening to the constitution itself. This is because such 'understandings' only remain understood as long as they remain sufficiently obscure to allow them to retain an approximate appearance of internal coherence and clarity, while at the same time accommodating several potentially conflicting and quite unresolved points of issue. The resolution of conflict in such cases is that of suspended irresolution — either consciously secured or, far more probably, unconsciously and unintentionally acquired. These packages of aggregated positions are preserved by studied inattention. They may include contradictions, tensions, anomalies, and inequities, but the fragility and, at times, total illogicality of such packages are kept intact through a convention of non-exposure, of strategic oversight, and of complicity in delusion — in short, through an instinctive reversion to not breaking ranks when confronted with the constitutional equivalents of the emperor's clothes.

In this paper, such understandings will be referred to by the term 'constitutional abeyances'. This name was chosen because it accurately reflects the element of dormant suspension implicit in what appears to be quite explicit constitutional arrangements. In portraying constitutions, there is normally a pronounced emphasis upon declaratory acts of creation, upon stipulated frameworks of institutional organisation, and upon enumerated allotments of power — all centring on an underlying premise of a constitutional settlement in which major sources of conflict over the nature of political authority and obligation have been decisively resolved and which the constitution embodies as a lasting monument.

Constitutional abeyances, by contrast, provide a much more equivocal view of constitutionalism. They do this by drawing attention to the continuing flaws, half-answers and partial truths that are endemic in the sub-structure of constitutional forms. Abeyances refer to those parts of a constitution that remain unwritten and even unspoken not only by convention, but also of necessity. More precisely, abeyances represent a way of accommodating the absence of a definitive constitutional settlement and of providing the means of adjusting to the issues left unresolved in the fabric of the constitution. Sometimes these issues will be trivial and insufficiently important to warrant the expenditure of the political capital required to resolve them; they are tolerated. On other occasions, however, the issues can be crucial; the only satisfactory way of defusing them is to inhibit their development and to place them in abeyance as a condoned anomaly, by which means they become a working anomaly within the constitution.

Abeyances should not be thought of as empty constitutional 'gaps' to be filled in through the normal course of legal interpretation and political development. Neither should they be seen as constitutional 'deals' by which particular issues are attended to through a conscious form of mutual accommodation between contending parties, nor as 'conventions' demarcating expected behaviour through informal but generally obligatory agreements. On the contrary, abeyances should be seen as akin to barely sensed disjunctions lodged so deeply within constitutions that, far from being susceptible to orderly compromise, they can only be assimilated by an intuitive social acquiescence in the incompleteness of a constitution, by a common reluctance to press the logic of arguments on political authority to conclusive positions, and by an instinctive inhibition to objecting to what is persistently omitted from the constitutional agenda.

Abeyances are valuable, therefore, not in spite of their obscurity but because of it. They are significant for the attitudes and approaches to the constitution that they evoke, rather than from the content or substance of their strictures. It would be no exaggeration to say that the habitual willingness to defer indefinitely consideration of deep constitutional anomalies, for the sake of preserving the constitution from the severe conflict that would arise from attempts to remove them, represents the core of a constitutional culture. When constitutional abeyances become the subject of heightened interest and subsequent conflict, they are not merely accompanied by an intense constitutional crisis, they are themselves the essence of that crisis. Such a crisis marks an interruption in the continuity of implicit truce and, as a result, throws everything into further flux and reveals the disarray that abeyances had previously prevented.

In this respect, constitutional crises can be of great value as they reveal in graphic form what before had lain in the relative tranquillity of obfuscation and neglect. It is for this reason that the present study of constitutional abeyances will concern itself with two constitutional crises of such magnitude and severity that the substructure and interior supports of the respective constitutions became dangerously exposed to corrosive scrutiny, thereby unleashing the reality of their internal contradictions and inner ambiguities and bringing down upon the constitutions in question the full force of all the disillusionment and frustration drawn from those misconceived expectations and assumptions that the constitutions had previously fostered through abeyances. In concentrating on these constitutional breakdowns it is hoped to illustrate the nature and importance of constitutional abeyances and, by doing so, to reinstate the analytical value of what is written and what is unwritten not as a mark of distinction between constitutions but as a way of identifying the different dimensions and conditions within constitutions. For this reason, the two crises selected for the study are the period leading up to the English civil war in the seventeenth century, when the English constitution could be said to be at its most unwritten; and the 'imperial presidency' episode of the late 1960s and early 1970s, when it could be said that the American constitution was at its most written.

Part II

Chapter two

Constitutional abeyances and crisis conditions: the early Stuart constitution

The Glorious Revolution of 1688 is invariably taken as the point at which England acquired the legal basis of its modern constitution. Together with the Bill of Rights (1689), the Act of Settlement (1701), and the Act of Union (1707), the Whig triumph of constitutional monarchy has become so established as the watershed in English constitutional development that it is almost impossible to conceive of anything resembling a constitutional settlement prior to the accession of William and Mary. Indeed, such is the attention given to the Glorious Revolution's climactic attributes that in many respects what preceded the settlement can be seen as nothing other than a pathologically unsettled period. The Glorious Revolution lends powerful weight to the general image of the seventeenth century as a turbulent succession of unbridgeable dichotomies and intransigent dogmas on the sources, forms, and uses of authority that appear to have led to an unavoidable power struggle by which a constitution was finally secured in the exhausted aftermath of civil war.

Appearances, however, can be deceptive. Instead of the intractable political conflicts or diametrically opposed doctrines of political authority that one is led to expect from the violent disorders of the time, the picture that emerges from both contemporary observations and historical commentaries is one characterized by common understandings and traditional codes of conduct. Ironically, this feature of an underlying protocol of socially amenable political practice is nowhere more conspicuous than in the critical period of the first two Stuart kings, James I and Charles I, which ostensibly marks the progressive dislocation of society into open strife. Far from bearing testimony to the absence of a recognizable constitution, the history of this pivotal period is exceptional for the way it reveals not only a strongly developed consciousness of an existing constitution, but also an acute sense of being obliged to work within its strictures. At the same time, this constitution could in no way be formally expressed, accurately ascertained, or even reliably understood.

Yet there was a constitution and its presence permeated early seventeenth century England. Nothing else could account for the extraordinary extent to which the terms, language, logic, and content of political argument were dominated by the appeal to law and by the constant quest to determine the meaning and extent of the law. This both reflected and reinforced the central significance of the law as a keeper of custom and as an imprimatur of authority. If that placed the law in the invidious position of being beset by inconsistencies and contradictions, this did not appear to adversely affect its significance. On the contrary, law became a ubiquitous medium of political exchange and a capacious source of political legitimization. Its binding capacity and political status may have remained open to dispute but the cultural preoccupation with law and legal sanction betrayed an attachment to constitutional forms and principles comparable to any modern constitutional system. Even in the absence of anything resembling a conclusive constitutional settlement and even in the presence of profound social divisions, there existed an elaborate and arguably sophisticated constitutional culture; a culture distinguished by hardened forms of usage and by recurrent patterns of obligation set within a matrix of shared convictions on the right ways of conducting government.[1]

This is not to say that the Stuart constitution was in any sense a precisely measured framework of public authority through which the exercise of power was controlled by institutional dynamics or by regularly enforced procedures and rules. Far from it. The governmental structure of early seventeenth-century England was notorious for its indeterminate lines of final authority; for its ambivalence on such central issues as precedents and prerogatives, rights and representation; and, as a result, for its inherent potential for disjunction, contradiction and eventual dissolution.

The ingredients for systemic conflict were in abundance. For example, there was a fundamental fault-line between the divine privileges and coercive prerogatives of an exclusive monarchy, and the competing conception of majesty in the form of sovereign laws, rights, and freedoms. Another basic tension existed between, on the one hand, the idea of lawful monarchy in the form of authority invested by law and powers conferred through legal custom, and on the other, the idea of subjects' rights which ostensibly confined the King's authority to a point — albeit an indeterminate point — compatible with the coexistence of legally sanctioned defences for property and other freedoms. To one distinguished historian, this represented 'the great constitutional problem which had never been resolved in the Middle Ages or in the Tudor period; the problem of controlling a king whose authority was legally limited but who could not be coerced by legal means'.[2]

A further flaw that disfigured the glaze of the Stuart constitution was the almost continuous manoeuvring for position by both the Crown and

Parliament as each attempted to gain what it regarded its rightful position in relation to the other. If Parliament had suffered a decline since the heady Tudor period (when at times it was called upon to govern almost in partnership with the monarchy) it nevertheless retained both its memory and its appetite for participation.[3] The early Stuarts, by contrast, saw Parliament as an unruly, unmanageable burden necessary mainly for the sake of financial solvency. Since the monarchy required public funds that could, according to custom, only be raised through the approval of Parliament and since Parliament could only be called into existence by the monarchy, both institutions were dependent upon and constrained by the other — with no adequately worked out format for reconciling the differences that arose between them.

In the same way that Parliament found it difficult to coerce the king, so 'the "absolute king" also lacked adequate ways and means of coercing the subject'[4] — so much so that the constitution could be said to have failed to establish the 'legal means by which the monarch could correctly and easily carry on kingly government without securing the co-operation and consent of his subjects'.[5] The exaggerated protocol and encoded vocabulary could not conceal the often venomous exchanges, as Parliament became more determined to give physical form to the force of custom and rights, while an increasingly exasperated monarchy became more truculent in the face of what it saw as a faithless and subversive body intent upon compromising monarchical authority.

The disjunction between categorical royal supremacy and independent Parliamentary power was further compounded by another source of ambiguity over the nature and form of authority, namely, the position of statute law. According to one interpretation, 'statute was the highest form of law in England, since an Act of Parliament could alter what was legal and illegal'.[6] In some quarters, this gave rise to a notion of legislative supremacy emanating from the joint authority of the King-in-Parliament. James Whitelocke argued out the merits of this case in a speech to the House of Commons in 1610.

> In the King is a twofold power, the one in Parliament, as he is assisted with the consent of the whole state; the other out of Parliament, as he is sole and singular, guided merely by his own will . . . The power of the King in Parliament is greater than his power out of Parliament, and doth rule and control it . . . If a judgement given in the King's Bench by the King himself . . . a writ of error to reverse this judgement may be sued before the King in Parliament . . .; in acts of Parliament . . . the acts and power is the King's, but with the assent of the Lords and Commons, which maketh it the most sovereign and supreme power, above all and controllable by none.[7]

According to another interpretation, statute law ought to be seen more in a supplementary and clarifying role; lawmaking could neither be construed as representing the highest act of government nor as being as important as other powers. This dispute devolved upon the central division between King and Parliament, as the Crown's counsellors insisted that it was the King who made laws in *his* Parliament, and that such laws were anyway the King's laws to be administered by the King's courts. Lawyers like James Whitelocke, on the other hand, claimed that as statutes were the highest law of the land and as they could only be made by the corporate entity of the King-in-Parliament, then the King and his prerogative powers had to be inferior to his legislative powers in conjunction with Parliament.

These differences were projected into a third level of complexity by the presence of a strengthening tradition of common law.[8] The revival and subsequent development of the common-law courts had been encouraged by the monarchy in Tudor times, but by the seventeenth century the Stuarts had begun to see them as antiquarian impediments to the drive towards modernized and efficient monarchical government. The close affinity of common law with the medieval concept of the supremacy of law over political will, and with the idea of historically sanctioned rights and procedures, posed a continual challenge to those monarchs like James I or Charles I who were seeking to build up and insulate their powers through the courts.

Common law, however, was a double-edged sword. It could just as easily condone the traditional prerogatives of the crown as it could throw into doubt the legitimacy of its activities and claims. Likewise, common law could be used to endorse the asserted rights of Parliament at the same time as it could be employed to render the authority of statute contingent upon common law principles. Either way, the common law became so entwined around contemporary issues and positions that it became a major component of the tortuous incoherence of early seventeenth century government. On occasion it even threatened to become an independent 'third force' in the constitutional disputes of the time. It never quite acquired this position but the authority of the common law was effective in encouraging the use of legal interpretation as both a method of political inquiry and as an instrument of political controversy in matters of law and history. Furthermore, in doing so, it provided yet another twist of discord in the Stuart constitution.

This time it involved the courts. The channelling of disputes over high matters of state into the courts gave judges the twofold task of preserving the impression of a settled pattern of legal traditions and principles, while at the same time seeking to find ways of accommodating the monarchy's claimed supremacy in law. This placed judges in an invidious position. Their formal role might be to preserve the integrity of the law, but they were also royal officers engaged in administering the King's justice and, therefore, needed to protect not merely the law but also themselves. This was defensible as long as cases directly involving the crown's prerogatives could be kept at bay. But, as the Stuarts were intent upon establishing in legal judgement an array of contested powers, the judges were projected into unaccustomed prominence. They could not be said to be blindly supportive of the crown but in the heated jurisdictional disputes of the period it was felt that there was an 'unduly intimate association between their work and government policies'.[9] Their technical arguments, use of precedent and general legal assertions, while quite valid, were always in danger of being seen as attempts to make the law conform to current royalist policies. The situation was hardly improved by the moot point of whether the King, as the fount of law and as the source of the judges' authority, could be expected to serve writs against himself.[10]

Individual judges like Edward Coke sought to sustain credence in the integrity of the common law and of the courts by reminding the crown that it was not so much the source of law as a protected beneficiary of it, but such gestures were in vain: Coke was summarily dismissed from the Chief Justiceship of the King's Bench in 1616 by James I. Coke's dismissal served as a salutary reminder to his colleagues to heed the exhortation of the Lord Chancellor, Francis Bacon, that judges should be 'lions under the throne'.[11] It also revealed the extent to which the traditional distinction between law and government had been compromised as James I and Charles I anxiously pressed their claims for legal authority into areas previously left open to negotiated and improvised arrangements. The manner in which judges were drawn into exposed parts of public controversy reflected the significance attached to the law in ascertaining the rightfulness of governmental action. More to the point, it served to highlight the apparently indeterminate and fractured structure of a constitution that all could agree upon as being authoritative, but which seemed ominously unstable and incoherent as to who or what it authorized.

At first sight, therefore, the Stuart ship of state seemed riddled with all manner of structural weaknesses and design faults. They might successfully have remained concealed as long as calm waters prevailed. But unfortunately the early seventeenth century conspired to produce a whole array of adverse conditions that were eventually to capsize the vessel, leaving its wreckage as apparently conclusive proof of its inherent unseaworthiness.

To say that the times were unstable is, at best, a gross understatement. Stuart monarchs were plagued with a host of problems, many of which were of their own making. There was, first of all, a climate of extreme anxiety over Catholicism — with its subversive and threatening connections to foreign powers and its history of opposition to both the established English church and its royal protector — and of nationalistic and religious paranoia, generated by suspicions that James I and particularly Charles I were crypto-Catholics, or at least victims of a popish conspiracy, intent upon toleration to the point of complicity in the counter-reformation. Charles I's actions moved the situation from that of dissent to outright rebellion. In England, he attempted to invoke his prerogative in order to impose a central uniformity upon a church that had become accustomed to an accommodating variation in theological doctrine, local organization, and liturgy. In Scotland, he provocatively applied the same policy to the more staunchly Calvinistic and independent church and, by doing so, precipitated an open revolt and the subsequent Scottish invasion of Northern England. At the same time, substantial disquiet was generated by the Stuarts' apparent vacillation in supporting popular Protestant causes abroad (e.g., the raising of Cardinal Richelieu's siege of the Huguenot citadel of La Rochelle, and the restoration of Frederick V to the Palatine which had been lost to Maximillian of Bavaria with the aid and support of the Hapsburg's Spanish army of Flanders) and the monarchy's evident affinity for diplomatic and marital alliances with the major Catholic powers, Spain and France.

The humiliating fiasco of the ineffectual Cadiz expedition (which was to have attacked the Spanish bullion fleet), the failure to lift the French siege at La Rochelle, and the collapse of the crown's alliances into unsuccessful wars with France and Spain did little to bolster confidence in the crown. Nor did the Stuarts show many signs of tackling the turbulence of the seventeenth century: rapid population growth, high inflation, periodic slumps, violent disorders, and radical religious and political sectarianism proceeded apace. Fiscally and administratively, the Stuarts were nothing if not irresponsible. Faced with stagnant financial, legal and administrative means of support, the monarchy resorted to prerogative adventurism, while at the same time increasing the government's social and economic responsibilities. Parliament responded by railing against royal abuses of power and channelling unrest and insurgency into formal confrontation. Given all these conditions, the viability and even existence of a constitution can be called into question. Arguably, whatever resilience the governmental system may have possessed in the Elizabethan era was, by the 1630s, quite dissipated. Looking back on the period, it seems as though the government's structure was destined to collapse under the weight of its inner contradictions.

There is much to commend this fatalistic view. In hindsight, it appears as though Queen Elizabeth I, in avoiding embarrassing constitutional questions and issues, had failed to bring 'the constitutional arrangements of the government into line with its functioning',[12] so bequeathing her successors the great, and apparently insurmountable, problems of the seventeenth century. Furthermore, the argument runs, because the critical issue of final and supreme authority had never been satisfactorily raised, let alone resolved, the incoherence of the government could not be corrected and in this sense it could be said that there was not only 'no theory' and 'no notion of a "constitution" ' but, in effect, 'no constitution'.[13] Perhaps this outlook is overly indebted to the Whig interpretation of history, with its emphasis upon the Glorious Revolution as the central catalyst in banishing royal absolutism in favour of rights secured under a Parliamentary government and constitutional monarchy. Whatever the reason, the perspective that casts a shadow of congenital disorder and protean formlessness upon the constitutional structure of early seventeenth-century England remains a mistaken and misleading one.

Despite the many appearances to the contrary, contemporary expressions of political principle and allegiance betrayed a marked belief in the existence of a pervasive constitutional order, the meaning of which was believed to be understood and honoured by all parties. To a remarkable extent for a society supposedly marked by convulsive dissent and chronic dislocation, the period preceding the civil war was conspicuous for the commonality of principles, attachments, and beliefs amongst the participants in the long-running dispute of the time. Society ran instinctively along the lines of order, traditional obedience, and deference in which the monarchy supplied the symbolism of an all-embracing patriarchal authority dedicated to the rights and laws of the kingdom, while at the same time possessing a customary prerogative to act on behalf of the people's general welfare. Custom, precedent, and law represented the common currency of debate and the common denominator of political thought.

> Everyone spoke the same language . . . With remarkable unanimity early seventeenth century Englishmen believed that they were bound to abide by the ancient constitution . . . In the sphere of practical politics the disagreement essentially lay in how to operate a constitution of whose nature few had any doubts.[14]

The crisis eventually arose not because of any absence of a constitution or because there was an insufficiently developed constitution, but because there was a discernible and workable constitution that acted as a point of reference by which to measure dissent and record innovation.

Nothing represents the vitality of a self-conscious constitutional culture better than a people's ability to work with anomalies and contradictions in such manner as to prevent them from becoming serious obstacles to the day-to-day running of government and from compromising the accepted integrity of government. This is not to say that differences are settled or resolved. On the contrary, they are suspended, held in abeyance, suppressed, and made workable by the general agreement not to expose the logical incompatibility of positions and doctrines to the corrosive forces of close scrutiny. Some interpretations regard such forms of concealment as signs of inner decay, incipient breakdown, and self-delusion. Michael Hawkins, for example, believes that

> the agreement on fundamentals was dangerous, since it was expressed in such generalities that it left the way open for widely divergent practical applications, and concealed a host of differences about the specific distribution of powers in the state . . . . A situation in which the crown and its opponents could accuse each other of misusing 'misty profundities' was potentially very unstable.[15]

In this view, the coexistence of rationally irreconcilable positions is untenable and is, therefore, fated to produce an explosive mixture and result. But interpretations of this sort, strengthened as they are by hindsight, assume that phenomena such as the royal prerogative, Parliamentary government, or common-law rights had the characteristics of bright primary colours set against one another. In reality, to those participating in the controversies at the time, such phenomena were seen more as muted shades of co-ordinated colour that could readily be accommodated to one another as long as they remained in subdued halftones. The anomalies and inconsistencies were discernible, but it was the strength of attachment to a code of constitutional obligation that permitted such discordance to be depressed by a willingness to shroud any issues on the ultimate essence of government in equivocation.

As Francis Wormuth points out, there was little or no impulse to clarify the organization of government according to a singular criterion of undisputed sovereignty. On the contrary, 'the seventeenth century thought of its principles of government in the plural: there were "fundamental laws", there were "constitutions" '.[16] They acquired a sense of harmony under the auspices of a largely mythical yet generally acclaimed ancient constitution. While this device afforded a perspective of common ground, its substantive imprecision and obscurity left the meaning of the Stuart constitution open to doubt and debate. 'Men felt strongly that their agreement on broad principles was sufficient to secure political peace.'[17] It was this capacious quality that distinguished the Stuart constitution and allowed it to survive and even prosper. Its assimilation of so many disputes concerning so many central issues for such a long period of time revealed the presence not just of a durable code of constitutional protocol, but also of a remarkably subtle and sophisticated constitutional culture. Far from being signs of weakness, therefore, the ambiguity and imprecision of the Stuart constitution were in actuality the hallmarks of its strength.

Just how aggregative the constitution could be and just how well constitutional practice could cater for ostensibly unmanageable positions is provided by the principle of divinely invested kingship.[18] There were several variations on this royalist theme, but in the main they centred upon the notion that kingly authority was directly derived from God and that, because of this, kings were responsible to God rather than to any purely temporal considerations. The theory was initially based upon the ancient idea that all power came from God and, therefore, any political authority by definition had to have a divine sanction and a religious purpose. By the end of the sixteenth century, however, what had been a very generalized proposition was being hardened and elevated into a rigorously defended device to protect the monarchy from those doctrines of civil disobedience, popular deposition, and tyrannicide that had been spawned in the religious wars of Europe. James I had been raised in the anxieties of the era and so when he assumed the English throne in 1603, he was already firmly lodged in the precepts and intellectual style of divine rule. Both in his books (*The Trew Law of Free Monarchies*, 1598; *Basilikon Doron*, 1603) and in his speeches, James made it clear that he believed himself to be God's lieutenant on earth.

> The state of monarchy is the supremest thing upon earth; for kings . . . sit upon God's throne, but even by God himself they are called gods . . . Kings are justly called gods for that they exercise a manner or resemblance of divine power upon earth, for if you will consider the attributes to God you shall see how they agree in the person of a king. God hath power to create or destroy, make or unmake, at his pleasure; to give life or send death, to judge all and to be judged not accountable to none; to raise low things and to make high things low at his pleasure.[19]

When James first arrived at the English court, he aroused serious concern; it was felt that his inflated view of the royal prerogative, already worked out in published forms, might constitute a direct threat to the established incoherence of government. James may well have pressed his claims to divine providence out of a sense of insecurity over his right to succeed, or because they conformed to his philosophical exposition on the monarchy. But whatever his motives and whatever the early reactions to his assertions, one thing is clear. James was not prepared to allow his basic outlook to become immutable and dogmatic. He refused to become a victim of his own philosophical system and to squander the adaptability required for political leadership for the sake of a myopic adherence to principle. In effect, 'he knew enough about men and affairs not to press absurd claims too far.'[20]

Despite his reputation for overbearance and doctrinal pomposity — a result, no doubt, of his conviction that he was an occupant of Christ's throne 'in this part of the earth'[21] — the manner of James I's kingship was in reality marked by its accommodation to the traditional spirit of disputed custom, contentious precedent, and competitive legal interpretation. James showed he could and would compromise even on the apparently most uncompromising position of divine rule. For example, he tempered the divine inviolability of his position by extending no further than to a defence against rebellion, deposition, and tyrannicide. To support the positive aspects of his position, James relied far more upon the less exclusive notions of natural authority, patriarchy, social order, and historical right. These allowed for the existence of fundamental customs that the monarchy had helped bring into existence and by which the monarch agreed to abide, while always reserving the right to act outside such laws as a sovereign power.

In this way, James kept his door open as an object of divinity and as a historically and socially sanctioned figure of order. At the same time, he kept other doors open to those who would challenge his position and policies.

> He was careful always to operate within the framework of the common law; he never imprisoned anyone without trial; he never levied money from his subjects without authorisation from Parliament or the courts of common law, he never promulgated a law of his own accord, even if he believed he could, and he was certainly more moderate and 'constitutional' than Queen Elizabeth.[22]

It is true that James insisted upon defining his position in 'terms which the far wiser Elizabeth had left to the imagination'[23] and that some of his 'subjects were surprised, not at their sovereign's ideas, but at his constant preaching of them'.[24] Nevertheless, it is also true that James possessed an ability to compromise despite his lofty propositions on sovereignty. It was this political astuteness and tolerance that allowed James to manoeuvre successfully within the grain of the constitution. Unfortunately, his skill in reconciling high theory with day-to-day policies was not inherited by his son Charles. John P. Kenyon notes that Charles 'was not as vocal as his father about the Divine Right of Kings, but he believed in it more firmly, and was not prepared to compromise as James had been'.[25] Charles had little understanding of the subtleties of working with a constitution that could remain viable only as long as its coexisting concepts were suspended in manageable irresolution. Charles's inability or unwillingness to square the face value of his categorical assertions about government with the prosaic substance of its equivocal nature accounted for much of the tragedy that surrounded his reign.

Just as constitutional practice could tolerate and even humour those who were most disposed to the florid pretensions of divine right, so the same accommodating spirit was at work amongst those who sought to challenge the crown. In spite of their reputation for revolutionary radicalism and ideological fervour, the Parliaments of the early seventeenth century were in reality far more conspicuous for their entrenched conservatism and instinctive self-restraint — and this was true even in the very act of protest and assertion. An illustration of this form of inhibited insurgency is the Petition of Right of 1628.

The petition arose out of the disarray in Charles I's financial and foreign policies. Controversy was particularly acute over the king's insistence upon collecting tonnage and poundage beyond the one year that Charles's first Parliament had authorized in 1625. Since 1485 the right to custom duties had traditionally been bestowed upon the monarch as a lifetime bequest by Parliament. Charles took his one-year limit as both a personal insult and a provocative attempt to suborn the authority of a newly appointed king. For its part, Parliament had during the Tudor period kept alive the basic principle that taxation was a voluntary and exceptional grant of supply given by the political community to its monarch to help supplement the crown's conventional resources (e.g. feudal dues, profits from crown lands) in times of crisis. Under the Stuarts, Parliament became increasingly concerned that the monarchy was acquiring the facility of financing itself through such new customs devices as 'the impositions'[26] and that these might well consign Parliament and its role of redress of grievances to the same dismal fate as that suffered by other assemblies in Europe. Parliament, therefore, was resolved to defend itself and the liberty of its property-owning members by keeping the monarchy as dependent as possible upon limited grants of supply.

To the crown, Parliament's position was akin to treachery. Faced with a chronic shortage of money to finance his numerous and ill-conceived foreign commitments, Charles was confronted by what to him was an obdurate Parliament intent upon exploiting his discomfort to build up its own privileges. It is quite true that members of Parliament did use their position to criticise the mismanagement of the war and the misuse of the crown's resources. They took it upon themselves to advise the crown on such high matters of state as foreign policy and church organization, and to contest the amounts and allocations of money required by the government. They even criticized the king's choice of councillors, as witnessed in the 1626 Parliament when the House of Commons launched impeachment proceedings against Charles's notorious favourite, the Duke of Buckingham. But Parliament felt its actions justified by a monarch who was seen as both philosophically reluctant to conform to legal measures and temperamentally incapable of accommodating himself to the collaborative spirit of agreements and promises.

The Commons were already dismayed by the expensive military fiascos suffered by the country during the 1620s and by the crown's support of the Laudian reforms in church ceremony and liturgy. But more importantly, at a time when there were strong impulses to subject the channels of political authority to legal definition, Charles I presented a picture of rigid and distant kingship awash in high prerogative and heavy-handed majesty mixed with low subterfuge and bad faith. It was a time of menacing requests for 'free gifts', of extravagant forced loans, of custodial punishment for those who refused to lend money to the crown, of royal interference with the judiciary, of arrests and detention without given cause, of the forcible billetting of troops onto local populations free of charge, of the imposition of martial law in the southern and western counties of England, of the continued collection of tonnage and poundage, and of peremptory dismissals of uncooperative Parliaments with closing speeches such as the one Charles delivered in 1626:[27]

> Remember that Parliaments are altogether in my power for their calling, sitting and dissolution; therefore as I find the fruits of them good or evil, they are to continue or not to be.[28]

It was against this corrosive background that, after only three years of his reign, the House of Commons was moved to present Charles with the Petition of Right.

At first sight, the Petition of Right looks like a dramatic frontal assault by Parliament on the nascent absolutism of the Stuart monarchy. The king was petitioned not to levy taxes without Parliament's consent, not to detain citizens without showing cause, not to billett soldiers and sailors on subjects without their agreement, and not to impose martial law upon the citizenry. After a struggle with both the House of Lords and Charles himself over the insertion of a 'saving clause' formally acknowledging that the royal prerogative would be unaffected by the measure, the House of Commons finally succeeded in overcoming all the objections and securing the consent of the Lords and even the king.

The Petition of Right has been interpreted as representing a watershed in the historical progression to Parliamentary government. Samuel R. Gardiner, for example, describes it as 'memorable' because it ranks as 'the first statutory restriction of the powers of the crown since the accession of the Tudor dynasty'.[29] And Harold Hume sees the petition as having 'curbed the power of the king to a greater extent than any document since Magna Carta'.[30] He concludes that through it 'the prerogative of the crown had unquestionably been limited'.[31] To all intents and purposes, therefore, 1628 does appear to mark the pivotal date on which the House of Commons departed from its customary position of deference, and undertook an explicitly radical challenge to the authority of the crown — a challenge that Charles I could not resist.

Nevertheless, like the assertions of divine right, the appearances of Parliamentary iconoclasm were not borne out in substance. For all its reputed audacity and innovativeness, the Petition of Right was in effect 'an extremely moderate document'[32] both in respect to its content and in the manner of its passage. First of all, the petition 'glossed over important issues'[33] such as impositions, and tonnage and poundage, which had been at the very centre of the controversy over crown taxation and Parliamentary consent. Even where the petition was more explicit in content, like the right against arbitrary and unspecified arrest, then it is important to note that it was not contesting the king's privilege of imprisoning subjects, including members of Parliament, but only the way in which he exercised this right.

Secondly, and most significantly, it was the form of the petition, together with the nature of the arguments made in its support, which more than anything else revealed the limitations under which Parliament laboured to subject the monarchy to a measure of control. It is noteworthy, for example, that the Commons chose the legal device of a petition rather than a bill by which to assert itself. Apart from the fact that a statutory bill of rights would not have won support in the House of Lords or the assent of the king, a statute would smack of a creative act of innovation by which relationships were to be changed. Nothing could have been further from the minds of the leaders in the House of Commons. Parliament chose a petition precisely because it was a way of confronting the crown without challenging it. A petition was a reiteration of the state of existing laws and practices and, as such, an invitation to the king through his assent to rededicate himself to their preservation. It was in essence a device for asking the king to recognize that legitimate grievances existed and to acknowledge that in future the law ought to be observed as it had been in the past by his royal predecessors. The strategy and objectives of the petition, therefore, were entirely conservative in character. Its supporters in the Commons sought to concentrate on what they took to be the ancient constitution and, by doing so, to allow the king's actions to condemn themselves by being at variance with it. The approach was deliberately oblique — so oblique, in fact, that Charles I found little difficulty in agreeing to the petition as he believed that by doing so he would not relinquish any of his powers.

Far from being the catalyst that precipitated a heightened Parliamentary consciousness of dissent and independence, the Petition of Right instead revealed the extent to which ingrained inhibition characterized the constitutional disputes of the period. The petition was perhaps more significant for what it did not contain. It was silent, for instance, on the issues of the crown's powers of calling and dissolving Parliaments, of imprisoning members of Parliament, and of interfering with its activities and procedures. Moreover, there was doubt as to the petition's legal status. It was difficult to ascertain whether it was inferior to, the equivalent of, or superior to a statute as a declaration of fundamental and unchanging individual rights.

The silence of constitutions

Particularly revealing was the extraordinarily circumspect manner in which the Commons discussed and formulated the petition. From the vocabulary, arguments, and explanations employed, it is clear that the spirit of the occasion was one drenched in conformity to the crown's patriarchal authority as a basic and incontrovertible element of national life. Those who pressed hardest for the petition proceeded from the traditional basis that the king could do no wrong, that it was his subordinates who were culpable and that his prerogative could in no way be jeopardized by the actions of Parliament. Even in 1628, after a period when Charles had been at his most persistently provocative, 'the opposition leadership carefully avoided any proposals which could be read as an invasion of prerogative rights'.[34] In spite of the aggravated circumstances, 'kingly authority was so firmly recognized and accepted that the Parliamentary opposition challenged it very slowly and hestitatingly . . . in 1628 they did not deny that such authority existed and should exist, they were determined only that it should not be written into the law of the land'[35] in such a way as to derogate the latter to the crown's prerogative.

It is quite true that Parliament refused to accept a 'saving clause' acknowledging the prerogative to be untouched by the petition. Such a clause was seen as tactically misplaced in a device to re-establish rights at a time when the king's prerogative was being enhanced through the courts. But it was also regarded as being strategically unnecessary as the prerogative was accepted as an inextinguishable part of the law and, therefore, could always be taken as read. What was just as significant as the rejection of the saving clause, however, was Parliament's conspicuous refusal to write the crown's prerogative explicitly out of the petition. Such a course of action would have been unimaginable to the participants in the process. Silence denoted Parliament's accommodation of the prerogative as an intrinsic constituent of the constitution. 'In the eyes of the Commons the legal power of the crown was no more restricted by the Petition of Right than it had been by existing law before the passage of this document.'[36] This was taken as being one of the chief signs of its success.

What is clearly discernible in the debates and manoeuvrings surrounding the Petition of Right is a manifest unwillingness on the part of the Parliament to reduce the issue to the stark terms of contested sovereignty. What might appear as weak equivocation or deliberate deception was, in reality, a feature of an underlying contemporary psychology which avoided pushing the cold logic of dissent to any sort of conclusion, and which resisted the sharpening of conflict if it threatened to produce unpalatable answers. This was a pattern of thinking that was accustomed to the grey subtleties of working with and through ambiguity, obscurity, and obfuscation. Present was what Christopher Hill called a 'stop in the mind'.

> Looking back, we describe the early seventeenth-century conflicts as a struggle for sovereignty . . . Contemporaries did not see it in this light . . . Pym denied 'sovereign power' to 'our sovereign Lord the King', but did not claim it for Parliament . . . The 'stop in the mind' ensured that the furthest that the Parliamentarians could go was to speak of the sovereignty of King in Parliament, or more often of a mixed monarchy, a balanced constitution. In case of conflict it was difficult historically, legally, and emotionally, for anyone to deny the ultimate authority of the king.[37]

The mind stopped at the distant approaches to Parliamentary sovereignty and even at the very appearance of questioning established power relationships. The belief was in traditional and legally sanctioned accords, regardless of the disputes and divisions which arose to obscure them. Sin lay in innovation. Redemption lay in antiquarian renovation. As such, the royalist councillors and Parliamentary leaders sought to outbid one another's conservatism and to outdo each other's grasp of the meanings of the past. The strategy even up to the 1640s was not to unpack conflict and to elicit new and final answers. It was to contain conflict by tolerating the indeterminacy of old answers and by lightening the burden of constitutional anomalies through mutual restraint and wilful neglect — in effect, to arrive at arrangements that would 'dowse controversy by circumventing knotty problems'.[38] The Petition of Right was one such arrangement. It not only typified the contemporary etiquette of protest but demonstrated the crucial importance of trust and reciprocity upon which such tenuous agreements inevitably depended for their effect.

Initially it appeared that Charles had accepted the terms of the petition in precisely the spirit in which it had been proposed by the House of Commons. The Parliamentary leadership believed that by approving the petition, the king had formally recognized the stipulated rights to be absolute liberties protected by law against any encroachment from the crown. The leadership assumed that Charles had tacitly affirmed the royal prerogative as a corporate part of a singular constitutional authority. Charles, therefore, would lose nothing through the petition because his prerogative rights, as legal rights, would be as secure as they had always been. The king agreed to the petition on the grounds that his prerogative would remain untouched. But his interpretation of that condition proved to be materially different from Parliament's. Charles acknowledged that in general the laws and customs of the realm should be and, under normal conditions, would be, observed. But as monarch, he would always retain those prerogative rights legally invested in him to transcend the law, in order to preserve the safety and welfare of his subjects. In other words, his prerogative was part of the common-law heritage and simultaneously separate from the law as an extra-legal sovereign authority.

Both the king and Parliament can be accused of being disingenuous, misleading, and even guilty of sharp practice on this and other issues. Parliamentary leaders portrayed the petition as leaving royal prerogative untouched when it was evidently designed to do just that. According to Lawrence Stone, their constitutional demands were 'clearly innovatory and aggressive' but ones that they sought to satisfy behind a 'smokescreen of a conservative ideology of a return to the past'.[39] Charles, for his part, agreed to the petition in order to gain the five subsidies that Parliament had used as an inducement. Thereafter, he set about revising the petition's strictures in accordance with his interpretation of the appropriate precedents. The king was seen to break his promises when he assumed as a matter of course that tonnage and poundage was not included in the petition's remit and announced that he would continue to collect the dues constitutionally owed to him. King and Parliamentary leaders alike were convinced of the righteousness of their positions. They were both implacably assured of their constructions of the constitution.

The petition provides a representative illustration of the way in which the two parties, in Charles McIlwain's words 'slid past each other',[40] never fully confronting one another's authority in direct conflict, but instead taking constant evasive action by resorting to inconclusive legal precedents. Distrust and suspicion festered. Under the leadership of Sir John Eliot, the more restive sections of the Commons secured passage of three highly inflammatory resolutions, including a description of anyone who either levied or paid tonnage and poundage as a treasonous 'betrayer of the liberties of England'.[41] The king responded by subjecting Parliament to the full force of monarchical authority. He reprimanded Parliament for turning its freedom into 'licentiousness' and for perverting the Petition of Right into 'lawless liberty'[42] and condemned the three resolutions as 'scandalous and seditious' measures made by an 'outlawed man, desperate in mind and fortune'.[43] He then dissolved Parliament until such time when 'our people shall see more clearly into our intentions'[44] and had Eliot and his associates arrested and imprisoned. Eliot eventually died in the Tower of London in 1632 and another Parliament was not called by Charles for eleven years. The king had allowed the petition to reveal the contradictions of the Stuart constitution to the unaccustomed and disquieting light of searching analysis. Charles resorted to first principles in the crisis and instinctively tried to restore the pattern of abeyances by shutting the ambiguities away again. During the 1630s, to an extraordinary extent he almost succeeded in doing so.[45]

It is easy in restrospect to construe this state of affairs as an irredeemable disjunction that could only lead to a hardened polarization of positions and, ultimately, to political disintegration. Charles McIlwain, for example, cannot see any other prognosis as plausible: 'from such

The early Stuart constitution

an *impasse* the only outcome and the only remedy was the same measure of revolution'.[46] While such a conclusion may rest upon sound logical propositions and modern conceptions of sovereignty, it is nevertheless based upon a misreading of the nature and durability of the Stuart constitution.

The notion that the hidden tensions were unendurable contradictions that had compulsively to be resolved was quite foreign to the early seventeenth century. 'To believe in both the divine right of kingly authority and at the same time in its limited nature was perfectly natural and consistent for many excellent seventeenth century minds'.[47] The minds of ordinary Englishmen were not so very different. They were not aroused by the need to define the separate components of government or to delineate the distribution of power between them. Their minds were not generally excited by whether or not the relationship between law and statute, or that between crown prerogatives and subjects' rights could be precisely ascertained. John P. Kenyon notes that whether the king was outside or above common law was a 'question that had never been settled, largely because it had so rarely been raised'.[48] Margaret Judson also senses the spirit of letting sleeping dogs lie: 'it is not easy to determine exactly how the royalists felt about the lawmaking power, for, like their Parliamentary opponents, they seldom discussed it'.[49] The constitution, therefore, did not just rest upon the feasibility of unanswered questions; it also survived by proceeding on the basis of questions remaining unasked. In general, 'as long as men agreed in substance, theoretical tensions aroused little conflict'.[50]

Far from being signs of terminal decline, the predilection for 'sliding past one another' had been a hallmark of the constitution's prudence and resilience stretching back even to the Tudor period. It did not embody a critical condition. It was a sign of utter normality. There were tensions and there were contradictions, but the constitution was still infused with the medieval ideal of organic harmony in which all the parts possessed the quality of basic inclusivity, in spite of occasional appearances to the contrary. It was not yet significant whether reference was made to constitutions or to the constitution. Sabine and Thorson are quite correct in stating that

> the older assumption of comity and harmony between these powers under the fundamental law of the realm could still be made, without considering the ultimate legal supremacy of any of them. The traditional rights and limitations which fixed, vaguely but with sufficient precision, the status of all parts of the constitution had not yet been strained to the breaking point.[51]

Although just such a breaking point eventually arrived, it is a misrepresentation to portray the Stuart constitution as one intrinsically predestined to collapse. The histories and commentaries of the period are at pains to point out that things could so easily have been different; that the development of the constitution could have taken a different course, or, just as likely, could have taken the same ambiguous course under different circumstances.[52] This is not to say that the practical processes of government were not subjected to the most severe military, religious, financial, and social stresses during the 1630s and 1640s. The magnitude of these might well have been so great that they would have overrun any form of government irrespective of personnel and organization. But in so far as constitutional confrontation was not merely the occasion, but an active generative cause of social and economic conflict, then it can be claimed that if the prolonged political crisis had been managed more adroitly in accordance with the customary spirit of the constitution, the outcome would not have been as foreclosed as it is often portrayed.

The Stuart constitution was heavily dependent upon the maintenance of a stable level of benign, bona fide ambiguity within which interests, ideas, and institutions became manageable and even reconcilable in practice despite appearing to be at cross purposes in form and logic. The constitution rested upon positions not being pressed beyond the bounds of what was tacitly and intuitively accepted. In this way, rights, honour, and reputation could be satisfactorily preserved. Not surprisingly, strong emphasis was always placed upon the value of subtlety, delicacy, and sensitivity in what was literally in these conditions the art of government.

Historians and commentaries agree that Elizabeth was unsurpassed in the skill and guile with which she handled Parliament, managed her court, supervised her finances and in general attended to her position. She was able to protect and cultivate her prerogative powers by a virtuoso performance in leadership and concession, rewards and punishment, charm and anger, threats and magnanimity, but above all by an acute sense of political astuteness and tact. Elizabeth set the standard against which subsequent monarchs were judged. While it is undoubtedly true that Elizabeth's manipulative flair has been exaggerated and that she did not have to face the sort of conditions that arose later in the seventeenth century, her reign nevertheless illustrates how the constitution could be made to work effectively with a monarch whose sureness of political touch did much to compensate for the indefinite nature of that constitution.

The early Stuarts were never able to match her skill. James I was too bound up in the broad sweep of monarchical power to appreciate the value of tactics, adroitness, and attention to detail. For example, James 'allowed the prerogative to be tested in the courts which Elizabeth would never have done'.[53] And yet, in spite of his pretentions to divine and distant kingship, James had the ability to step behind the edifice and to engage in the collaborative process of negotiating agreements with others who also possessed rights and powers. James might have had his eyes set on high monarchy, but 'his bark was worse than his bite, and no sensible man could take his claims too seriously'.[54] He retained the ability to, in his own words to Parliament, 'wink and connive at the execution of some penal statutes, and not to go on too rigorously as at other times'.[55] No such levity could ever have been expected from Charles I.

Charles Stuart was noted for his remoteness and rigidity in the face of conditions that required contact and adaptability. Even amongst those who emphasize the socio-economic causes of the civil war, there remains a strong sense that the critical conditions of the late 1630s and early 1640s were aggravated, if not directly provoked, by the personal ineptitude of the monarch.[56] Charles fluctuated unnervingly between accommodation and imperiousness, between constitutional pledges to restrict his authority and pledges to the constitution to enlarge his authority, and between promises made and promises discarded. Such fluctuations produced a disjunction between, on the one hand, the constitution as conceived by many of his leading and most vociferous subjects and to which Charles paid intermittent lip service and, on the other hand, the constitution that authorized the king to transcend constraint in the service of his subjects' welfare. Charles's evasiveness and even deviousness over which conception of the constitution he was conforming to at any one time, together with his indifference towards giving adequate explanations of his changing positions, engendered a level of suspicion and distrust that can make the final breakdown of the constitution seem like the inevitable conclusion of an ineluctable process. But for the aptitude, conduct and policies of Charles, the course of the Stuart constitution might well have been markedly different.

It is possible to speculate in all manner of ways on such a subject, but what remains quite evident is the enormous reserves of popular attachment and allegiance to the established order of patriarchal authority, even in the critical period of the 1640s. The 'stop in the mind' concerning notions of Parliamentary sovereignty or violent rebellion was as much in evidence in 1642 as it had been in 1628 when Charles's threat to dissolve Parliament in response to the Petition of Right did not produce a groundswell of republican insurgency, but instead 'caused many Parliamentary leaders to weep'[57] tears of grief as misunderstood subjects. In the end the result was a crisis in the monarchy, but there was nothing irrevocable about the degeneration of the process of government into open disarray. On the contrary, there was considerable potential for the settlement of outstanding disputes by recourse to old loyalties and customary practices. That this potential was not effectively tapped and was instead wastefully dissipated should not be seen as proof of a terminal disorder.

The silence of constitutions

The tensions and anomalies implicit in such a disorder are better seen as inherent characteristics of a sophisticated constitution which, under more skilful leadership and more normal conditions, had the capacity to provide scope for the expression and resolution of conflict. With careful handling, its obscurities could be made to work and even flourish — so long as they are kept obscure and the idea of winners and losers, victories and defeats, advances and retreats remain as muddled as before. It was the threat of innovative clarity that posed the greatest danger. This fact was well understood by Thomas Wentworth when he warned the House of Commons in 1621, 'lett's not with too much curiousity enter theis things . . . lett us not question *archana imperii*'[58] and again in 1628, 'I hope it shall never be stirred here whether the king be above the law or the law above the king.'[59]

That such warnings and recommendations needed to be made at all can be taken as testimony to the redundancy of such a constitution. Indeed, it can even be claimed that evasiveness of this order was tantamount to proof that no constitution worthy of the name existed. But it was precisely because of its lack of definition, its indeterminate lines of authority, and its agreed abeyances that the constitution succeeded not only in accommodating differences in difficult circumstances, but in fostering a constitutional culture of exceptional vitality and durability. Instead of seeing the Stuart constitution as one plagued with weaknesses, therefore, it should more appropriately be conceived as one of strength — in having continued in adverse conditions for as long as it did; in having had the capacity to have gone on longer in the right hands; and in requiring no less than a civil war to bring it to an end.

Chapter three

Constitutional abeyances and crisis conditions: the imperial presidency

At first sight, there would appear to be no point of comparison between the Stuart and the American constitutions. The constitution that early seventeenth-century Englishmen had inherited was an incoherent assemblage of unresolved tensions and genuine inconsistencies that only remained workable through cultivated evasion and a simultaneous attachment to varying criteria of analysis and legitimacy. The American constitution, by contrast, is portrayed as the exemplification of modern constitutionalism. It is a codified framework of institutions, powers, procedures, and rights which has become invested with an accepted authority, thereby elevating the constitution to 'the supreme law of the land'. Unlike the Stuart constitution, the American constitution seems to possess the capacity to define the principles and organization of public authority in terms which not only closely correspond to, but seem directly to account for, the actual exercise of power. In other words, the United States constitution has the reputation of providing a comprehensive and systematic structure of government embodying a constitutional settlement in which such major issues as institutional powers, legal rights, and even sovereignty have not had to be suspended or held in abeyance, but have been conclusively resolved through the format of legal stipulation.

A number of the US constitution's characteristics, and the political developments closely associated with it, have lent substantial weight to the notion that American government is known, understood, and accounted for. First is the fundamental fact that it is a written constitution. Agencies are enumerated, powers are delineated, rights are defined. Its documentary nature is significant in that it suggests, by its very nature, the presence of a unified and coherent government structure. Furthermore, it also predisposes the mind to accept the constitution as a document built on the resolution of fundamental disputes concerning the nature and structure of public authority. By implication, such disputes would need to have reached a sufficient level of settlement before a constitution could have been set down and committed to print. More important, however, is the sense that the constitution's brevity and longevity indicate that the settlement must have been a substantive and decisive one. The United States constitution ranks as the oldest written constitution in existence, and certainly as one of the briefest. As such, it is naturally envisaged as reflecting a social solidarity on the means and purposes of government — a solidarity that could only have remained so solid with a constitution thought clear enough to be satisfactorily free from debilitating anomalies, ambiguities and disjunctions.

A second factor contributing to the apparent absence of the indeterminate in the American constitution is the way the constitution was written. It is commonly suggested that the constitution bears the hallmark of systematization that comes from the rationalistic dispositions and objectives of its authors. Men like James Madison, Alexander Hamilton, and Benjamin Franklin were imbued with the confidence of the Enlightenment, with the belief in the ordered regularity of a harmonious nature which held out the prospect of eliciting universal laws of human behaviour and social dynamics.

This image of a universe of systematic cause and effect permeated the eighteenth century and is widely thought to have been particularly salient in the US, where in 1787 the Founding Fathers were confronted with the need to design and construct a system of government from scratch.[1] That they grasped the opportunity and believed that a workable form of government could be rationally contrived through the assimilation and application of empirically derived principles of political behaviour was a significant testament to the Enlightenment's faith in the accessibility of government's fundamental nature. More to the point, the very fact that the American constitution was a 'conscious creation of the mind'[2] — particularly of the eighteenth-century mind, with its predilection for Newtonian models of mechanical interrelationships — creates an even stronger impression of an exact and integrated framework of government. So well-integrated was this framework that the constitution's structural and dynamic characteristics can easily be made to seem the natural legacy of a 'massive effort of political engineering'[3] and 'probably the most important instance we have of the deliberate application of a mechanical philosophy to human affairs.'[4]

This leads us to a third factor in the American constitution's professed format of systematized unity, namely, the status of the separation of powers and of the associated checks and balances as the government's chief structural and operational characteristic. Irrespective of whether the constitution was as rationally designed and as scientifically motivated as it is reputed to have been, the complex series of functional and spatial restraints on the internal organization of government has bequeathed the constitution with every sign of being a self-regulating mechanism. Indeed, the constitution appears to be so systematic and self-contained that it is common for the language of Newtonian mechanics to be called upon as terms of description.[5]

These analytical allusions to mechanics are seen as neither far-fetched nor implausible, but as justifiable and accurate commentaries on the actual condition of American politics and government. The widely accepted accounts of the constitution as a 'system of checks and balances and interlocked gears of government . . . designed for deadlock and inaction'[6] is typically used as prelude to urgent calls for the structural reform of government. Kevin Phillips, for example, has criticized its 'archaic constitutional provisions', including the separation of powers, for causing a 'destructive warp of power . . . [and] distorting the logical evolution of technology-era government'. He joins many others in advocating a 'fusion of powers tying Congress and the executive together, eliminating checks and balances and creating a new system'.[7] That this appeal is made on such grounds is a commentary on the perceived inability of the government to adapt to modern conditions and requirements. Ironically, however, the very futility of such demands for constitutional reform adds even greater support to the notion that the constitution has no substantial gaps, that there is little or no room for major adjustment, and that there is no chance whatsoever of breaking out of a system made intractable by its own regularized dynamics.

Implicit in the constitution's apparent immunity to change lies a fourth factor, the instinctive, widespread reluctance to tamper with a constitution valued and even venerated as complete in itself. The constitution is often portrayed as having been bequeathed in its final form from the moment of its inception. This affective attachment to the constitution can take many forms. On occasion, the cult of the constitution can reach religious and even mystical proportions. Daniel Boorstin, for example, believes that the Founding Fathers equipped the United States

> at its birth with a perfect and complete political theory, adequate to all our future needs . . . Our mission, then, is simply to demonstrate the truth — or rather the workability — of the original theory . . . . Constitutional history can, and in many ways has, become a substitute for political theory.[8]

On other occasions, the constitution is venerated because of its role in the nation's historical and political development. The document assumes the identity of the nation itself. It has come to represent, for example, 'the lifeblood of the American nation, its supreme symbol and manifestation . . . so intimately welded with the national existence itself that the two have become inseparable'.[9] Whatever the reason behind the conservatism surrounding the constitution, the effects are the same: to infuse the constitution with an impregnable authority and, in doing so, to give it an implicit quality of being a totality not only of historical experience, but also of political provision.

A fifth component in the constitution's pedigree further enhances the document's image of inherent meaning and definition. This ingredient consists of the way that the American tradition of natural or fundamental law has been incorporated within the American constitution and maintained through the medium of constitutional interpretation. The traditional idea of a pre-existing and predominant code of constant and universal legal principles, to which enacted law deferred for authority and substance, was not superseded by the constitution. On the contrary, the strictures of higher law were transmuted into it. This has had the most profound repercussions in the political system, not least upon the role and power of the judiciary. But perhaps the most extensive impact was on the nature of the constitution itself: by becoming a recognized repository of fundamental law, it has fostered the belief that the constitution is an inexhaustible source of law in any area and on any subject.[10] According to Henry S. Commager, the Founding Fathers proceeded on the basis that the function of men was not to make the law, but to discover and publish it.

> Constitutions were but transcripts of natural law, and the ideal toward which all rational lawmakers aspired was a government which should reduce the merely human factor to a minimum — a government of laws not of men.[11]

This outlook has been sustained for many reasons and through many devices. It has resulted in the constitution being perceived and used as a densely packed plenum of legal content made continuously ascertainable through human reason and interpretation.

On the basis of these five factors, there has arisen in the United States a phenomenon that could be termed 'flat constitutionalism'. This refers to the way in which the American constitution is commonly viewed, understood, and used as a document fixed in print, formed in content, and uniform in the basis of its authority. In contrast to the Stuart constitution, so apparently fatally flawed with its cross-cutting dimensions of meaning and authority, the American constitution is distinguished for its unidimensional quality. The reason is straightforward: the constitution was written as a single document in a short period of time by a single collective act of creation. But the result is more complex. Because the constitution is characterized as emanating from a single source, it has assumed a continuity by which any subsequent development can be related back to a fixed point of departure and explained as a determinant of its past. This does not mean that the American constitution has remained static, but it does mean that while the constitution has widened and developed in form and interpretation, it is seen as having done so along a single historical continuum preserved from competing dimensions of power, authority, or sovereignty.

Reinforcing this notion of a conclusive and continuing constitutional settlement is the infusion of higher law principles and authority into the constitution. It is conceived as a timeless and autonomous 'set of wheels and mechanisms'[12] and granted a social status which equates it with the American experience of nationhood. Because of the American consensus that the constitution possesses a finite, grid-iron nature, it is perceived as assimilating change only on its own terms and then only 'within the four corners of the document'.[13]

The net result is to confer upon the constitution a reputation for absolute political resolution and legal integrity. While the Stuart constitution stands condemned for its unsustained multi-dimensionality of divine rule, common law, and Parliamentary rights, the American constitution is celebrated as a model of a fully developed, clarified, and established authority and, therefore, as a document free from the elaborate devices inhibiting free inquiry and obscuring constitutional contradictions on which the government of the early seventeenth century depended for its survival.

Yet, despite its reputation as a self-evidently unified system of political authority and organization, the American constitution is not as immune from internal anomalies and disjunctions as it is often perceived. On the contrary, under closer examination the coherence of its content and legitimacy is far from being unassailably secure. One obvious indication of this is the prodigious amount of conflict over the scope of the constitution's legitimate sphere of authority. Much of this conflict can be explained away as the competitive interplay of a checks and balances system, or as the natural consequence of a written constitution requiring textual interpretation. Nevertheless, there remains a residuum of less conspicuous and more underrated conflict for which we cannot so easily account. We are left with a profound scepticism concerning the coherence of the American constitution, with the strong suspicion that the constitution is by no means the fully worked out and decisively resolved foundation of government that it is normally believed to be.

Fortunately for the constitution (and not least for the stability of the country) such inconsistencies are rarely perceived, let alone publicly acknowledged or subjected to close scrutiny. Only on rare occasions do the deeply embedded disjunctions rise up to disturb the tranquil surface waters with the prospect of coexisting yet incompatible and irreducible elements of political principle. But when they do occur, these disfunctions are marked by severe constitutional crises. Because they are so rarely exposed, the constitution's normally obscured divisions and anomalies have all the more force when they are brought to the surface.

Major crises in American government, therefore, are of great value not just because they reveal the presence of previously unsuspected forms of conflict, but because they disclose something of the manner by which such anomalies are managed under normal conditions. They also demonstrate that the American constitution is not so strikingly different from many other constitutions and that there are even significant similarities and points of comparison between it and pre-modern constitutions like that of the Stuart government. Going even further, we can argue that the Stuart constitution can offer surprisingly valuable insights into the United States's constitutional culture and, in particular, into its cultivation of constitutional abeyances.

The American experience with abeyances was probably shown to its greatest effect in what ranks as the most severe constitutional crisis in American twentieth-century history: the 'imperial presidency' episode of the 1970s which culminated in the Watergate scandal.[14] This many-layered, multi-faceted crisis was significant in two main respects: firstly, for the actual substance of the charges laid against the Nixon administration for its unlawful mismanagement of government business; and secondly, for the way in which the confrontation was conducted between the presidency and the other major institutions engaged in the crisis.

The several related scandals that were subsumed under the collective term 'Watergate' climaxed a process of progressive disenchantment with presidential power which had been in evidence since the closing years of the Johnson administration. Public anxiety had been induced by the presence of increasingly isolated chief executives intent upon ruthlessly following their own policies against considerable opposition and on assuming for themselves a mantle of higher obligation to the public and to the nation. Through these devices, they developed an invulnerability to opposition, even to the extent of throwing into doubt the legitimacy of dissent.

The persistence and intractability of Nixon's policies, particularly in the crucial field of national security and foreign policy, gave rise to the accusation that the president was usurping constitutional powers. This had resulted in a 'new balance of constitutional powers',[15] by which the presidency had become transmuted into an 'imperial presidency' with an apparently dictatorial capacity to inflate and abuse its powers at will. The reason for the disquiet was not merely the scale of presidential power. It was the growing realization that this power was threateningly different in nature from the powers normally conceived to be invested in the other major institutions of government. It seemed to an acutely anxious public that the presidency had acquired a set of exclusive and unassailable prerogative powers, intrinsic to its executive status and imperative to its executive responsibilities. The spectre of this presidential hegemony excited renewed public interest in the dynamics of the constitutional system, and subsequently prompted the political challenge to the Nixon presidency which came to fruition during the Watergate crisis.

Watergate became a crisis largely because it reopened one of the darkest and most brooding issues at the heart of the constitution. It made manifest and exposed to the corrosive light of public examination an issue which had never been satisfactorily resolved by the constitution. Contrary to both appearance and reputation, the nature and role of the executive within a fully constitutional system had only ever been successfully deferred to an inconclusive state in which the executive's position was determined by a constantly shifting pattern of needs, conditions, precedents, traditions, and personalities. The Watergate crisis succeeded in opening up the question of executive power to intensive analysis and critical evaluation with a brutal insurgency and dangerously inquisitive appetite for precision which were quite alien to the conventional manner of accommodating the presidency within the constitution's sphere of legitimacy. President Nixon may well have provoked the crisis through his actions and style of government, but the severity of the crisis was clearly a product of the iconoclasm implicit in subjecting an office such as the presidency to a form of scrutiny to which it was wholly unaccustomed and which it was quite unable to withstand for any sustained period of time. Although it was the Nixon administration that appeared to be under the most direct assault, therefore, it was the evolved structure of protective ambiguity, cautionary obscurity, and conventional reticence that had previously surrounded the presidency which represented the more significant casualty of the attack.

During the imperial presidency episode, the trauma visited upon the customary layer of constitutional abeyance concerning executive power was made all the more intense because of the previous record of success that such abeyance had had in deflecting attention from the subject. The instinctive cultural evasiveness over the constitutional implications of modern executive power had essentially been the product of two central factors.

First was the actuality of the presidency's acquired position and power in modern American society. Since the New Deal and the Second World War, the president's role and responsibilities had become so broadened that the office not only reached unprecedented levels of institutionalization, but achieved a central significance in the conduct of policy-making and in the direction of policy objectives. The presidency, in effect, became such an integral part of the post-war system of American government that the office's energy and initiative were commonly equated with the substance of government as a whole. 'Presidential government' came to signify the contemporary shift towards a modern positive state with its attendant requirements of government intervention and regulation.[16]

As a corollary to this first point, the power of the office was also seen as an unavoidable consequence of the United States's position as a world power in an insecure and threatening international arena. Responsibility for reacting to the complexities of foreign policy and national security seemed to devolve naturally upon the president, thereby giving the incumbent an established prominence and a pronounced element of indispensibility.[17] The presidency came to rest upon its intrinsic capacity to react to an increasing number of critical, or potentially critical, issues that could not be adequately dealt with by any other agency of government. These responsibilities, combined with the organizational requirements of a state servicing the myriad demands of an advanced industrial society, transformed the presidency within a generation from an executive functionary into an expression of national consciousness, social purpose, and superpower responsibility. The presidency became crucial to the effective functioning of government, for without its active and coordinative role, the whole framework of policy and administration was thought to be in jeopardy. Such was the contribution made by the office that to all intents and purposes 'the President was the government for millions of Americans'.[18] The primary assumption was that 'the President and the state were the same thing, that President was state personified'.[19]

The second great pillar of presidential power was the prescriptive support lent to the office by both professional commentators and the general public. Superimposed upon the declared needs of executive action and the recognized imperatives of executive responsibilities, grew a positive, and even enthusiastic, encouragement to presidents to seize opportunities for power and to maximize the president's sphere of operation. The growth in presidential power was sanctioned as the key requirement in moving the nation towards its historical destiny and galvanizing the country into forming a coherent order of national purpose and social progress.

As a result, the presidential office became celebrated in American politics as a redemptive force striving heroically in adverse conditions to marshal those resources of national and social progress that would otherwise have remained separated and isolated within an otherwise dangerously static political system.[20] 'Historians, political scientists and journalists . . . generally held that a strong presidency was a necessity'[21] in order to ensure the future of the nation and the freedom of its people. Such was the importance attached to the presidency's role as catalyst that Richard Neustadt was led to conclude that 'what is good for the country is good for the president and vice versa'.[22] Good presidents were seen as great presidents, and great presidents were identified and sanctified as strong presidents — and by strong was meant

> their mastery of events, their influence on history, their shaping of the country's destiny, their capacity to draw talented men to their side,

their ability to magnify their own department, at the expense of the other branches.[23]

Such was the cultural sanction afforded to presidential power that the office's status served not only to symbolize the contemporary social consensus and national unity on major objectives, but also to translate that solidarity into an active instrument of mobilized political expression. The presidency became synonymous with the concepts and physical entities of both 'the people' and 'the nation'. Just as 'the state of the Presidency could be regarded as the state of the nation',[24] so presidents assumed the almost exclusive proprietary right to speak for, and to act on behalf of, the public by portraying themselves as the 'personification of the people'[25] and of its common ideals, values, and aspirations.

The cult of the modern presidency that had been woven around the strictures of national necessity and the inducements of popular demand, and galvanized by the self-advancement and media saturation of the presidents themselves, generated what at first sight appeared to be a robust and durable mantle of legitimacy. Presidential apologists could point to the office's enriched democratic credentials, derived from the national electoral process and the successful cultivation of the notion that the president could be relied upon to use the power entrusted to him on behalf of the public interest. Authority was also claimed on the grounds that it was incumbent upon the executive to react to the emergent challenges of an advanced industrial society and to the exigencies of superpower rivalry by employing those capacities intrinsic and exclusive to the executive, in order to ensure society's continued viability. Presidential prominence, therefore, could be taken as the imprimatur of a successfully adaptive system of government. By responding to these new conditions, the presidency showed itself to be not just the chief adaptive force within the system, but the chief means by which the system at large revealed itself to be efficiently responsive. When the idea that overriding conditions and circumstances necessarily required presidential predominance was joined to a popular attachment to the traditional themes of precedent, historical continuity, and custom, the result was a potent, if incoherent, structure of authority.

This authority had a distinct *de facto* quality: in essence, it was derived from a mainstream consensus on the major objectives of society and, therefore, on the general configuration of government. It was a public philosophy that condoned presidential power rather than rationalized it.[26] Very little attention was given to the nature, basis, and possible ramifications of such power. There appeared no need to question its authority or to cast doubt on its validity. On the contrary, it was assumed to be within the rule of law and to be thoroughly amenable to normal constitutional processes.

The silence of constitutions

The Supreme Court afforded presidential power the mantle of constitutional legitimacy by generally deflecting the issues raised by the scale and nature of executive power away from concentrated legal attention. This practiced form of abeyance generally took the shape of designating those cases concerning presidential power as 'political questions' to be reserved to the 'political branches of government' for resolution.[27] Such judicial self-restraint prevented the Supreme Court from becoming embroiled in cases of heightened party and political interest that might well have endangered its own standing within the governmental system. But it also meant that the cases likely to arouse the most intense controversy were precisely those kept at bay, and suffused in conflicting political and constitutional arguments. That the Supreme Court was able to relegate questions concerning executive power to other agencies, and thereupon to constitutional oblivion, was a reflection not only of the Court's own political subtlety, but also of the social equanimity surrounding the presidency at the time. The Supreme Court's reticence further encouraged the public to view the powers of the modern executive as intrinsically the same as those of other political centres of power and, as a result, as being similarly susceptible to the normal interplay of that system's checks and balances.

Presidential power, however, did not acquire its constitutionality solely by default. On the limited occasions that the Supreme Court felt compelled to intervene and apply constitutional definitions and sanctions to the office, the results generally worked in favour of executive power. More often than not, the Court was led to affirm the office's expanded role and responsibilities in contemporary American society. Nowhere was this licence more in evidence than in the area of foreign policy and national security.[28] This was the field in which executive obligations were greater, more urgent, and more important than any other. Moreover, they were more elusively indeterminate and resistant to prior demarcation or clear definition — turning as they did upon the president's irrefutable duty to meet a crisis 'in the shape that it presented itself . . . without waiting for any special legislative authority'.[29] The need for an integral and purposeful agency to provide urgent and authoritative responses to threatening world conditions and to maintain a supervisory grasp of the changing requirements of foreign policy came to be universally acknowledged as representing the very essence of the executive's governmental function, and the subtleties and dangers of international relations were recognized as being almost wholly executive in character. The Supreme Court therefore tended to give the presidency a very wide berth in connection with the burdens of the office's foreign-policy and defence responsibilities. It largely acquiesced in the face of what appeared to be the modern presidency's self-evident right to discretion in this most imperative of circumstances. In doing so, the Court gave tacit approval to the presidency's 'stewardship theory' of implied or reserved executive powers to be deployed as conditions warranted and to be validated constitutionally by the principle that it was not only the president's 'right but his duty to do anything that the needs of the nation demanded . . . unless such action was forbidden by the constitution or by the laws'.[30]

When the Court did feel the need to make pronouncements in this field, it found it difficult to detach such factors as convention, precedent, tradition, practice, and circumstance from the purely legal criteria of constitutionality. As a consequence upon entering the field, the Court was compelled to acknowledge and, thereby, to validate both the existence of a shadowy structure of evolved executive prerogative and discretion, and the means by which such a structure had come into existence — i.e. 'of rights, duties and obligations growing out of the constitution itself, our international relations, and all the protection implied by the nature of the government under the constitution'.[31] Under such conditions, the Court was only too well aware that any attempt to confine the executive within tightly defined constitutional boundaries risked being either conceptually implausible or politically inappropriate, or both.

Sometimes the Supreme Court conceded a form of defeat at the outset and would intervene for the sole purpose of legitimizing executive prerogative and even of extending its scope. In the case of the *United States v. Curtiss-Wright Export Corporation* (1936), for example, the Court went to great, and arguably excessive, lengths to rationalize the pre-eminence of the presidential office in the conduct of the country's relationships abroad. Although the Court paid lip service to the executive's required 'subordination to the applicable provisions of the constitution', it stressed the president's 'very delicate, plenary and exclusive power . . . as the sole organ of the federal government in the field of international relations'[32] and thus came perilously close to investing the office of the president with a specifically extra-constitutional status.

On other occasions, the Court gave the impression of turning against the presidency and invoked the checks and balances system in response to an excessive use of executive power. But even in these cases the Court remained cautious and circumspect in the face of the executive's need for discretionary powers and its capacity for eluding legal barriers. The Court felt a responsibility, on the one hand, to avoid erecting crude and crippling legal obstacles in a field requiring finesse and subtlety, whilst on the other hand it hastened to prevent the rule of law from being undermined through the imposition of unenforceable legal strictures upon an executive function. In deciding against an individual action of an individual chief executive, the Court could in the process affirm, by implication, the constitutionality of broad swathes of discretionary power accumulated in the presidential office.

The silence of constitutions

This occurred in the celebrated case of *Youngstown Sheet & Tube Company v. Sawyer* (1952).[33] In this case, the Supreme Court appeared to censure President Truman for his seizure of several major steel mills during a labour dispute. Amidst a blaze of publicity, Truman was seen to lose the case by a majority decision of six to three. Nevertheless, in reaching its decision, the Court qualified its position with such a variety of provisos and caveats that it was by no means clear at the end whether the Court had struck a blow for long-term constitutional restraint. Apart from the fact that there were six opinions in which individuals and groups of justices argued out their positions on different grounds, seven out of the nine justices carefully steered a course away from the sensitive, yet nebulous, area of the executive's implied powers. In the course of invalidating Truman's action as a specific abuse of executive power, the Court tended to confer legitimacy upon the undefined residuum of contingent presidential power in other areas and under different conditions. For example, in pronouncing Truman's seizure of the steel mills as an illegitimate turning inward of his commander-in-chief's power upon a domestic economic struggle, Justice Jackson was prompted to concede that he would 'indulge the widest latitude of interpretation to sustain' the president's 'exclusive function to command the instruments of national force, at least when turned against the outside world for the security of our society'.[34]

Whether by accident or design, whether by a concerted absence of definition or by a conscious affirmation of prerogative powers, the Supreme Court cannot be said to have really challenged the mainstream social legitimacy of the modern presidency during the course of its development. On the contrary, it quietly and discreetly endorsed it. Commentators such as Richard Funston, for example, now allude to an 'affinity between the Supreme Court and the Presidency'.[35]

> For a number of reasons, the public has desired a strong executive. Generally the Supreme Court has functioned to legitimate this desire by rationalizing it in terms of constitutional principles. The Court has often engaged constitutional philosophy to shore up presidential actions that were otherwise legally suspect. Instead of creating ways to restrain Presidential power, the Court has labored to reinforce the presidency.[36]

At no point has the Supreme Court asserted any disquieting propositions that the presidency might be qualitatively distinct from the rest of the government and therefore constitute a threatening force or an aberration within a constitutional system. The logic and rationale behind the American constitution has always been weighted towards the limitation of governmental authority.[37] The onset of the modern presidency might be thought to have posed a direct challenge to such an ethos. With its discretionary licence, its exclusive spheres of authority, and its separate roots of identity and power, both the nature and scope of executive force might have been viewed as something no longer strictly within the constitution, or of it, or even accountable to it.

Yet the period was marked by a remarkable equanimity over presidential power — an equanimity born out of an abiding trust in the leadership and judgement of individual presidents and the belief that executive authority was thoroughly compatible with the constitution and its institutional dynamics. Presidents such as Harry Truman preached that 'as the pages of history were written they unfolded powers in the presidency not explicitly found in Article II'[38] and yet were 'derived from the constitution, and . . . were limited of course, by the provisions of the constitution'.[39] Supreme Court justices like Felix Frankfurter reasoned that 'a systematic, unbroken, executive practice, long pursued to the knowledge of the Congress and never before questioned, engaged in by presidents who have also sworn to uphold the constitution, making as it were such exercise of power part of the structure of our government, may be treated as a gloss on "executive power" vested in the president'[40] by the constitution. And constitutional scholars such as Edward S. Corwin gave assurances that the president's extra-constitutional prerogatives were integral to the maintenance and survival of the constitution. In this way, the circle could be squared; 'the president's very obligation to the law became at times an authorization to dispense with the law'.[41]

In the past, doubts about the legitimacy of presidential power had been resolved by curbing it. But the modern era was marked by the demise of any comforting fluctuations in executive advances and retreats. The power of the modern presidency was characterized as an established feature of the political system and integral to its viability. Moreover, as the magnitude and complexity of the government's responsibilities increased, so the presidency appeared to be engaged in a linear and irreversible progression of development. And yet, in spite of what appeared to be 'the inevitability of the upward course of the presidency',[42] there arose conspicuously little public concern over the presidential office and even less sustained objection to its power. If anything, the need for, and the legitimacy of, the presidency were positively condoned to the extent where many recognized, and even enthused over, the presence of 'presidential government' in the United States.

Whether public attitudes underwent a radical change, or the scale of presidential power reached an unacceptable level, the net effect was that in the late 1960s and early 1970s the presidency suffered a decline in stature. Just when its prestige and power seemed most intact, the office was suddenly surrounded by disaffection and agitation. What used to be accepted as an inevitable, trustworthy, and benevolent force in American society began to be viewed as a disquieting centre of exclusive power, intractable policy, and political unaccountability. The scale of distrust and incomprehension seemed in direct proportion to the earlier condition of acquiescence and assurance.

Evidence of the excesses and abuses of presidential power provoked a quite incongruous and thoroughly alarmist overreaction. The air became thick with references to an 'imperial presidency',[43] 'Presidential autocracy',[44] 'executive hegemony in government',[45] 'militarized authoritarian government', and even to an 'imperial dictatorship'.[46] Arthur M. Schlesinger, Jr., claimed that the president had become 'the most absolute monarch (with the possible exception of Mao Tse-tung of China) among the great powers of the world'.[47] Even more uninhibited was Henry Steele Commager, who warned that 'had Mr Nixon succeeded in his pretensions and ambitions, the character of the American presidency would have been decisively and perhaps irrevocably altered, and with it the character of the American constitutional system'. Commager concluded that 'such a shift in the centre of political and constitutional gravity would have led logically to totalitarianism'.[48] The hyperbole betrayed a sort of culture shock. An office which had been the object of so much public conviction now stood revealed as capable of political abuse. And, more importantly, a plethora of deep-seated conflicts within the constitutional substructure had become exposed to the sulphurous atmosphere of eroded trust and institutional confrontation.

Previously these structural flaws had been obscured and thereby made manageable by a range of assumptions, devices, and condoned practices through which the power and position of the executive had acquired a makeshift, yet durable, authority. The fact that many of the executive's privileges and prerogatives had not been constitutionally marked out or satisfactorily resolved to a level anywhere near that of valid finality had remained, by common acquiescence, a largely moot point. For most of the period during which the modern presidency developed, the ambiguous position of executive power within the constitutional system was kept in that condition by a generally accepted protocol of inattention and evasion. Participants conformed to constitutional abeyances, content in the knowledge that the nature and extent of such a power could be accommodated most effectively through a *modus vivendi* of mutual understandings, political flexibility, and reciprocal trust. When this normative network of conduct between the presidency and the Congress broke down, it generated an atmosphere of extravagant charge and counter-charge as the conflicting parties reached for fundamental constitution principles to support their position.

The collapse of the abeyance system meant that a serious crisis became a grave one. Both parties became painfully disabused of the reach of their own power and shocked at each other's now sharpened and dogmatic conception of their own rightful authority. To President Nixon, Congress was proving itself to be an irresponsible and politically motivated destroyer of established constitutional practice. In the eyes of Congress, President Nixon presented the disconcerting spectacle of executive potential transformed into a genuine and impregnable prerogative power. Believing that it had been deceived and exploited by the president, Congress reacted with hostility. Their ire was only heightened by their realization that they had deceived themselves into regarding the presidency as inherently subject to normal constitutional dynamics and accountable to the usual channels of accustomed understandings and diversionary arrangements.

The move to breach abeyances and plunge into the unresolved and insoluble underworld of constitutional fundamenta was occasioned by a whole range of issues. War-making authority, executive agreements, emergency powers, impoundments, and executive privilege all became constitutional flashpoints that served to invoke intense political controversy and, thereby, to incite rigorous constitutional scrutiny. Of these, it was probably the issue of impoundment which best represented the transitional process by which a power, that had been exercised in an attentuated, provisional, and negotiated manner by previous presidents, was transformed by President Nixon to one of exclusive executive authority. This was an authority to be exercised regardless of underlying motives, political intentions, or even the scale of its deployment.

By custom, the practice of impoundment was an element of executive discretion by which congressionally authorized expenditure could be deferred or even rescinded.[49] At first sight, it appeared to conflict with the constitution and, in particular, with the functional rationale of the separation of powers. For the president to impound funds passed by Congress, for example, was arguably tantamount to an infringement on Congress's legislative and spending powers, to a failure of the president's constitutional duty to faithfully execute the laws, and to a unilateral presumption of a line-item veto. Nevertheless, a case for legitimate executive discretion could be made on three counts. First, it could be claimed that implicit in the president's general executive obligations was the managerial authority to conduct his administration in the most efficient and economical way possible, even to the extent of amending the pattern of expenditures in the light of changing circumstances. For instance, if a government service could be satisfactorily performed at a cost lower than that for which it had been budgeted, or if there was no longer a need for a particular government programme, it could be assumed that the executive was obligated to prevent such unnecessary expenditure.

The second source of impoundment discretion lay in Congress's own actions in affording the executive statutory powers over the control and direction of government spending. The Anti-Deficiency Act of 1950, for example, included the following recommendation.

> In apportioning any appropriation, reserves may be established to provide for contingencies, or to effect savings whenever savings are made possible by or through changes in requirements, greater efficiency of operations, or other developments subsequent to the date on which such apportionment was made available.[50]

Furthermore, Congress has on occasions permitted the administration to impound funds of state and local governments or of federal contractors who were in breach of federal regulations. On other occasions, Congress has further reinforced the notion of executive spending discretion by passing budget ceiling measures in which the president has received congressionally delegated authority to make specified cuts or blanket reductions.

The third constituent of the executive's impoundment power was that of precedent. Presidents could refer to their predecessors' actions in refusing to spend appropriated funds; by doing so, they sought to erect a claim to authority on the grounds of accumulated precedent, historical experience, and established usage. As President Thomas Jefferson had deferred expenditure for gun boats in 1803, the executive's claims to inherent power could stretch back to the formative years of the republic and the constitution.

The claim of historical precedent was indeed one of real substance. In 1876, President Ulysses S. Grant impounded what he regarded as unduly wasteful expenditure on rivers and harbours schemes. In 1931, Herbert Hoover imposed a 10 per cent cut in federal spending under the pretext of creating budgetary reserves through 'savings'. During the Second World War, Franklin Roosevelt used the emphasis on defence to slow down the implementation of domestic programmes, so that by the end of 1943 as much as $500 million earmarked for public-works schemes had been impounded. Harry Truman impounded funds for air force and naval projects and John F. Kennedy held back money for the RS-70 bomber project. Under Lyndon Johnson, impoundments reached a level of $10 billion; in his economic message to Congress in 1966, he stated that he would withhold, wherever possible, appropriations that exceeded his budget recommendations.[51] Taken together, these and many other precedents lent weight to the proposition that congressional appropriations essentially represented permission for expenditure rather than a mandate to spend specified allocations of money within a designated period of time.

From the combination of executive obligation, statutory authorization, and aggregated precedent, it might be thought that the impoundment power had slowly but surely been clarified and become firmly lodged within the presidential office. It might seem that Congress, either by legislation or by acquiescence, had sanctioned impoundment and even affirmed it as an implied presidential prerogative power. Nothing could be further from the truth. At no point had Congress unequivocally endorsed the executive's impoundment power, let alone formally recognized it. On the contrary, it had always treated it as a temporary privilege; the president could make reductions only where and when they were necessary — and only where and when they could be construed as being supported and sanctioned by Congress. Far from being a clarified prerogative, it remained by common consent a prima-facie power, always open to interpretation, negotiation, and challenge.

In all these cases, sections of Congress contested the president's use of impoundments, even to the extent, on occasion, of passing qualified measures restricting the scope of the impoundment power. The spirit in which such disputes normally took place was one of institutional conciliation and political negotiation. Both sides' claims were acknowledged and remained intact for the purposes of accommodation. President Jefferson, for example, sought to allay fears of executive usurpation by making every effort to assure Congress that the impounded gunboat funds would be spent the following year when improved vessels would be available. In 1967, President Johnson responded to political pressure and released $1.2 billion in impounded highway funds. In the Revenue and Expenditure Control Act of 1968, Congress permitted Johnson to make a $6 billion cut in budgetary outlays, but the president worked closely with Congress in the wording of the resolution, in the priorities that were set, and in the prerogatives to be reduced. To further reassure Congress, Johnson relied on temporary deferrals rather than permanent rescissions.

But perhaps the most well-known example of impoundment negotiations came with the Kennedy administration decision to block funds for the RS-70 bomber project. Even though the president possesses a superior constitutional claim to impoundment powers over military expenditures due to his position as commander-in-chief, Kennedy engaged in a campaign of conciliation and persuasion to induce the House Armed Services committee to drop the mandatory language in its legislative measure. After a walk in the White House rose garden with the president, the chairman of the committee, Carl Vinson, agreed to substitute the word 'authorized' for 'directed'. In a previous letter to Vinson, Kennedy had described this form of language as being 'more clearly in line with the spirit of the constitution'.[52]

It is fair to say that prior to the Nixon administration 'presidents exercised [the power of impoundment] with considerable restraint and circumspection'.[53] Although precedents had been established, Congress had never recognized impoundment as an exclusive executive power or even as an established *de facto* privilege. For their part, presidents were sensitive both to the need for discretionary impoundment and to the need to assuage congressional fears about the extent of its usage. In this context, it remained in everyone's interests to confine differences over impoundment to the political interplay between the institutions involved. The basic constitutional position was unresolved, but both sides recognized that there was much to be gained in keeping it unresolved. Both institutions could therefore keep their ultimate claims intact, negotiate from positions of suspended yet retained constitutional righteousness, and come to productive political agreements without arousing the divisiveness and dislocation of contesting constitutional positions. Impoundment was essentially a political power dependent upon the 'political context within which the president decided to impound funds'.[54] The constitutional position was accordingly held in abeyance through the collusion of the major participants.

This spirit of suspended legitimacy changed dramatically with the onset of the Nixon administration. According to Thomas Cronin,

> Before President Nixon, impoundments were rather infrequent, usually temporary, and generally involved insignificant amounts of money. Only occasionally were earlier impoundments controversial. Still, the precedent was set for the future. Nixon stretched the use of impoundment to limits previously not attained.[55]

Unlike his predecessors, President Nixon viewed precedent as a concrete bequest rather than as a provisional basis for argument. He thought, therefore, he had inherited what in actuality he needed to acquire. With this belief in the executive prerogative of impoundment, and faced with rising budget deficits and what he took to be a partisan Democratic Congress pursuing irresponsible and discredited policies, Nixon launched an impoundment campaign against excessive federal spending. Compared to previous presidents, Nixon's impoundments were of 'an entirely different order' in terms of their 'magnitude, severity and belligerence'.[56]

First of all, they were of a magnitude greater than that of any other administration; by 1972, approximately 20 per cent of controllable expenditures taken from over one hundred programmes were being held by the Office of Management and Budget. Secondly, impoundments were being made in spite of Congress's clear approval of expenditure. For example, in 1972 President Nixon's veto of the Federal Water Pollution Control Act Amendments was overridden, and yet over half of the $4.5 billion allocated to the programme was witheld a month later by presidential order. Thirdly, and quite unprecedentedly, the Nixon administration impounded money in an effort to terminate whole domestic programmes instead of individual projects (e.g., rural environmental assistance programme, water bank programme, rural electrification loan programme). Fourthly, impoundments were used as a statement of administration intent to abolish programmes and, in so doing, to precipitate the formal action required for their abolition (e.g., the Office of Economic Opportunity). Fifthly, the administration employed impoundment as a device by which to remove additional expenditures subsequently attached by Congress to the administration's original budget proposal (e.g., water and sewerage funds). Lastly, the practice of impoundment was often conducted in what was seen as a secretive and devious manner, verging at times on sharp practice. Nixon would often rely on legislation like the Employment Act (1946) and Economic Stabilization Act (1971) for his impoundment powers — not because these powers were specifically granted in such laws but because they were not expressly denied or explicitly forbidden and therefore could be taken as denoting tacit congressional assent to executive impoundment on general economic and fiscal grounds.[57]

Nixon's use of impoundment was seen in many quarters as highly provocative. It was widely interpreted as a deliberate re-ordering of spending priorities set within the budget by a Congress controlled by the Democratic Party; as part of the administration's assault upon those programmes sponsored by past Democratic administrations; as a weapon for the Republican administration's general posture of reducing federal expenditure; as a device for building up financial reserves in preparation for an economic stimulus in the election year of 1972; and, most significantly, as a clandestine means of acquiring an item veto denied to the presidency in the constitution. The audacity of Nixon's impoundments was more than matched by the level of aggravation they induced in his political opponents.

> The pattern became clear. The president was going to veto all authorizations and appropriations which violated his budget ceilings or his ideological pronouncements. Authorizations passed over his veto would be ignored, and appropriations passed over his veto would be impounded. When it was necessary to stop an entire programme viewed as a 'failure,' an entire appropriation would be impounded. The president's opponents were befuddled not only by the breadth of his actions, but by their lack of leverage.[58]

Nixon was accused of amending and redirecting laws passed by Congress, of defying the will of the legislature, and of failing to faithfully execute the laws of the United States. Far from using impoundments reluctantly, and as an unusual device for producing bona fide savings and economies, Nixon appeared to be deploying the power as a normal instrument of state in the service of his administration's policy objectives.

The situation soon deteriorated into confrontation. Nixon became

The silence of constitutions

ever more intransigent and insistent upon his impoundment powers. As early as 1969 and 1970, Congress refused to grant the specified impoundment powers it had previously given to President Johnson in a number of budget ceiling measures. Nixon took this as an affront to himself and to the institution of the presidency. This set the tone of the distrust and polarization which lingered throughout the Nixon years on this issue. It also determined Nixon's truculent and aggressive posture towards attempts to define his position more closely in this area. When Congress passed a number of specific bans on, and disincentives to, impoundment in designated areas, Nixon countered by regarding the absence of restriction in the remaining mass of legislation as tantamount to congressional assent to the general practice of impoundment.

In 1972, Congress passed the Federal Impoundment and Information Act requiring the administration to justify its impoundments. The Act was meant to revive the old framework of negotiation and accommodation, but it was greeted as a tacit recognition of the president's impoundment powers and it was followed by a fresh wave of impoundments in 1973. During this period, Congress countered by resorting to the high ground of constitutional fundamentalism. It began to interpret impoundment in the stark terms of the separation of powers doctrine. Senator Sam Ervin's Separation of Powers Subcommittee held hearings into the issue in 1971 and again in 1973. Ervin himself sponsored a bill (S. 373) 'to insure the separation of federal powers and to protect the legislative function'[59] by requiring the president to apply for congressional permission for any impoundment action. To Ervin and many others in Congress, Nixon's impoundments were doubly provocative: they were not only excessive, but conducted as if he 'seemed to be claiming unlimited constitutional power to nullify appropriation laws'.[60] In other words, even in the most basic and manifestly elemental area of the legislative process, where the powers of Congress seemed most intact and the powers of the presidency seemed most vulnerable to a strict interpretation of the constitution, President Nixon behaved in a way that betrayed a belief in an overriding prerogative authority.

It is true that the Nixon administration deployed all manner of statutory devices to support its claim to impoundment authority. But in the acrimonious atmosphere of the time, these all too often seemed like mere pretexts for a determined use of power. At worst, they appeared to be simply outlets through which an established power was exerted. Despite the legal expositions, there was little doubt that Nixon believed that he had a proprietary right to follow his predecessors in impounding funds. Early challenges to this right were dismissed by him as legislators playing 'games'.[61] Later and more earnest assaults received Nixon's clear and imperious riposte. At a new conference on 31 January 1973, he unequivocally affirmed 'the constitutional right for the President of the

The imperial presidency

United States to impound funds . . . that is not to spend money, when the spending of money would mean either increasing prices or increasing taxes for all the people — that right is absolutely clear'.[62]

Even the more cautious spokesman for the administration, Deputy Attorney-General Joseph T. Sneed, betrayed the administration's belief in a vested executive right to impoundment. In his measured defence of the administration's position before the Separation of Powers Sub-committee, Sneed sought circumspectly at first to relate the impoundment power clearly to statutory provision. Nevertheless, the presumption of prerogative was discernible in spite of Sneed's assiduous efforts to conceal it. Because impoundment was 'such a long-continued executive practice, in which Congress had generally acquiesced', Sneed concluded that it 'carried with it a strong presumption of legality'.[63] When the president was given general responsibilities in the economy, he had by right 'substantial latitude to refuse to spend or to defer spending for general fiscal reasons'.[64] Sneed doubted whether Congress could legislate against impoundment even in the domestic area if it were to have a detrimental effect on inflation. 'To admit the existence of such a power,' Sneed revealingly retorted, would deprive the President of 'a substantial portion of the "executive power" vested in him by the constitution'.[65]

Sneed tried his best to avoid the question of fundamental authority, but in the end the actions and beliefs of the White House forced even him to concede the presence of a prerogative power. Other presidents may well have believed that such a prerogative existed and were prepared to exercise it in a guarded *de facto* manner. But they were too astute to declare the existence of such a prerogative, or to act as if it had belonged irrefutably to the executive as a *de jure* right. President Nixon, however, clearly believed in his rightful ownership of such a power. The power itself was assumed to be beyond doubt; only the conditions of its usage remained in question.

In some respects President Nixon's position was understandable and even logically defensible. He felt that the impoundment power was typical of the many intrinsic prerogatives accruing to the president as the nation's chief executive. He also felt that Congress's renewed interest in such a power was typical of the irresponsible and partisan assault that was being conducted against his administration in order to undermine Republican policies and suborn the rightful authority of a Republican president. Nixon's sense of grievance over what he saw as a double standard is clear from his memoirs.

> Presidents since Thomas Jefferson had considered it their prerogative, and indeed their responsibility, to withhold the expenditure of congressionally appropriate funds for projects that were not ready to

begin or if inflation was especially severe and putting more money into the economy would make it worse. This is known as impoundment . . . . The Democratic Congress had not challenged my Democratic predecessors for their heavier use of the practice, so I saw the 1973 impoundment battle as a clear-cut partisan attack on me.[66]

This 'attack' on his presidency stung Nixon into an aggressive defence and a belligerent exercise of those powers which he believed at base to belong to him as president. In doing so, he broke the delicate fabric of suspended finality and functional obscurantism, that had previously held impoundment authority effectively in abeyance.

Relying upon precedents as a *force majeure*, Nixon plunged the issue into the unstable fundamentalism of ultimate legal authority, explicit institutional demarcation, and final constitutional truths. Nixon's provocative truculence led to a sharp polarization of positions between the White House and its opponents in Congress. At stake were important domestic programmes, now detrimentally affected by impoundment, and, at least in the congressional view, the administration's abuse and exploitation of constitutional abeyance. These abeyances were dependent upon mutual trust and themselves the register of such trust. The administration's headlong rush away from amicable negotiation within a framework of acceptable anomalies, and towards the high ground of historically sanctioned prerogative, therefore provoked the sort of backlash that only comes from the disillusionment of preconceptions.

Used with restraint and circumspection, impoundment had been used for decades without precipitating a major crisis. But during the Nixon years, restraint was replaced by abandon, precedent stretched past the breaking point, and statutory authority pushed beyond legislative intent . . . . The Nixon administration never demonstrated an understanding of what lies at the heart of the political system: a respect for procedure, a sense of comity and trust between the branches, an appreciation of limits and boundaries. Without good faith efforts on the part of administrative officials, the delicate system of nonstatutory controls, informal understandings, and discretionary authority could not last.[67]

In this summing up of the impoundment issue, the legal commentator Louis Fisher is, in effect, describing the breakdown of the constitutional abeyance which had previously protected impoundment from close scrutiny and intensive dispute. Its demise marked the transformation of an almost private ambiguity into a rancorous imbroglio of sweeping assertions, irreconcilable claims, and insoluble contradictions. The collapse of the constitutional abeyance immediately unleashed a host of dichotomies in respect to institutional function, legal right, public authority, and historical legitimacy. The resultant impasse of strident charge and counter-charge revealed not merely an unanticipated depth of difference between the presidency and Congress or a previously unsuspected degree of scope for abuse, but, more significantly, a genuine absence of constitutional finality on the issue.

Ultimately, the subject of impoundment was only satisfactorily dealt with by *not* resolving it. The Budget and Accounting Act of 1974, passed during the nadir of the Nixon administration, appeared to mark Congress's recapture of the purse strings. But in reality the Act brought about as much of the old status quo as it was possible to retrieve in such strained conditions. By providing Congress with a veto power over presidential impoundment, the Act revived something of the previously agreeable range of indeterminancy, in which both organizations had a joint role in impoundments and so could operate adaptively whilst preserving their institutional honour and integrity.[68]

This was also a solution that the courts had encouraged and endorsed through their refusal to pass judgement on the central issue of whether or not the presidency possessed an inherent constitutional power of impoundment.[69] The judiciary's reverence for constitutional abeyances and its sensitive appreciation of their productive political value was a well-established legal tradition. In the impoundment controversy, the courts were occasionally led to invalidate specific cases of impoundment for specific statutory or technical reasons. But in doing so, they left the door open for their favoured and astutely realistic solution — namely the eventual reconstruction of a constitutional abeyance to cover the troublesome issue of impoundment.

A similar pattern of polarized positions and eroded abeyances occurred in other areas of constitutional dispute. The controversies surrounding executive privilege, war powers, and executive agreements all contributed to a condition of manifold legal turmoil in which the unresolved nature of some of the constitution's key components were laid bare. In particular, the nature of legitimate executive power within a constitutional order became the subject of intense interest and concern. The president was thought to have superseded his powers and to have created an imbalance in the distribution of political authority. And in a much wider sense, the executive's power placed much of the American public in the disquieting and uncomfortable position of contemplating the existence of an institution with the functional and political ability to transcend the normal dynamics, and even the statutory restrictions, implicit in the principle of constitutionalism. Nixon's actions, and those of his associates, revealed the full extent of the anomalies, inconsistencies, and margins of indeterminancy within the constitution, and the result was a crisis in the conventional American conception of constitutionality.

The silence of constitutions

The audacity and intransigence of the administration in exploiting the grey areas of constitutional inconclusiveness — very often over and against congressional protests — threw into relief the presence of an executive with proprietary rights, exclusive authority, and vested prerogative powers. This was nothing new. An executive power, qualitatively irreducible to purely legal definition and structurally impervious to much of the normal operation of checks and balances, had always been present within the constitutional framework. Yet it had rarely been glimpsed in full flight. For much of the period covering the modern presidency, the office's inherent nature had been carefully cultivated by its incumbents, but also just as carefully obscured through the judicious use of negotiation and accommodation, and through the encouragement of a consensus surrounding the requirements and purposes of the office in modern conditions. With the amenability of a presidential style geared so much to consent, presidents were able to preserve and even extend the constitutional abeyance surrounding the office, whilst at the same time exploiting the opportunities for power afforded by the generalized neglect and implicit trust embodied in just such an abeyance.

Given the explosive potential for discord over the status of executive power and authority within a constitutional republic, it was a mark of the sophistication of American constitutional culture that the office had been so successfully integrated into the ethos of American constitutional government. This had largely been achieved by the condoned obscurity and strategic inattention afforded to the presidency. That spirit of abeyance, which had enabled Americans simultaneously to embrace differing and conflicting principles of government, was severely interrupted during the Nixon years. But it was an indication of the American attachment to abeyances — in spite of the society's reputation for democratic candour and constitutional clarity — that the issue of the imperial presidency was satisfactorily resolved by legislation and court decisions which restored the potential for constitutional inexactitude and indeterminancy, and, by doing so, enhanced the future viability of effective abeyances.[70] The net effect, therefore, was not to eliminate prerogative powers. On the contrary, it was to make them safer by rendering them more open to the camouflage of obfuscation in terms of their content and more liable to a process of negotiation in the conditions of their exercise.

Chapter four

Constitutional gaps and the arts of prerogative

In observing the constitutional crises surrounding Charles I and President Nixon, it is difficult not to be struck by the parallels between them. Both Charles and Nixon believed that they faced a radical conspiracy to undermine the established order of government and subvert their rightful authority. Both felt constrained to take extraordinary measures in response to what they felt were security requirements and foreign obligations. Like Charles I, President Nixon 'used methods which, though politically irritant, seemed legally unassailable; he used them with an indiscreet reliance upon sheer power and mere law'.[1] Like President Nixon, Charles engaged in a 'prodigal dissipation of the natural sources of support'[2] by failing to engender a spirit of consent and trust towards his policies and personal style of government.

Both also made it quite evident that they had little respect for the assemblies with which they were expected to work. Charles I made it clear that Parliament was to him an unruly body, thoroughly unworthy of the status it had mistakenly assumed for itself. But, as Charles reminded them in 1628, Members of Parliament should not feel alarmed by his manner and should not regard him as threatening them in any way, for, as he said, 'I scorn to threaten any but my equals'.[3] President Nixon had little time and even less regard for Congress. It was an institution that in his eyes had become 'irrelevant'[4] because it was 'cumbersome, undisciplined, isolationist, fiscally irresponsible, overly vulnerable to pressures from organized minorities, and too dominated by the media'.[5]

Charles and Nixon were strongly influenced by the reputations and political successes acquired by their predecessors working within what appeared to be the same respective constitutional systems. The model for the Stuarts was Elizabeth I, whose reputation for political skill, tactical astuteness, and attention to detail in the arts of government was second to none. Charles could neither grasp that the end result of Elizabethan success could not be divorced from Elizabethan methods and talents, nor appreciate that the conditions within which the monarchy functioned

The silence of constitutions

were in a process of change. Nixon too mistook his personal maladroitness and the changing outlook on the presidency as a direct and unwarranted attack upon his Rooseveltian inheritance.

> The 'Imperial President' was a straw man created by defensive congressmen and by disillusioned liberals who in the days of FDR and John Kennedy had idolized the ideal of a strong presidency. Now that they had a strong president who was a Republican — and Richard Nixon at that — they were having second thoughts and prescribing the re-establishment of congressional power as the tonic that was needed to revitalize the Republic.[6]

Ultimately, Charles and Nixon aroused so much agitation and disaffection that the focus of attention passed from specific issues to the central question of royal power and of presidential power. The subsequent constitutional turmoil was similar in the two cases in that both disputes turned upon the issue of which party could be accused of departing from tradition in favour of constitutional innovation. Charles and Nixon both claimed that it was not they but Parliament and Congress which had threatened stability by encroaching upon custom and law. Both lost their arguments and were effectively deposed.

Interesting and illuminating as such parallels may be, they should not allow us to be distracted from the central purpose of this exercise. The objective has not been simply to study the points of comparison in the respective pathologies of the two cases, but to allow the crises to demonstrate something of those constitutional properties that normally lie in a dormant state of condoned insolubility. Under the stress of a constitutional crisis, such previously hidden characteristics come to light. They thereby reveal their contribution to a constitutional order and their significance in a culture supporting a constitutional system of government. By examining crises, therefore, it is possible to discern with greater clarity the means by which constitutions function effectively under more normal conditions.

In particular, the study of crises enables the contribution of those attitudinal devices known as abeyances to be discerned and evaluated. Far from being a sign of decay, the presence of abeyances can denote an advanced constitutional culture adept at assimilating diverse and even conflicting principles of government within a political solidarity geared to manageable constitutional ambiguity. It is possible to go even further and to assert that if a constitution does not have a capacity to accommodate contradictions or to acquiesce in the coexistence of apparently incompatible positions, it may well be a weaker and less adaptable constitution for that deficiency.

An underlying assumption of historical accounts is that what are here called constitutional abeyances are a political phenomenon peculiar to the Stuart or pre-Stuart period. That is to say, abeyances are limited to a pre-modern era in terms of both time and space. Moreover, the presence of such abeyances is seen as indicating that the English constitution at that time was thoroughly outmoded and incapable of sustaining itself. This view seems to be confirmed by the collapse of the constitutional order into violent civil war. In retrospect, this appears to represent an inevitable consequence of the disorderly, unsustainable mixture of royal absolutism, Parliamentary power, and common-law rights that were a feature of the Stuart period.

Nevertheless, such a view overlooks the presence of a relatively well-formed and universally acknowledged constitutional order, an order that rested upon a broad agreement of principles and upon a common, if ambiguous, understanding over the manner and substance of government. The constitutional abeyances, by which 'the insoluble question of sovereignty lay dormant'[7] were not a sign of a degenerate or moribund constitution. True, the constitution placed a large premium on the tact and subtlety of its adherents, but it was not formless in content or character, or unworthy of the name 'constitution'. That is altogether too easy a conclusion and one which ignores the way the seventeenth century's consciousness of an existent constitution acted as a tangible network of expectations, as a code of acceptable conduct, and as a legitimate frame of reference in the matter of disputes. Much of the controversy surrounding Charles's actions was derived from the widespread feeling that they had transgressed the customary lines of the crown's prerogative. In other words, if there had been no firm conception of a constitution, or no sense of that constitution's prescriptions or strictures, it is difficult to account either for the agitation which Charles's behaviour generated or for the legalistic currency of debate which permeated the disputes between the crown and Parliament.

In the heightened political atmosphere of the early seventeenth century, abeyances might well have been a risky way to run a constitution, but it was far from being ineffective. There was nothing implicit in the deferral of issues to warrant the conclusion that such a constitution was untenable in principle and ultimately unworkable in practice. It may have been so in hindsight, but it was not so at the time. And there was nothing in the abeyances themselves that provided incontrovertible evidence of a terminal decline. On the contrary, bearing in mind the pressures and strains laid upon the constitution in the reigns of Elizabeth and James I, it would appear that the strategy of abeyances could and did allow for long periods of stability and governmental effectiveness. The Stuart constitution was an imprecise and elusive entity; yet in the right hands it was a relatively resilient one. That resilience depended upon the constitution's capacity for remaining *acceptably* imprecise and *agreeably* elusive. It depended upon an intuitive appreciation of the common benefit and general safety to be accrued from a constitution with the capacity to subdue conflict through equivocation and measured ambivalence.

In this context, the value of abeyances did not lie in keeping the Pandora's box shut on the manifest furies of opposed principles. For a considerable time, abeyances helped to inhibit both the formation of more explicit and exclusive doctrines of sovereignty, and the development of sharper and more polarized institutional antagonisms. These abeyances might have enabled the constitution to continue for an indefinite period. The negotiating skills of Elizabeth and James had managed to keep differences negotiable. They had stunted or foreclosed conflict through their ability to adapt to changed circumstances.

Parties on all sides saw the advantages of not making the differences between them as apparent as they could be, or as developed as they could have become. Intuitively, in a constitutional culture geared to order, tradition, and deference, it was widely felt to be both *unnecessary* and *dangerous* to break abeyances and resort to the futile divisiveness of first principles, implacable rights, and intransigent defences. *Unnecessary* in so far as the common currency of constitutional terminology allowed for different meanings to be attached to similar concepts within a range of congruence, thus permitting effective accommodation under the guise of organic harmony. The ambiguity in meaning enabled different parties to acquire benefits for themselves and, in doing so, to generate an empathy for one another expressed in the collaborative undertaking to maintain the slack and its ability to match constitutional validity to a variety of separate interests and causes. And *dangerous* in that should abeyances be pressed too far or exploited by one or another party, it would lead to an aggravated form of political discord that might be difficult to control and which would render practically impossible the restoration of the nuances of trust and understanding to their previous condition.

Realizing the strategic value of abeyances and appreciating the 'stop in the mind' upon which they depended for their affect, Charles I's actions were doubly provocative. They aroused irritation in their own right, but they also generated a much deeper hostility because of the way they became attached to claims of exclusive authority. Moreover, Charles sought to take what had been previously assumed to be provisional, negotiable, or emergency powers and to transform them into a permanent and legalized form. Charles was seen to be acting against the spirit of the constitution by first threatening the constitution's abeyances and then by harvesting their considerable potential for affording power to any party ruthless enough to exploit their delicate ambiguity.

Parliament, for its part, also adopted what were constitutionally innovative positions. Even though these were claimed to be defensive measures to restore Parliamentary and property rights to their traditional status, they were just as prejudicial to the spirit of abeyance as the king's own impetuous quest for forceful clarification. In this atmosphere of distrust — in which Charles I fluctuated between devious duplicity and imperious heavy-handedness and in which Parliament increasingly found itself in a position of resistance — the old device of obscure but mutual inclusivity began to wither away. It wilted under the weight of merciless scrutiny, dogmatic assertion, and extended claims to the benefit of whatever residual doubt that remained available.

Appropriately, the final collapse of the abeyance system witnessed the onset of a civil war. The iconoclastic wish for singular, emphatic, and conclusive concepts of government and sovereignty was quite incompatible with the graded subtleties of constitutional abeyances. But by no means could it be said that they were tossed lightly aside. On the contrary, it had taken an event as momentous as a civil war for them to be relinquished.

It can be supposed that this abandonment of abeyances for certainties was greeted by a mixture of great reluctance and grave trepidation. There had never been any pre-meditated intention to provoke a civil war. Few had ever envisaged a governmental order much different from the one that already existed. On the contrary, the attachment to abeyances betrayed a hope, a desire, and a trust that different positions and principles were assimilable — but without really knowing how and without the need or the desire to find out for certain whether or not they were. The tears spilt by Parliamentary leaders in 1628 when Charles threatened to dissolve Parliament before giving a satisfactory answer to the Petition of Right, therefore, can be seen as a sign of abject sorrow. But it is reasonable to suspect that they were also tears of fear at the prospect of a breakdown in the spirit of abeyance, and even tears of anger at such a spirit being so tragically and needlessly placed in jeopardy.

Turning to the American constitution, there would appear to be no comparison between it and the defunct Stuart constitution. The latter's disjointed package of apparently competing concepts of power would seem to belong to a pre-modern era — supplanted since by a climactic settlement characterized by a thorough codification of institutional powers and a clear stipulation of the criteria of legitimate political authority. The American constitution is commonly assumed to be the model of such constitutional modernism. It may be seen as a derivative of the principles and impulses emanating from the Commonwealth era,[8] but a very distant derivative and one that has been refined to produce a constitution with all the appearances of a stable, coherent, and consciously designed prospectus for government. And yet, under closer examination, the American constitution reveals the presence of a much greater degree of disorder and inconsistency than its reputation conveys. Indeed, under crisis conditions, it is possible to discern contradictions of an order of magnitude comparable to those witnessed in the Stuart constitution. The imperial presidency episode provided a further twist of irony in that the anomalies exposed bore a marked resemblance to precisely the tensions between prerogative and Parliamentary rights which had purportedly been 'resolved' during the course of the seventeenth century. Confounding the American constitution's reputation for legal constraint and dynamic self-regulation, the seventeenth century's syndrome of the rule of law struggling with executive authority was found to be alive and well and living in the United States — albeit in altered circumstances and under assumed names.

Through an accumulation of precedent and custom, the presidency had gradually enhanced its power and status within the American system. This represented enough of a trend for Edward Corwin to conclude that the 'history of the presidency had been the history of aggrandizement.'[9] The rise of the presidency betrayed to an increasing extent the presence of a force qualitatively different from other government agencies. Less than any other branch of government, it did not conform to the conventional conception of institutional checks and balances.

But the objections were few. The value of the office was seen as its capacity for immediacy, responsiveness, and discretion. To the extent that the presidency could provide services which the other elements of government could not, and that these services were regarded as imperative to the nation's security or to the public's welfare, the potential autonomy of the office was overlooked and even given tacit approval. Executive leadership was condoned as necessary and legitimate. The presidency was believed either to be relatively emancipated from legal and constitutional strictures by popular consent, or to be inherently and invariably elusive through the integral properties of executive power. 'Presidential government' therefore was instinctively recognized as both a descriptive truth and a prescriptive value.

The nebulous quality of the presidency's position in being an explicit part of the constitution, while being implicitly excluded from much of its structured and legal matrix — and even arguably from its very ethos — reached a point at which commentators and scholars felt obliged to take note of it.

Some alluded to the office as being ultimately unknowable in that the nature of its power was not susceptible to any operational instruments of analysis. Grant McConnell, for example, believed that the presidency was 'not a given quantity and never a known factor in any political equation'. Its powers could 'never be stated with certainty and precision'.[10] Others went further and ascribed to it a pronounced element of mysticism. Arthur Schlesinger described the 'rise of presidential mysticism'[11] as the process by which the president became 'a superior being requiring reverence and awe'.[12] To Clinton Rossiter, the office had become a 'breeding ground of indestructable myth';[13] to Alfred de Grazia, the office had 'an overlay of myth and magic';[14] to Emmet John Hughes, the presidency only became explicable 'when looked at as a political mystery rather than a political institution';[15] and to Theodore White, part of the 'crowning myth of the presidency' was that 'the supreme office would make noble any man who held its responsibility'.[16]

Such explicit admissions of incomprehension and inexplicability were reminiscent of the *arcana regis* which the royalists used during the early Stuart period to oppose Parliamentary incursions upon the king's prerogative. At that time, the royalists referred to the monarchy's power as a mystery which only the king and his closest councillors could understand. The crown's intentions, objectives, and judgements were not to be questioned as the mystique of their veracity and legitimacy could only be satisfactorily grasped by the crown itself. While it is quite true that presidential scholars in the main did not seek to defend or promote executive power on such grounds, they did describe and rationalize presidential power in terms of mystique. To that extent, the net effect was the same in so far as the presidency became closely associated with an idiosyncratic form of power which seemed to possess not only a self-generative property of its own, but also a conceptual and political immunity to the established order and purpose of constitutional organization.

The mystique surrounding the presidency was not limited to the substance of executive power. There was another source of mystery closely connected to, yet distinct from, the perceived nature of the office. This was the mystery of the generally positive attitude shown towards the office in spite of its ambiguous relationship to the conventional understanding of a constitutional system. In other words, the mystery of the content of presidential power was compounded by the further mystery of how the former came to be accepted and assimilated, given Americans' dedication to constitutional principles and their traditional anathema to rank, privilege, or any form of exclusivity.

Some of this attitudinal conundrum can be explained away by reference to beliefs in the president's ultimate accountability to the constitution's checks and balances, or to the sanction of the electorate, or to the rule of law. Explanations of this sort are not altogether convincing as they would not normally have been thought through in such a logical and conclusive manner. If they had been, they might well have succeeded in raising more doubts and anxieties than would otherwise have been the case. Many of these explanations only became plausible in any real sense when they were combined with trust and faith. The presidency was believed to be ultimately reducible to law on the basis of trust. The office was recognized as being qualitatively different, yet it was faithfully believed to be somehow amenable to the normal dynamics of constitutional restraints.

What must be explained, and what therefore ranks as the main explanation of the mystery, was the source of that trust and faith. The answer lies in the system of protective abeyances that had been built around the presidency during the modern era. To put it bluntly, there was, to use Christopher Hill's description of the prevailing attitude during the early Stuart period, a 'stop in the mind'.[17] The anomalies, tensions and doubts concerning presidential authority were for a considerable time laid to rest by a series of understandings that inhibited scrutiny, deflected inquiry, and dissipated concern. The presidency's domination of foreign policy and national security arrangements was simply a fact of life. Even the prospect of an accelerating presidential concentration of power and authority was not regarded as being particularly controversial. In much of the literature, it was greeted with utter equanimity.

Because there had been this 'stop in the mind', when the period of studied disinterest came to an end with the onset of a challenge to the presidency in the late 1960s, the effects were all the more convulsive. After the first tentative, reluctant, and even deferential probings by Congress had been rebuffed, the system of abeyances began to be assaulted by the righteousness of both the Congress and the president. It was not long before the full scale and nature of executive prerogative, which had been evolving quietly and largely undisturbed for thirty years, was suddenly subjected to the unaccustomed intrusion of glaring publicity and critical evaluation.

Fuelled by the sort of acrimonious misunderstandings and misconceptions that inevitably arise from previous arrangements based upon imprecision and ambiguity, the 'stop in the mind' turned to a rush of the mind. As a result, both parties emerged at cross-purposes with one another. Without the other's reciprocity, each became beached upon a conspicuously formalized and stipulated position of what it had supposedly always believed to have been the true and underlying state of affairs concerning the presidency's power. Each did so with an assurance and an exactitude, logic, and resolution which had not before been claimed and which was quite unfitted to the reality of the situation. Nevertheless, given the extreme polarization of positions, and given the constitutionally fundamentalist nature of the debate, it was the authority of the presidency's position that was placed in the more dangerously exposed condition.

While Congress resorted to evangelical cries for a return to the old and simple truths of the constitution, President Nixon was left trying to invoke the more intangible, but nonetheless well-established, ramifications of legitimate executive power. Nixon appealed to the authority of precedent, custom, interpretation, practicality, conditions, and needs.

Constitutional gaps and prerogative

He believed that the government was being subjected to extreme duress by subversive forces and that the assault upon the presidency was symptomatic of the critical nature of the challenge to rightful authority. Under these conditions, the president felt entrusted and obligated to preserve the integrity of the government, even if that meant he had to renounce normal constraints and to employ extra-constitutional or illegal means to achieve his objectives. In this venture, he took as his guide the record of those of his predecessors who had followed Lincoln's dictum — 'that measures otherwise unconstitutional might become lawful by becoming indispensable to the Constitution through the preservation of the Nation'.[18] Under these conditions, the intention served to intensify the crisis and to unearth the highly ambiguous relationship that existed between the presidency and the law.

Along with his modern predecessors, Nixon proceeded on the principle that statute and even constitutional law depended upon the maintenance of conditions conducive to the rule of law. Accordingly, laws could be provisionally suspended during emergencies when the president had the capacity and the responsibility to protect the public welfare and to defend the nation's security. In this sense, law was being supplanted or superseded by an overriding authority where pre-eminence was a direct product of extraordinary circumstances. Nixon clearly believed that he possessed this authority — albeit rather overactively, as he thought that the presidency could actually determine the content of law. This was made evident in the televised exchange between President Nixon and David Frost on the issue of national security:

Frost: When you were concerned about street crime and so on, you went to Congress and got laws passed. Wouldn't it have been better here though to have done what you were going to do legally, rather than doing something that was illegal — seizing evidence in this way. In retrospect would it not have been better to combat that crime legally rather than adding another crime to the list?

Nixon: Basically, the prosposition you have just stated in theory is perfect. In practice, it just won't work. To get specific legislation . . . to have entries for the purpose of obtaining information would not only have raised outcry but it would have made it terribly difficult to move in on these organizations because basically they would be put on notice by the fact that the legislation was on the books that they would be potential targets. An action has either got to be covert or not.

Frost: So what in a sense you are saying is that there are certain situations . . . where the President can decide that it is in the best interests of the nation, or something, and do something illegal.

Nixon: But when the President does it, that means that it is not illegal.

Frost: By definition?

Nixon: Exactly. Exactly. If for example the President approves something, approves an action, because of the national security, or in this case because of a threat to internal peace and order of a significant magnitude, then the President's decision in that instance is one that enables those who carry it out to carry it out without violating the law.[19]

The presumption of legality behind ostensibly 'illegal' presidential actions was placed in a more concrete context by John Ehrlichman in his testimony to the Senate Select Committee on Presidential Campaign Activities. He stated that both he and President Nixon believed that the burglary of Daniel Ellsberg's psychiatrist's office, for the purpose of obtaining damaging personal information on the person who leaked the Pentagon Papers to the press, was an action quite consistent with the president's constitutional power to protect the nation's security.[20]

Taking into account the weight of prior understandings and historical precedent, it is far from clear that such sentiments and actions were constitutionally unsound or invalid. Like Charles I, President Nixon believed that he was conforming to the constitution as *he* understood it and as it had been translated into practical effect by his predecessors, and by the general assent given to their actions. Like Charles I, however, President Nixon was seen not only to invoke prerogative as a pretext for undermining the legitimate opposition of his critics, but also to press that prerogative quite arbitrarily and unjustifiably into areas of doubtful competence — and by doing so to raise executive prerogative into a starkly prominent and unpalatable form. In Nixon's hands, executive prerogative was given too high a profile in circumstances too controversial for it to be condoned through the normal channels of abeyance. Conditions and attitudes had changed in the ferment of the early 1970s. Like Charles I in the 1620s and 1630s, Nixon was seeking to exercise powers according to a conception of the constitution that had become outdated. The earlier tolerance and acquiescence had abated leaving the presidency open to more conventional forms of observation and evaluation.

It is true that President Nixon can probably be blamed more than anyone else for provoking a crisis in the presidency which served to dissipate its protective abeyances. What he cannot be held accountable for was the underlying reality of what duly became exposed, namely, a form of evolved power, the nature of which appeared to be manifestly at variance with the declared ethos and controlling principles of the constitution. So much at variance was this presidential power that, after years of executive prerogative being effectively concealed from the consciousness of the American public, the shock at the veil of obscurity being raised was for many a traumatic experience, and one for which they were thoroughly unprepared. This was reflected in the exaggeratedly alarmist rhetoric used at the time. References to 'autonomy', 'imperialism', and 'totalitarianism' betrayed not just an inadequacy of political vocabulary, but an inability to come to terms with a phenomenon that appeared to be so contrary to the American experience. Abeyances up to that point had perhaps worked too well. When they failed, they revealed the presence of a problem that had long been thought to have been resolved by the Founding Fathers at the time of the writing of the constitution.

During the constitutional convention, John Jay had asked the question 'shall we have a king?'[21] Although the suggestion was rejected unreservedly as inimical to the very principle of a free government, the Founding Fathers' success in divorcing themselves from the past and designing a thoroughly secularized and republicanized executive office has always been open to question. True, they sought to ensure that the office would have none of the social connotations of blood, rank, title, or privilege that had for so long been the staples of monarchy. Nevertheless, it is arguable that in the structure and power of their designed executive, the Founders never quite managed to transcend their own epoch and to detach themselves from monarchical models elsewhere. It would perhaps be more surprising if they had done so. Edward S. Corwin, for example, is left in no doubt that the presidency was 'designed in great measure to reproduce the monarchy of George III with the corruption left out, and also . . . the hereditary features'.[22] And although the Founders had 'rejected the concept of the divine right of monarchy', it is clear to George Reedy that

> when they sat down to write a constitution . . . they were incapable of thinking of government in any terms other than monarchy . . . Someone must have ultimate and final authority. Therefore, their conclusion, although not stated in these terms, was a solution which placed in office a monarch but limited the scope of the monarch's activities.[23]

The influence of cultural heritage may or may not be decisive. More salient are those structural, operational, and functional characteristics that are shared by both monarchical and executive offices, and which provide a common set of entrenched and constant factors. In other words, there is an implicit unity in the nature of monarchy and the nature of an executive office such as the presidency. Even John Locke, who gave such heavy emphasis to the superiority of law and of lawmaking within his contractual and majoritarian conception of government, felt obliged to concede the need for a prerogative power lodged in an executive office. In the *Two Treatises of Government*, he recognized that

> the Good of the society requires, that several things should be left to the discretion of him, that has the Executive Power. For the Legislators not being able to forsee, and to provide, by Laws, for all, that may be useful to the Community, the Executor of the Laws, having the power in his hands, has by the common Law of Nature, a Right to make use of it for the Good of the Society, in many Cases, where the municipal Law has given no Direction . . . . Nay, 'tis fit that the Laws themselves should in some Cases give way to the Executive Power, or rather to this Fundamental Law of Nature and Government . . . . This Power to act according to discretion, for the publick good, without the prescription of the Law, and sometimes even against it, is that which is called *Prerogative*.[24]

Locke suggested that the only way such a prerogative could be controlled was by *ex post facto* public judgement. Thus, it can be argued, as Arthur Schlesinger has done, that although

> the idea of prerogative was not part of Presidential power as defined in the constitution . . . there is reason to believe that the doctrine that crisis might require the executive to act outside the constitution in order to serve the constitution remained in the back of their minds.[25]

This conclusion is unduly cautious. It would have been well nigh impossible for the Founding Fathers to expunge such thoughts from their minds. They would not only have been thoroughly familiar with Locke, but in having read and absorbed his works they would have been only too aware that prerogative powers would necessarily be integral to the executive office, irrespective of declaration or definition.

It is more likely that the Founders recognized both the problem and its insoluble nature, and that, accordingly, the constitution was designed along the lines which Locke had suggested as being the only available recourse — namely *ex post facto* redress. The conclusion of Joseph M. Bessette and Jeffrey Tulis, therefore, is the more plausible one in that they acknowledge the 'constitution effectually institutionalizes a version of this principle by its openness to and even encouragement of Presidential initiative balanced by the ability of Congress and the Court to act decisively after the fact to endorse or oppose Presidential actions'.[26] The problem of executive prerogative was resolved — but only in formal terms. The substance of the problem remained, although largely occluded by the formal arrangement.[27]

The conundrum of executive prerogative within a constitutional system has not been solved by the passage of time. The circle still resists being squared. Occasionally, as in the 'imperial presidency' crisis, anguished cries of monarchy are heard in the American capital. But generally these are employed as loose terms of abuse at the lavish accoutrements of the modern presidency.[28] The more serious attempts to analyse presidential power in terms of monarchical attributes normally come from British observers,[29] whose views are seen as being excessively derivative from their own cultural preoccupations with monarchy. But to dismiss all such analysis as either poetic licence or mistaken identity is to trivialize the comparison and to overlook the functional, cultural, and political substance of monarchy that is recognizable in the presidency.

Although the Founding Fathers rejected the idea and the physical embodiment of monarchy, this does not mean that monarchical attributes are not, and cannot be, present in the presidency of a constitutional republic. 'A popularly elected monarch'[30] need not necessarily be a contradiction in terms. Being chief executive can entail such political significance and engender such cultural symbolism that its functional character can ramify into a social phenomenon. Modern presidents have deliberately and consistently sought to cultivate the imperative and unfathomable qualities of the office. This has been a political strategy in its own right but one very much based upon the traditional and integral characteristics of the executive arm of government.

In fact, a good deal of the presidency's authority is drawn from the old monarchical principle of the office being indispensable to the efficient functioning of the system as a whole. Executive power is taken as being exclusive to the executive department. 'The power cannot be delegated . . . . It can be abandoned . . . but nobody else gets the power; it is just lost for the time being.'[31] As such, the presidency is normally respected as an element of government needing to be preserved and protected for the sake of the government in general. This facet of the presidency is complemented by the monarchical mystery that is normally attached to the office. 'The presidency has a mystique which Charles I would have recognized',[32] and presidents have shown themselves to be quite prepared to use the mystique as a political resource with which they have been invested and which can be exploited to generate an even greater sense of executive authority.

Whether the imperative or mystical elements of the presidency have been drawn more from what was originally invested in the office by the Founding Fathers, or more from the features inherent in the functional nature of an executive agency, the net effect has been to render some aspects of the presidency comparable to some aspects of monarchy. There are features and properties common to both. What may be logically inadmissible in a constitutional democracy like that of the United States is seen to be practically and politically assimilable in the form of the presidency's integral — if unexplained and normally unexamined — role in the modern system of American government. When the habits of mind and attitude, however, are interrupted and the presidency attracts critical scrutiny, the result can be one of shock, incomprehension, and utter confusion. In the imperial presidency, the trauma was especially severe as it had been so long since the office had been the subject of constitutional scepticism. The disjunction which was implicit in the constitution, and which had been made more acute and yet more concealed by contemporary attitudes to the presidential office, came to a dramatic head in the 1973–4 period.

The result was a vote of impeachment by the House Judiciary Committee, the resignation of President Nixon, and a widespread impression that the constitutional system had worked to order. But, despite appearances, the controversy surrounding the Nixon presidency was far from decisive. It failed to produce a definitive resolution to the challenge of executive power in a constitutional framework. Indeed, for much of the critical period, the different parties were not fully engaged upon the central question of whether executive power could be contained by constitutional means. The situation was reminiscent of Charles McIlwain's description of the entrenched righteousness of both the royalists and the Parliamentarians when he said that their arguments 'slid past each other'[33] with each side citing its own set of precedents and resorting to its own exclusive conception of legitimate authority.

Congress pressed forward with its rights, its privileges and its legitimacy suddenly emblazoned as key components in the system's framework of institutional dynamics. So too did the courts, which felt their authority and their conception of constitutional demarcation and legal restraint under threat. President Nixon, for his part, was content in the knowledge that tradition, precedent, and practicality generated an authority necessarily immune from indictment. Like Charles I who, at the lowest ebb of his reign, challenged the authority of Parliament to place him on trial,[34] so President Nixon's response to the adverse decision on the *United States v. Nixon* case was not to comply with the judgement but to question the jurisdiction of the Supreme Court. 'He wondered if, in fact, to preserve the power of his office, he didn't have a constitutional duty to reject the court order.'[35]

While it is true that President Nixon was finally humbled into submission and resignation, his departure did not represent a reduction of the presidency into a uniform set of categories compatible with the other branches of government. Nixon's resignation, together with the profusion of restrictive legislation that accompanied his decline, certainly lends weight to the idea that the generative and discretionary properties of the office had been decisively laid to rest. Not long after the crisis there even arose consternation over the 'tethered presidency' and the 'imperiled presidency'.[36] And yet, by closely examining the legislation passed at the time, it is clear that much of it not only recognizes the discretionary privileges of the presidency, but formalizes them into law.[37] Furthermore, by recalling how the special functional qualities of executive government can be differently construed and evaluated under different circumstances, it is evident that the presidency has not been decisively and permanently humbled. It has not been transmuted by mere acts of legislative will into a framework of legal and material attributes, fixed to constitutional definition and to the regulatory interplay of checks and balances. The idiosyncratic dimension of executive action remains intact. Even in the convulsive circumstances of 1973–4, when conditions seemed so conducive to a climactic settlement concerning the presidency, the net result was circumspection and equivocation. The potential for presidential prerogative continued undiminished.

It is arguable that the critics and reforms of the Watergate era did not intend to intrude upon or to prejudice the presidency's prerogative. What is important to grasp is that it would be difficult to conceive just how they would have delimited the executive's capacity for prerogative power should they have wished to do so. In retrospect, it is clear that the system did indeed work. The system of abeyances was resurrected and the highly disruptive issue of executive prerogative was put back to sleep again. After surfacing suddenly and dramatically, the historic problem and its historic insolubility was re-examined in chronic discomfort until the 'solution' of placing it in abeyance was rediscovered and accepted to the satisfaction and considerable relief of all those concerned.

From this study of the American constitution under severe stress, it is evident that the constitution is not the comprehensive and coherent frame of reference which its written format normally leads one to suppose. The associations and connotations linked to a written constitution like that of the United States invariably centre upon the assumption of a determinable content and character. If constitutional government can be equated with limited government, and if the United States can be regarded as the most constitutionally limited government of all, then it is possible to conclude that the American constitution must be the most settled in terms of structure and meaning. Such a logical deduction, however, would be inappropriate in these circumstances. As the imperial presidency episode reveals, the American constitution is far from being the paragon of high resolution coherence that its written and declaratory nature so often confers upon its reputation.

In reality, the American constitution is pitted and flawed by anomalies, inconsistencies, and cross-cutting dimensions of constitutional meaning and authority. Like the Stuart constitution, the American constitution is susceptible to a wide variety of interpretations occasioned by the disjunctions inherent in the historical origins and development of the American republic. And again like the Stuart constitution, these disjunctions can be so severe and intractable that the American system cannot survive by laws and conventions alone but is dependent upon the far subtler device of abeyances. The methods, customs, and understandings which were closely associated with the Stuart constitution, and which were commonly thought to have been exclusively associated with that constitution, provide very adept instruments of analysis into the functioning of the American constitution. Ironically, what used to be derided as evidence of the untenable nature of early seventeenth-century English government can now be seen to offer extraordinarily useful insights into a comprehension of what is, ostensibly at least, a highly modern constitutional arrangement.

The irony does not stop there. The abeyance in constitutional outlook that used to characterize the Stuart constitution is not merely present at the highest levels of contemporary American government. It is also there in a more successful and effective form. Where the Stuart constitution could be said to have failed because it was unable to sustain its abeyances, the American constitutional culture appears to be far better equipped for keeping deep and unsettled issues at bay through its structures of abeyance. Indeed, the American constitution has a positive genius for subduing conflict, or potential conflict, into agreeable indeterminancy and suspended finality. Many of its major features are testaments to its ability to make ambiguity manageable and, by doing so, to prolong and develop it into a protective mantle valued in its own right as a constitutional device.

Federalism, for example, can be seen as a form of constitutional abeyance as it embodies a constantly changing conception of the ambiguity implicit in the coexistence of national integration and political decentralization. Americans are accustomed to having both without a sense of unendurable contradiction. Another abeyance deflects critical attention away from what outsiders might regard as the dichotomy between popular sovereignty and the fundamental law which provides the American system with so much of its special character. This duality achieves its most conspicuous manifestation in the Supreme Court exercising the power of judicial review in invalidating the acts of democratically elected legislative assemblies and executive officers. Such a power assigned to judges can be seen to be an aberrational affront to the precepts and principles of democratic authority, which the United States has always professed to be the basis of its political system. Nevertheless, it is an aberration that has traditionally been swallowed whole and assimilated into the American political tradition in an undigested and unresolved state. Abeyances swathe the whole issue of judicial review. They have succeeded in rendering the matter acceptably incoherent by engendering an appreciation of the safety and value to be accrued from not seeking to resolve the insoluble, and instead to proceed on the basis of muddled inconclusivity and compulsive evasion.

Constitutional gaps and prerogative

What is remarkable about American abeyances is that, in contrast to those of the Stuart constitution, they survive and prosper in an environment geared so emphatically to social and political inquiry. Even in the face of the most prolific and intensive analyses of government, the United States's constitutional abeyances have been well able to sustain themselves in inhospitable conditions. This may partly be due to the self-cancelling quality of the multiplicity of research. It may also be due to a basic faith in the unanimity of the American historical experience and in an inbred assurance in the ultimate inclusiveness of the phenomena and principles drawn from that experience and present within its resultant social consensus.

Nevertheless, it is more likely that the real reason for the durability of abeyances within the United States constitution is what Robert McCloskey describes as Americans' 'native tendency to harbour conflicting ideas without trying, or caring, to resolve them'.[38] Addressing himself specifically to the conundrum of popular sovereignty and fundamental law, McCloskey acknowledges that

> it may be possible to harmonize these seeming opposites by logical sleight of hand, by arguing that the doctrines of popular sovereignty and fundamental law were fused in the constitution which was a popularly willed limitation. But it seems unlikely that Americans in general achieved such a synthesis and far more probable . . . that most of them retained the two ideas side by side. The propensity to hold contradictory ideas simultaneously is one of the most significant qualities of the American political mind at all stages of national history, and it helps substantially in explaining the rise to power of the United States Supreme Court.[39]

McCloskey accurately ascribes the viable coexistence of democratic principles and the practice of judicial review in the American system to the functional properties of ambiguity. Alexander Bickel makes the same point in his description of judicial autonomy being 'sustained, not by a self-consistent theory, but by an ambivalent practical accommodation'.[40] What at first may have seemed a vice — when the constitution was 'conceived in ambiguity as well as in liberty'[41] and when important issues were 'treated in ambiguous clauses that passed problems on to posterity'[42] — subsequently became transformed into a virtue. Ambiguity developed into an integral component of the constitution's supportive apparatus.

Although the points made by McCloskey and Bickel pertain to the specific controversy of judicial review within a democratic framework, their observations can be applied with equal validity to other disjunctions within the constitution. Abeyances can only really thrive in a constitutional environment of genuine, long-lasting, and thoroughly acceptable ambiguity. It was the ability to live satisfactorily with ambiguity that not only encouraged the creation of a disjointed, and even divided, system of governmental powers, but also permitted that structure to become and to remain operational through the attitudinal strategy of abeyances.

The separation of powers system, therefore, probably represents the ultimate expression of the unresolved and unsettled nature of the American constitution, and, at the same time, the chief means by which the constitution can be made to work. This is to say that there is no better way of discerning the potential for fundamental conflict within the constitution than by observing the system of the separation of powers. Along with the other historical forms of divided power, the separation of powers scheme is dedicated to balanced government, which is another way of saying that its various components are not aligned towards a common and universal conception of authority. It has even been claimed that a balanced government is a device for evading the whole issue of sovereignty and thus for accommodating more than one form of sovereignty in an uneasy and necessarily ambiguous coexistence.[43]

The United States is no exception. In terms of abstract analysis, the American system can appear to be rife with incoherence and contradiction and, as a result, replete with the ever-present possibility of severe constitutional conflict. And yet in dividing powers and functions, the constitution also provides the stimuli and incentives to political participants to turn away from the manifest disjunctions and fundamental discord inherent in the institutional composition of the constitution.

The sheer intractability of the incoherence, together with the disruption (not to say disintegration) required to sort out much of the contents, provide the practical antidote to conflict over constitutional fundamentals. There is simply more to be gained by cultivating and protecting abeyances and in preventing political issues and institutional differences from inciting intransigent divisions and entrenched constitutional dogmatism. In not extending claims to their logical but provocative conclusions; in not seeking to maximize advantages irrespective of their repercussions; and in promoting 'comity' by which positions are acknowledged and honoured in the cause of achieving a means of cooperation within a context brooding with adversity, political participants can transform immobilism into productive interplay. The unremitting dissonance of a separated powers system, therefore, can condition those who work within it to the need to strive continuously against a background of conflict and dispute, in order to achieve any sense of common purpose.[44]

This system leads not just to political incentives to inhibit the degeneration of conflict into open disarray, but also to an acquired capability to defuse the constant potential for dispute and to complement it with a level of cooperation required for effective action. This capability is subsequently strengthened by a normative attachment to avoiding actions and positions and counter-claims. Like those who worked within the Stuart constitution, most of the participants in the American system come to know enough about the protocol of understandings and expectations to make the system work satisfactorily, in spite of itself. But they also come to know what would arise if comity were to break down and if conflict were to deteriorate and become attached to the normally dormant, but potentially convulsive, disjunctions within the sub-structure of the constitution. The result would be that, in the hopeless search for clarification, rationalization, and finality, the constitution's abeyances would be breached and the sensitive core of the constitution's deep-seated anomalies would be dangerously exposed. The incentives to work with the constitution's inconsistencies, therefore, are supplemented by the deterrent effect of the explosive risk connected to the full revelation of those elements of the constitution that remain unresolved and, arguably, unresolvable.

The reluctance to press forward to clinch the constitutional position, and the evasion over final constitutional truths in the distribution of powers within the system, are habits of mind that are normally instinctive, private, and unobservable. Nevertheless, one can occasionally see glimpses of them in action. They are particularly noticeable in those constitutional cases that place the Supreme Court uncomfortably amidst issues of an exceptionally sensitive political nature, e.g., the legitimacy of a state's electoral system, or the nature and extent of the President's prerogative in the direction of foreign policy.

In the past, the Court has refused to decide such cases and has deflected the issues back to the more explicitly political branches of government for resolution. The Court describes these cases as 'political questions' which can bring the judiciary into close proximity with an aroused public divided into active partisan conflict. Controversies such as these are seen as clearly falling 'outside the conditions and purposes that circumscribe judicial action'[45], both because judicial intervention would be inappropriate and because of a 'lack of satisfactory criteria for a judicial determination'[46] of such issues. The Supreme Court's reticence in becoming embroiled in the 'political thicket'[47] has often led it to be accused of timidity or of expedience. The Court's record in such cases, however, is representative of a much more generalized reluctance 'to pass upon a constitutional question . . . if there is also present some other ground upon which the case may be disposed of'.[48] 'Political questions' merely make the Court's habit of 'leaning over backward to find technical . . . reasons for leaving important constitutional questions unsettled'[49] a far more conspicuous procedure than would otherwise be the case in less contentious circumstances.

In some ways, the Court's prudential evasion of political questions and its avoidance of making constitutional judgements in fields of heightened public interest may be seen as an astute form of both self-restraint and, thereby, self-defence. But it can be argued that the Court possesses a highly developed understanding of the properties of the constitution and of its need for protective abeyances. It may well be that the Supreme Court is simply placed in a position and given an opportunity to articulate the attitudes and habits of mind which are integral to abeyances in a way that is not afforded to other participants in the system. Whatever the reason, the Court's outlook on the constitution has often betrayed precisely that intuitive reluctance — to plumb the depths of the great constitutional divides — which characterizes so much of the general spirit and conduct of ordinary politics in the American constitutional order.

In the prelude to his decision in the Youngstown case, for example, Justice Felix Frankfurter's reticence to pronounce upon such a severe constitutional dispute and to jeopardize the abeyance surrounding the issue of presidential power is clearly discernible.

> A constitutional democracy like ours is perhaps the most difficult of man's social arrangements to manage successfully . . . . The relation between the President's powers and those of Congress [is] a most delicate matter that has occupied the thoughts of statesmen and judges since the Nation was founded and will continue to occupy their thoughts as long as our democracy lasts . . . . Clashes between different branches of the government should be avoided if a legal ground of less explosive potentialities is properly available. Constitutional adjudications are apt by exposing differences to exacerbate them.[50]

Frankfurter's sentiments are symptomatic of the whole ethos that lies behind constitutional abeyances. The objective is to preserve the cushion of indeterminancy and, by doing so, to keep the channels of institutional and political interplay as open, and as free from profound constitutional dislocation, as possible. Frankfurter represents that spirit, necessarily common amongst participants in the American political process, which senses that the lines of constitutional demarcation are both indistinct and inconclusive and that it is better for them to remain so.

The purpose of this essay has been to draw attention to the phenomenon of constitutional abeyances. What at first appeared to be a property of a pre-modern frame of government like that of the Stuart constitution emerges as an integral component of the American political system at the very deepest level. In spite of the highly developed sense of constitutional examination and appraisal which characterizes American attitudes towards government and in spite of a political system that both stimulates and facilitates constitutional inquisitiveness, it is nevertheless matched by an instinctive acknowledgement that 'the great ordinances of the constitution do not establish and divide fields of black and white'.[51] Contrary to its reputation for being written and therefore coherent in structure and purpose, the American constitution is in reality as notorious as the Stuart constitution for its flaws, anomalies, disjointedness and for those elements that remain unexpressed and indefinable.

The protective abeyances which provide such a secure edifice of obscurity reach their highest level of efficiency in the system of constitutional checks and balances. The conceived interplay between different institutions and different functions under the rubric of checks and balances conceals questions — of either the prescribed or actual distribution of power within the government — as proficiently as it obscures issues over the variety and compatibility of different forms of authority coexisting under the guise of a single constitutional order. The cult of balanced government in the United States has succeeded in presenting the prodigious anomalies and contradictions within the system not just as a necessary condition, but as a virtuous one as well. They are portrayed as the vital raw material of those homogenized dynamics which generate the self-regulatory mechanistic stability widely proclaimed to be both an irrefutable physical truth and an unassailable political value in the American political ethos. The closed mechanical system of continuous cause and effect has become so established as an instrument of political conceptualization, analysis, and evaluation that the system's property of perpetuating the indeterminate and the unresolved is assimilated as a concomitant of mechanical equilibrium, instead of as evidence of major constitutional disjunctions. As the conventional, and popularly endorsed, construction of political reality, the self-contained dynamics of checks and balances can accommodate all manner of conflict in terms of its own nature by predisposing any interpretations of conflict as being ineluctably in accordance with its own mechanical rationale and objective.

For example, the indeterminancy surrounding the precise and legitimate form of control over the country's foreign policy can, and has been, translated into a thoroughly coherent mechanical construction. The clash between the statutory authority of Congress and the prerogative authority of the presidency has been described by Edward S. Corwin as 'an invitation to struggle for the privilege of directing American foreign policy'.[52] In reality, it is highly unlikely that it was anything of the sort, as there is precious little evidence that the divergent views of the Founding Fathers were ever fully reconciled on this point. The description, which has become a piece of conventional wisdom on the subject, in fact represents an *ex post facto* rationalization and disguise of what was, and what remains, an abeyance on the unsettled state of the powers and rights over foreign policy. Corwin's dictum, nevertheless, stands as the persuasive account because it is so thoroughly in accord with the predominant paradigm that imputes not merely harmony from dissonance, but an intentional and pre-determined harmony from an intentional and pre-arranged dissonance.

The United States has been particularly adept at accommodating the numerous divisions which lie at the root of its constitution. Through universalizing and systematizing its fault-lines into a comprehensive mosaic of multiple abeyances, it probably ranks as the system most able and best equipped to work successfully with abeyances. One could argue that the number and scale of its disjunctions is matched by the effectiveness of its strategy of abeyance, by which it can evade the consequences of what remains unresolved in the depths of the constitution.

But in acknowledging the United States's exceptional status in the field of constitutional abeyances, we must acknowledge the abeyances of other systems. The British system, to return to our point of comparison, has a reputation for having reached climactic constitutional settlements, but continues nonetheless to be afflicted by substantive uncertainties. The Commonwealth era of popular sovereignty and strident radicalism that followed the civil war, the abolition of the House of Lords, and the deposition of Charles I was followed by the Restoration Settlement of 1660. 'The irony was that the Restoration Settlement broadly restored the constitution of 1641, which Charles himself had agreed to observe and had later proposed as the basis of a settlement.'[53] To that extent, the Settlement also represented a conscious attempt to re-introduce the ambivalence and related need for abeyances which had characterized the Stuart constitution.

Later, in 1688, the Glorious Revolution was reputed to have further clarified and limited the constitutional status and power of the monarchy. Other climactic measures followed in the nineteenth cetury that could be thought to have conclusively modernized the British constitution according to the principles of Parliamentary supremacy and democratic authority and, in doing so, to have finally resolved the issue of sovereignty. Yet, the constitution remains uncodified, in many respects undeclared and often uncertain as to the precise relationships between its component parts.[54] For example, the exact degree of discretion afforded to the crown remains a matter of constitutional conjecture. Where the House of Lords's relationship with the House of Commons is concerned, 'the position of the two Houses . . . has never been precisely settled'.[55] Furthermore, 'the relations between the law stated by the House of Commons and the common law stated by the courts have never been determined'.[56] Therefore, even in the British constitution — renowned as it is for the clarity and penetrative qualities of Parliamentary sovereignty — abeyances linger on in a normally unobtrusive manner. The techniques of abeyance may be different from those of the American system, but that the abeyances themselves exist and are sustained by an accustomed acquiescence cannot be doubted.

At the beginning of this essay it was argued that any differentiation of the American constitution from the British constitution on the grounds of their written and unwritten qualities was unfounded and invalid. Just as the American constitution could be shown to be supplemented by customs, usages, and conventions, so the British constitution could be regarded as written, albeit unassembled in a singular and authoritative document.

For this reason we have discarded the 'written-unwritten' classification on the grounds that what was written or unwritten in the two constitutions was ultimately reducible to something that was positively known and that could be acted upon in a definite sense. Custom and practice might not be documented, formally recognized or officially sanctioned. But their content is discernible and susceptible to description and to concrete understandings. In the subsequent haste to dismiss the old classification, however, there was always the risk of overlooking the possible value of the 'written' and 'unwritten' categories in other contexts and in different forms of deployment.

This essay has been dedicated to salvaging from that classification what is arguably its most useful insight. It has sought to prevent the positivistic swing towards the unwritten being construed as nothing more than the written in a different and unnecessary form. Instead, the study has looked again at the phenomenon of the unwritten in constitutions and has concluded that it contains far more than merely that which can be objectified into material definition. It is proposed that it is precisely those unwritten components of a constitution that represent its most integral features and its most fundamental properties. They remain integral and fundamental, furthermore, because of their need for protective obscurity and because of their inherent resistance to explicit expression. In effect, the unwritten part of a constitution is its most significant element because it accommodates the constitution's encoded system of abeyances by which any constitution ultimately survives or perishes.

By concentrating on the gaps and fissures in a constitution, it is possible to sense the silent strength of a collective and instinctive impulse to condone glaring anomalies. In the future, such anomalies may be cited as stark evidence of how the British and American constitutions were at root unsustainable and liable to degenerate from logical incoherence into open disorder. After 300 years, the Stuart constitution is habitually looked upon in such a comfortably assured manner. But, as this essay has sought to show, the Stuart constitution was potentially durable because of a supportive constitutional culture which enabled participants to work with, and through, the contradictions and divisions that only in hindsight appear unsustainable. More significantly, there is also evidence to show that something of the Stuart constitution and, in particular, of its cultivated attitudes of agreeable indeterminacy, wilful neglect, and studied evasion are present and functioning in modern constitutions like those of Britain and the United States.

The Stuart practice of resolving conflict by not confronting the nature of divisions to anywhere near their logical and analytical conclusions can be discerned quite clearly in modern constitutions, with their similar repertoires of abeyances and 'stops in the mind'. That which is unwritten, therefore, cannot always be rendered expressible or even distinguishable — let alone be admissible to precise knowledge. What is unknown in this sense, however, is not necessarily contrary to the ethos of constitutional government. On the contrary, it would appear that abeyances can be portrayed as not only being central to the objective of limited government, but also indicative of a conscious political community geared to inhibiting conflict through a protocol of diversion and circumvention. It may well be that such a normative solidarity is built upon individual groups and parties being, in Arthur Koestler's phrase, 'accomplices by omission'. But there is no reason to suppose that such a solidarity is less resilient than any other; and no reason why such a body of instinctive and precautionary attitudes should not be given the recognition that is normally reserved for the more definitive and explicit contributions to the maintenance of a constitutional order.

Gaps in a constitution should not be seen as simply empty space. They amount to a substantial plenum of strategic content and meaning vital to the preservation of a constitution. Such interstices accommodate the abeyances within which the sleeping giants of potentially acute political conflict are communally maintained in slumber. Despite the absence of any documentary or material form, these abeyances are real, and are an integral part of any constitution. What remains unwritten and indeterminate can be just as much responsible for the operational character and restraining quality of a constitution as its more tangible and codified components. Those constitutional analysts and scholars who dismiss the 'written-unwritten' classification, therefore, are right to do so. But they are right for the wrong reasons. They are correct in drawing attention to the way that both written and unwritten constitutions can be reduced to rules already written or to customs, conventions, and usages that are always susceptible to being written. Nevertheless, they are incorrect in overlooking those elements within both written and unwritten constitutions which remain in abeyance and thereby remain dependent upon an instinctive, indefinable, and thoroughly unwritten code of practiced obscurity and accepted ambiguity.

Part III

Chapter five

The theory of abeyances and modern constitutional unsettlement in Britain and the United States

Prior to the 1970s, the British constitution could still be portrayed as an entity of assured meanings and principles. It was seen to possess a distinctive identity which belied its unwritten format and which prevailed through the dissonance of rapid political and institutional change. At its heart lay a limited number of potent political axioms that were seen to be expressed so forcefully into institutional devices that it became a matter of habit to presume that the common-sense experience of everyday political life necessarily embodied an interior state of constitutional coherence.

The most important and most self-evident of these controlling axioms included principles such as parliamentary sovereignty, the rule of law, constitutional monarchy, cabinet government, individual and collective ministerial responsibility, parliamentary democracy, party government, judicial independence, and constitutional convention. In so far as the relationships between them were closely examined, they were generally viewed as being in one way or another mutually inclusive and forming a spontaneously integrated arrangement. That such a concoction of principles and formalities was habitually assumed to satisfy the criteria of a constitutional settlement to the extent of precluding the need for a written constitution bore witness to the belief that the British system had been touched by historical providence.

History has traditionally been seen by the British as a substitute for a properly conceived and fully worked out constitution. History has performed this function in two important ways. First, it provides a standing explanation for the absence of a tangible constitutional entity governing the distribution and exercise of power, and regulating the relations between the state and the citizen according to clearly discernible rules. History has rendered such a deficiency intelligible by proffering reasons for the British constitution's uncodified agglomeration of laws, usages, customs, and traditions. From this perspective, it is clear that a succession of authoritative sources of legal powers, rights, and restraints have been made available, and have been built

The silence of constitutions

up by accumulation, throughout British history.

The basic historical context of the constitution is provided by the antiquity of common law. The multiplicity of inherited legal legacies concerning private rights and crown prerogatives were originally subsumed under the idea of a *de jure* sovereign kingdom of ancient liberties fashioned and recognized through judicial decision. Declaratory refinements to common law through landmark statutes (e.g., the Bill of Rights of 1689, the Act of Settlement of 1701) expressing new social and political priorities culminated in the elevation of the principle of parliamentary sovereignty into the 'one fundamental law of the British constitution'.[1] With the various Representation of the People Acts (in 1832, 1867, 1884, 1918, 1948 and 1969) together with the Parliament Acts (1911 and 1949), Parliamentary sovereignty subsequently became compounded with the thrust of an electorate expanding in numbers, demands and levels of organization. Parliamentary democracy thereby became 'the essential principle which underlay the whole of the British constitution'.[2] It was clear that this democracy was one of party majorities in the House of Commons drawing upon their electoral authority to provide both party government and party accountability through the devices of ministerial and cabinet responsibility, and ultimately through the sanction of a parliamentary or electoral defeat.

In this sense, history can plot the reasons for the lack of a codified constitution. It is possible, for example, to refer to the common-law tradition to explain why civil liberties in Britain are still based upon a negative concept, whereby a citizen's rights are implicitly reserved up to the point where they are expressly limited by act of Parliament, or by common law itself. Since silence has always denoted an individual's presumptive proprietorship of rights and liberties, this tradition has been instrumental in deterring the movement towards any sweeping codes of positively defined rights.

Another historical explanation for Britain's unwritten constitution is afforded by the traditional principle of Parliamentary sovereignty, which has been logically and practically repugnant to the very notion of a superior fundamental law applied through the courts and made to render statute law subordinate to a higher legal authority. Since one Parliament cannot bind its successors, any codified constitution brought into existence by a Parliament would remain at best a provisional and precarious statement of intent, conditioned by the interests and behaviour of future Parliaments. The historical authority of Parliamentary sovereignty, therefore, means that Parliament would need to write any proposed constitution, but it also means that Parliament could rewrite it at anytime.

On other occasions, it is purely historical circumstances that can account for the lack of development in constitutional law. W.D.B. Mitchell, for example, believes it was 'one of our misfortunes that we had our overt revolutions early'.[3] Because the revolution of 1688 came before the development of the modern state, it effectively bequeathed a traditionalist set of common-law courts and private-law concepts to later generations in differing circumstances. When the need for a more advanced administrative law and for greater legal control of the government's burgeoning activities became apparent, the old common-law practices proved to be wholly inadequate to the task. The retarded development of public law provoked a corresponding increase in the dependence upon full Parliamentary supervision in the nineteenth century. As a result, 'the respect for, and belief in, the efficacy of Parliamentary controls moved courts to assume an attitude of restraint'[4] at a level even greater than before, thereby providing the basis for the judiciary's characteristic reticence in appraising the motives, merits, and morals of government decisions in the twentieth century.

The second important sense in which history can be said to have replaced substantive constitutional principle in Britain is the way in which the constitution is referred to and comprehended as a historical process. Through this device, the melange of past practices, contemporary usages, and accumulated sources of authority can be rationalized in hindsight as the fitful and improvised course of political evolution. Evolution is a process that incorporates the purposelessness of arbitrary chance and circumstance with the generative properties of time to produce an involuntary pattern of adaptive improvement. What might be seen a mere compilation of past developments and traditional practices, therefore, can also be viewed as an integrated expression of historical experience conferring a unified meaning upon political existence.

The British constitution was very much conceived in this evolutionary light during the late Victorian and Edwardian era (1870–1914), when the stature of Britain and her political arrangements were at their height. Combining the contemporary interest in Darwinian natural selection with the more traditional conceptions of a 'national character' and an 'ancient constitution' and the Whig notion of progressive history, the prevailing view of British government was one of a culmination of historical advance. Difficulties had been overridden, challenges had been resolved, and changes had been assimilated without any profound disturbances to the productive continuity of British history. Britain had emerged from history not only with national power and economic wealth, but with a unique record of governmental stability drawn from an apparently idiosyncratic capacity to adapt to the demands for popular participation whilst retaining the heritage of its established structures of traditional authority.

> Not only were many books written about it [i.e., British government], but most of the commentators assumed that there could scarcely be any improvements. . . . The conventions and practices of the late

Victorian period were not considered as merely true for that time, they were regarded as proper or normal. When further changes occurred, they were noticed with reluctance and tended to be regarded as departures from the norm, the main features of this system still dominating the textbooks in use after the Second World War.[5]

The chief means of apprehending the British constitution thus became rooted in the inescapability of the past. This fact was brought to the attention of generations of prospective students by commentators such as J. Harvey and L. Bather, who still phlegmatically forewarn their readers that 'since the British constitution is largely the result of a process of adaptation covering a period of over a thousand years, a historical background helps considerably.'[6]

To the question of why Britain has no properly declared constitutional settlement, therefore, history could provide two kinds of answer. First, it could give the reasons for the absence of an overriding constitutional entity. Secondly, it could explain why there was no *need* for a normal constitution. Evolution moves in mysterious ways, its wonders to perform, and the British constitution was such a wondrous embodiment of the layered accretions of British history that it could not and should not be confined to documentary sanction. Historical experience was simply transposed to political experience through which, and only through which, the British constitution could be said to exist.

The chief difficulty in this reliance on historical and political experience to define the nature of British government, however, is that it generates the most chronic problems in establishing the meaning and identity of the constitution. Without the anchorage of any fixed legal principles of superior obligation, the British constitution becomes an exercise in inductive reasoning. Its forms and principles have necessarily to be inferred from particular usages and circumstances. While other countries have climates, Britain simply has its weather. The British constitution has the same amorphous ubiquity and the same facility to elude generalized categories of definition. It stands as an improvised bundle of laws, customs, and institutions defying collective definition but nevertheless assuming an irrefutable authority as an embodiment of historical progression and social obligation. As a result, it is more customary to record the fact of the constitution's existence than to describe the properties of its character.

It is this emphasis upon the deed rather than the word that has generated the peculiar British dependence on great authoritative works of interpretation to divulge something of the substance and meaning of the British constitution.[7] Significantly, these books of revelation, which have no formal authority whatsoever, are nevertheless the only form in which the British constitution approaches the coherence and clarity of a systematic point of legal reference. Yet in the end they are only interpretations. They resemble Monet's series of impressionist scenes of Rouen Cathedral painted at different times of the day to capture the visual changes in the masonry. Monet's objective was to record the several ways that changing light and atmospheric conditions amended the form and colour of the same subject — so much so in fact that the solidity and exterior reality of the cathedral were drawn further into doubt with every additional record of Monet's experience.

The British constitution is similarly lost in a translucent haze. It can acquire a definitiveness of form by means of a concerted interpretation, but it can just as easily lose that definition through the proliferation of differing interpretations given to it. The very existence and meaning of the historical bequest is thereupon thrown into such doubt that in some quarters the only solution has been to abandon altogether the idea of apprehending the constitution and, instead, to acknowledge that it is nothing other than a record of what politicians do, or even simply what happens in British politics.[8]

Presented with this surfeit of historical authority and with the corresponding absence of a clear identity, it is customary to resolve the subsequent disarray by emphasizing popular traditional attitudes towards the constitution. The functional substance and historical legacy of the constitution is then normally conveyed through the medium of intuitive outlook and social manners. This process is almost invariably one of inference and implication rather than of explicit declaration. But it is no less effective for that.

In the usually awkward first chapters of textbooks on British government it is often the case that authors tend to list a succession of historical events and developments as an explanation of the British constitution, only to find that by the end that they have propelled themselves into a blind alley in which the historical record makes no coherent sense at all. Relief comes in the form of established habits of British behaviour and sentiment that act as the works managers of the constitution and that effectively rationalize the diversity of its forms and principles. The constitution's silences, conventions and unwritten mysteries are taken as signs of the social continuity and homogeneity which accommodate such apparent deficiencies and make them viable instruments of government.

If Arthur Balfour's dictum is correct that 'we are a people so fundamentally at one that we can afford to bicker',[9] then it is that historical unity which can be seen to work through the plethora of institutions and practices and to fashion the British way of government. It is that assurance of political solidarity which fosters the characteristic bravura of relying upon conventions and customs, and of daringly sustaining the huge powers of the Prime Minister and cabinet with hardly an acknowledgement in statute or common law. While this penchant for imprecision can lead to highly convoluted and arcane debates about what is or is not a convention, the working arrangements of British government are seen in the final analysis to be 'like the most fundamental rules of any constitution in that they rest essentially upon general aquiescence'.[10]

This emphasis upon the solidity of political attitudes tends to set in motion a set of circular arguments. The basic proposition is that because the constitution is in many respects undefined, this property becomes in its own right a measure of the settled status of British government — which in turn is interpreted as meaning that there has been no need to provide the constitution with a greater degree of definition and precision. Just as silence is seen as denoting a presumptive agreement, so basic unanimity is seen as allowing for constitutional silence. Accordingly, the constitution becomes the projection of that sort of implicit reciprocity that can be deferred to without formal agreement or declaration. The end result is one of a constitution for a people with no need for a constitution and, therefore, with a constitution which embodies that lack of need.

The most celebrated and most enduringly persuasive example of this circularity was provided by Albert Venn Dicey in his standard work entitled *Introduction to the Study of the Law of the Constitution*.[11] Dicey fully acknowledged the Austinian orthodoxy of Parliamentary sovereignty which could make or unmake any law and which precluded the right of any court to set aside parliamentary legislation in deference to any notion of a fundamental law. The second of Dicey's controlling principles of the British constitution, however, was the rule of law, by which public authorities would be constrained from acting beyond their statutory powers by the courts. Judges and juries would reveal the general principles of the constitution as a result of 'judicial decisions determining the rights of private persons in particular cases brought before the courts'.[12] Dicey tried to fuse the clearly unconstrained legal potential of Parliament with the notion of a rule of law which — if it were to mean anything apart from the truism that Parliament conferred any power by law — had to incorporate some autonomous standard of legal principle and political legitimacy. He combined the two elements by proceeding on the understanding that those liberal principles which would reveal themselves in the judgement of juries would be the self-same principles informing the decisions of the sovereign Parliament. In other words, Dicey propounded the idea that Parliamentary sovereignty and the rule of law were mutually inclusive and mutually supportive principles based upon a common core of nineteenth-century beliefs concerning individual freedom and private rights.

Dicey's assimilation of the seventeeth century's settlement establishing the principle of Parliamentary sovereignty was conditioned by the imputation of an underlying dimension to that settlement, in which both Parliament and judiciary were seen as the joint guarantors of a corpus of common-law rights. Parliament could be entrusted with the custody of sovereignty as it could be expected to exercise self-restraint and to preserve those common-law traditions that were always receiving elucidation and refinement in the law courts. Dicey's thesis has been subjected to sustained criticism over the last fifty years, not least because his libertarian passion for legal rights prevented him from appreciating the 'difficulty of reconciling the power of Parliament — which at a whim could destroy it — with the rule of law'.[13] Nonetheless, the Diceyan perspective is still significant for providing the traditional paradigm of the British constitution; for the way that its language and concepts continue to resonate through any discourse on British government; and for epitomizing the genre of deducing a necessary constitutional settlement from the appearance of settled attitudes to the basic but undocumented manners of government.

The characteristically British emphasis on attitudes and outlooks congruent with the operational arrangements of government can be seen as a sign of constitutional weakness. In contrast to the United States's constitution, with its obvious physical form and documentary nature, the British constitution is an extrapolation from the postulated presence of political beliefs and behaviour compatible with the existence of a settled constitutional structure. Ronald Butt, for example, is quite correct when he points out that 'no constitution, written or unwritten, is worth more than the political temper of the community allows it to be worth' and that ultimately the 'capacity for constitutional development depends . . . on the political spirit of the nation.'[14] The British constitution, denuded of any formal textual attire, has been rightfully instrumental in fixing attention on the underlying need for political beliefs, practices, and traditions appropriate to the maintenance of a constitutionally legitimate government. In this respect, Britain's traditionally upward view — moving from social attitudes to connotations of a constitution incorporating agreed political structures and legal arrangements — is to be thoroughly commended for its analytical veracity. But this virtue is more than outweighed by a concomitant vice.

The major problem and chief objection connected with this British trait is that it normally proceeds on the understanding that settled forms of political conduct are evocative of a fundamental and comprehensive constitutional settlement, allowing for manageable conflict within the tranquillity of an accepted and assured constitutional framework. Whilst it is entirely appropriate to concentrate on political attitudes rather than on the superstructure of constitutional accoutrements, it seems quite inappropriate and unjustified to assume an equivalence between a condition of amenable political conduct and the existence of a settled constitution.

From any careful examination of the history of the British constitution, it is clear that 'the building has been constantly added to, patched, and partially reconstructed, so that it has been renewed from century to century; but it has never been razed to the ground and rebuilt on new foundations.'[15] It has already been acknowledged that the net result can be passed off as the necessary condition of trial and error required for evolutionary improvement. On closer inspection, such a view seems excessively short-sighted. The variety in both the structures and foundations of the British constitution is of such magnitude that it is difficult to reach any conclusion other than that the British form of government is riddled with dualities, disjunctions, and anomalies. Far from embodying a sense of British history's inner coherence, the British constitution is replete with great yawning gaps of unsettled sources of authority and unresolved issues of procedures, powers, and rights. When the British constitution is logically examined and broken down into its component parts, it quickly becomes apparent that the constitution's silences become far more comprehensible than its substantive elements.

The functional value of silence and of other forms of distraction in affording protection to the unresolved and arguably insoluble disjunctions implicit in the British constitution can be gauged by the severity of those disjunctions themselves. For example, there still exists no adequately worked-out relationship between common law and statute law, or between the legitimacy of natural law concepts in the rule of law and the legislative supremacy of Parliament. Civil liberties in such a reputedly modern and positive state are consequently left in a residual limbo of common-law rights made sustainable only by inference through the absence of statutory restrictions.

One form of improvised coexistence is readily compounded by others. The principle of equality before the law, for instance, has to accommodate not only local government and police officers who possess powers denied to the ordinary citizen, but also the legal immunities enjoyed by trade unions and by the crown. Another blind spot of the constitution is its simultaneous acknowledgement of the legal process in restraining official power and of the countervailing power of corporate bodies (e.g., trade unions, local government, churches, civil service, professions) which can deploy their influence in the service of balanced policies and of protected individual freedoms. These two elements of government can act in unison to restrict the ambit of the state, but they can also act against one another and are always potentially contradictory.

> For one is individualistic and the other corporate. One is legalistic and the other political. A danger, especially in a world of organisational power, is that individual liberty and moderation will be

shoved aside by the urgencies and passion of the group struggle.[16]

This theme is connected to another of the constitution's major fault-lines, namely, the status of democratic authority in a system which progressed to its democratic form through a succession of incremental changes to a structure that continued to incorporate much of the historical imprint of the pre-democratic age.

Part of the price paid for not having had anything that could be described as a climactic revolution has been a condition of chronic ambiguity over the British constitution's democratic credentials. It is still an elementary fact that the 'emanation of sovereign power from the people of the United Kingdom, and its conferring upon Parliament, is a fact to which the Constitution itself is blind'.[17]

This omission has led to a depth of confusion over the rightful relationship between the monarchy, the House of Lords, and the House of Commons in the relative attribution of sovereignty. It has generated obscure conceptual devices such as Dicey's differentiation of 'political sovereignty' (i.e., the electorate) from 'legal sovereignty' (i.e., the Parliament). It has perpetuated the idea that members of Parliament are appointed trustees of the nation rather than representatives of their separate constituencies; that the electorate votes for an independent House of Commons rather than for a government; and that the House of Commons is privy to a host of privileges to protect its members from what they may regard as excessive and improper influence by outside parties exercizing what might be argued elsewhere to be their right to ensure adequate representation and redress of grievances. Lastly, the constitution's blindness towards the electorate has led to a quite disproportionate reliance upon customs and conventions to contrive a system of rules by which the power of an elected majority in the House of Commons might work its way through government and receive recognition of the authority conferred upon it by the people.

Given these ambiguities and anomalies, it might be thought that the soaring principle of Parliamentary sovereignty would provide a thorough rationalization of the fractured and disjointed nature of British government. And yet behind the edifice that proclaims Parliamentary sovereignty to be 'the dominant characteristic of our political institutions'[18] lies a similarly disorganized lack of settlement. Parliamentary sovereignty appears to be the supreme guiding principle of British government, drawing on the authoritative arrangements established in the Glorious Revolution and affording Parliament the clear and pre-eminent power to accomplish anything attainable by law through the medium of its own legislative processes. In more popular terms, Parliament can do anything it wishes to the constitution except bind succeeding Parliaments. Parliamentary supremacy, therefore, is taken to be a given fact conditioned only by the constraints of public opinion and electoral forces operating upon the House of Commons.

The reality of Parliamentary sovereignty, however, is much more ambiguous. It is not so much a declaration of political power as a tradition of legal principle, the exact origins and legitimacy of which remain firmly wrapped in obscurity.[19]

> What it amounts to is that the courts have adopted the practice of accepting validly made Acts of Parliament as being superior to other legal rules . . . The sovereignty of Parliament is therefore itself an example of case law. It is also one on which there are remarkably few cases, so that some doubt exists as to its precise implications.[20]

Parliamentary sovereignty, therefore, is a legal convention determining the action of judicial authorities. Paradoxically, while the legally assured supremacy of Parliament has made the courts the foundation of Parliamentary power, the same principle has deterred the judiciary from developing an evaluative function in respect to government legislation, and has instead reduced the role of the courts essentially to one of ensuring that Parliament's laws are correctly applied. The judiciary's resistance to developing a body of constitutional law applicable to Parliament has not only secured the independence of the courts, but has also ensured that issues are debated and resolved on political rather than legal grounds.

Another consequence of the legal basis of Parliamentary sovereignty is that the principle lies embedded in a mass of common law. Parliament cannot supersede common law, but nonetheless, in a system apparently dominated by the positive enactments of a sovereign entity, the surrounding hinterland of common law traditions provide a further dimension to the anomalies in the British constitution. The most conspicuous example of this peculiar dimension lies in the perpetuation of crown prerogative, the customary powers and privileges exclusively reserved to the crown by right of its regal authority.

Crown prerogative includes the power to summon and dissolve Parliament, make treaties, control the disposition of the armed forces, to declare war, give pardons, appoint ministers, judges, and privy councillors, confer honours and control the administration of the civil service.[21] Originally, the monarchy retained many of its medieval prerogative powers after the Glorious Revolution. Yet with the advent of ministerial dependence in the eighteenth century and the widening of the franchise in the nineteenth century leading to the onset of cabinet government, ministers became politically responsible to Parliament, but still legally responsible to the crown for their powers and actions. The net effect has been for ministers to co-opt the crown prerogative for their own ease of government and to rely on their majority support in the House of Commons to prevent any Parliamentary intrusion into the free masonry of government decision-making. Thus the crown has become a euphemism for central government, while the prerogatives have remained largely the same in content.

There is no question that Parliament could at any time limit and even abolish crown prerogative, but it has generally chosen not to. Even when it has attempted to exert a measure of control, the precise relationship between statute law and crown prerogative has remained as problematical as before — a problem further compounded by the chronic uncertainty surrounding the relationship between crown prerogative and the position of the courts. The difficulty of reducing crown prerogative to Parliamentary or legal supervision is, apart from the problem of motivation, largely a function of their nature in that they embody the requirement of executive discretion in areas of especially sensitive decision-making. It would be difficult to legislate controls in fields of policy which do not conform to ordered patterns of legal prescription. As things stand, it is 'not easy to discover and decide the law regarding the royal prerogative and the consequences of its exercise'.[22] Nevertheless, Parliament's general avoidance of even minimal supervision of crown prerogative and, on occasion, conscious efforts at self denial in this field has had the effect of transferring the 'nebulous inherent part of the mystery and sanctity of the crown'[23] to the Prime Minister and cabinet — leaving Parliament in a position of despatching its powers of legal definition and political accountability to the capaciously indefinable and unaccountable void of the crown prerogative. To give two examples: the political advice upon which the sovereign makes decisions on appointments, patronage, and Parliamentary dissolution has been formally ruled as out of order in Parliamentary proceedings; and the Parliamentary Commissioner for Administration is prevented from making investigations in practically all the areas covered by crown prerogative.

The prerogative powers epitomize what Gillian Peele describes as the 'oddly schizophrenic' nature of the British tradition. Regarding the ideas of the state as 'foreign and unfamiliar', executive powers are made amenable by being categorized under the device of the crown; but in the process, they constitute a 'degree of discretionary power available to the executive which is formidable indeed'.[24] Indeed, it is so formidable that, in the opinion of one outside observer, 'no other western democracy has accumulated over time such an awesome array of powers designed to assure the integrity of government and to prevent or suppress civil disorder'.[25] The recourse to the crown prerogative's reliquary of abstruse privileges is entirely typical of a system of government dependent upon usages and improvisations rather than on conclusive settlements.

These disjunctions and anomalies are not minor inconsistencies. They are vast chasms of constitutional 'unsettlement' compounded by a depth of difference in the various constructions given to the nature and purposes of government. In Britain, the exact source and location of sovereign power remains elusive and undisclosed, thereby affording enormous potential for dispute. There exists, for example, well-documented Tory and socialist interpretations of types of representation, forms of democracy, and categories of liberties within the British system of government.[26] Ideological divergences extend inevitably to the very concept of a constitution. On the one side, the libertarian tradition emphasizes entrenched individual rights made enforceable against governmental authority by courts working on the principle of limited government. On the other side, the socialist tradition stresses the constitution's facility for an interventionist state by way of Parliamentary sanction and electoral mandates.

The possibilities for chronic division and unmanageable conflict are rife. The ameliorative properties of a binding constitutional tradition can seem remote when one party regards the other as subverting the constitution in an egalitarian crusade to crush civil liberties, property rights, and individual autonomy beneath a socialist state, while the other sees its role as freeing society from 'the tentacles of the natural lawyers, the metaphysicians and the illusionists' who always give the impression that 'the working of the constitution is something all done by mirrors',[27] and who continue to act as the dissembling instruments for conserving the status quo by wrapping political conflict up in the arcane trickery of legal argument and the rule of law.

The existence of a unified constitutional tradition can look even more remote when one considers the gulf between the outlook of Tory democracy — which has traditionally refuted the proposition that the voter is the 'active and originating element'[28] in government — and that of the radical and dissident perspective, which has often justified the tactics of extra-Parliamentary action and violent defiance of the law on the grounds of an institutional corruption of democracy, denying the use of power from the populace who rightfully possess it.[29]

Despite all these raw materials for profound discord and the pungent possibilities for exploiting the yawning gaps in the constitution, the British system has nevertheless been marked by a general disinclination to translate political drives into constitutional argument. British politics have traditionally been characterized by a missing constitutional dimension. Political discussion reveals a basic discomfort with the language of constitutional dispute and an 'unfamiliarity with discussing the constitution in broad conceptual terms'.[30] According to Gillian Peele, the way in which the British debate issues which elsewhere would be regarded as thoroughgoing constitutional issues (e.g., a bill of rights or the role of the House of Lords) displays the depth of the United Kingdom's attachment to *ad hoc* solutions and its lack of interest in general constitutional issues. . . . Many examples could be given to bear out the assertion that the British are reluctant to treat what are manifestly constitutional issues in terms of general principles.[31]

The British antipathy to abstract and penetrating theorizing about the state in an open, accessible, and commonplace manner has often been thought of as a peculiar deficiency born out of exceptional historical circumstances by a people sufficiently at one to superimpose that unity upon an otherwise shambolic constitution, thereby providing it with the appearance of some order and coherence.

This condition, however, is no deficiency at all, but a representation of something fundamental to the viability of a constitutional culture. The British are different in the sense that they have had to face the fact that, even in the midst of an apparently thriving constitutional system of government, constitutions do not solve, and cannot be expected to solve, the basic underlying questions of authority and power. The British are only too well aware that at a fundamental level they do not have a constitutional settlement. Much remains to be sorted out, worked over, and thought through. But just as much remains to be left thoroughly unresolved.

The British constitution's weakness, therefore, is its realism. But this is also its strength, for it means that British politics have had to acknowledge the incompleteness of the constitution and to work around its formidable gaps. This takes technique, practice, and subtlety. It is not enough to pass off the problem, and the achievement in overcoming it, by simply resorting to the tautology of one people reciprocally inferring the existence of one constitution. It has been noted above that the circle breaks down on both counts. There is not a single concrete constitutional entity; neither is there an absence of deep social and ideological divisions.

Yet, for the most part, the British constitution is seen as workable and self-sustaining. In some quarters, this can only be explained by reference to a profound mysticism. Seductive though this is, it is not an explanation so much as a denial of one. The real explanation approximates to a feature of British government which is prosaically commonplace; the only element of mystery lies in the fact that it is hardly ever recognized for what it is. Its value is likewise normally never taken into account or appreciated as integral to the British constitution. The feature in question is the British system's facility for devising and maintaining an elaborate structure of constitutional abeyances by which politics can be conducted without constitutional crisis.

Judging by the basic tenor of the textbooks on British government in the 1950s and 1960s, it is clear that the constitution's great gaps of 'unsettlement' were not central to the normal conduct of politics. Indeed, they were quite peripheral to the customary flow of political dispute. 'The fragmentation of constitutional thought'[32] was accepted with equanimity as the conflicts of constitutional principle seemed to move in different and disengaged dimensions. On the surface, British politics was characterized by a basic acquiescence in what were seen to be the constitution's 'charming historical anachronisms and anomalies'.[33] The constitution was taken as an inescapable legacy of Britain's historical development bequeathing forms and sanctions that could be valued from the neutral standpoint of their very longevity.

On the other hand, the constitution was accepted as a set of contemporary improvisations by which the fundamental disjunctions in structures and principles might be satisfactorily circumvented. A.H. Hanson and Malcolm Walles are entirely typical of the generally sanguine outlook at the time.

> Even the class oriented politics which the two-party system now reflects has failed to undermine the essential political homogeneity of the British people . . . Such consensus is possible because class conflict, although real and occasionally reaching a high level of intensity, has never become sufficiently intense to break the barriers of constitutional rule and political convention.[34]

What is not made clear, or recognized in any form, is that much of the substance in the terms 'constitutional rule' and 'political convention' relates implicitly to the British system's capacity for holding its chronically unresolved questions in abeyance where they can be studiously neglected.

It would be well to remind ourselves at this point that abeyances do *not* refer to a solid set of shared beliefs or to some notional compromise between definite positions. They refer to the habit of keeping unsettled questions in a state of remote irresolution through acceptable forms of obfuscation. For much of the post-Second World War era, the standard construction of British government still conformed to the late Victorian ideal, which obscured so many of the constitution's disjunctions through a thick overlay of acquiesence that it was thought to have simplified the constitution through recourse to a single common postulate. According to the Westminster model, the electorate transposed its authority to the party possessing majority status in the House of Commons. This authority was in turn deposited with the cabinet, the members of which were both individually and collectively responsible for departmental administration and for government policy. So long as the Prime Minister and cabinet could retain the confidence of a majority of MPs, then most of its proposals would be enacted and its governing position would be maintained by the public's consent conveyed to the membership of the Commons.

Such a conception of government had the virtue of simplicity and clarity. Everything in government could be construed in terms of a nexus of general consent connecting government institutions and organizations in respect to both authority and accountability. The Westminster system generated its own fictions (e.g., the formal distinction between policy decisions and the execution of policy; the assumption of detailed financial supervison of government by Parliament; the close ministerial control of departments), but, in the main, it satisfied the need for a comprehensive substitute for a fully developed constitutional settlement by rationalizing everything within government through the cloying imprimatur of an ultimate electoral sanction. The Parliamentary party model was favoured by the moderate left because it facilitated the 'execution of a broad ranging programme of reform' in respect to 'economic intervention and planning and the development of social services'.[35] It was also endorsed by the British right because it 'emphasised executive authority and executive strength'.[36]

The appeal of the Westminster model was not a reflection of its integrity as a thoroughly worked-out system of government. It was a measure of its effectiveness in delimiting controversy over the system's innermost gaps and in clearing away much of the constitutional clutter that would otherwise have become entangled in the wheels of party politics. Just how successful the Westminster model's structure of protective abeyances had been in preventing the potential for discord can be gauged by what transpired in the 1970s. During that decade, Britain underwent what has generally been described as a constitutional crisis. Like other critical periods for other constitutions, the crisis of the 1970s was in many ways marked by the destabilizing exposure of constitutional issues which had previously been held in abeyance. Also, like other crises, it was this breakdown in constitutional abeyances which to a large extent determined the nature of, and the reactions to, the crisis.

'The British constitution used to be the envy of the world',[37] with the Westminster version of Parliamentary government seen as the model both for European democracies and post-colonial regimes after the Second World War. And yet by the end of the 1970s, the British structure of government was in the throes of a deep and systemic crisis in which all the anchorages had become dislodged so that there was 'hardly any element of the constitution which [did] not come under attack'.[38] The earlier confidence which had made the British constitution so familiar that it had become 'rather boring to discuss'[39] evaporated into deep anxiety. The spectre haunting Britain was that it possessed 'an old and tired political order' which had begun 'to look obsolete'.[40]

The 1970s were marked by economic stagnation, inflation, unemployment, and industrial and social under-investment, which degenerated at times into open defiance of the law and even of Parliament's very right to legislate in the field of industrial relations. The Heath government's ventures into price controls, incomes policies and trade union law reform — set against a backdrop of an oil crisis, an economic recession, spiralling production costs, declining living standards and, ultimately, a miners' strike that led to a three-day working week amidst a swathe of power cuts, bankruptcies, and proposed 'private armies' — generated a pathological atmosphere of profound scepticism and discord.[41] In February 1974, Edward Heath appealed to the electorate on the grounds of 'who governs the country?' The government lost the election, but the onset of a Labour government with a wafer-thin majority of seats served only to lend weight to the suspicion that the answer to Heath's question was 'no one'.

Two changes of government in less than four years, with each administration intent on reversing the major enactments of the other, was not the norm of stability which had previously characterized the British system. Furthermore, the British electorate was showing signs of alarming volatility. In the 1950s, the standard swing between elections had always been in the region of 2 per cent. Although voter turnout declined in the 1970s, those citizens who did overcome the growing state of indifference, or frustration, or alienation, were far more likely to switch party allegiances to provide rapid swings of over 6 per cent in by-election and general election results.

This new mutability in party attachments undermined both the parties themselves and the two-party system', in that it became possible for third parties suddenly to attract large numbers of floating voters. The subsequent upsurge in the popular support given to the Liberal party and to the Welsh and Scottish nationalist parties in 1974 led, in turn, first to a heightened awareness of the inequities of the old first-past-the-post system and, secondly, to the intensified demands for electoral reform to allow the national profile of party support to be projected more accurately upon the membership of the House of Commons.[42] Such appeals for proportional representation were particularly apposite at the time, as the minority Labour governments (1974–9) tenaciously proceeded on the assumption that any party in power necessarily possessed a full mandate and that the party which controlled Parliament was entitled to the sovereignty that traditionally accompanied it. The net effect of these pressures was a permanently precarious government seeking to act out its powers, whilst at the same time presiding over conditions which were throwing the anomalous and anachronistic basis of those powers into caricatured relief.

The stature of the Labour government, operating as it did on the basis of *ad hoc* Parliamentary coalitions, was that of a crippled government. It continued to face the same disintegrative social and economic forces which had brought the Heath government down, while the centre consensus was further eroded and political positions and ideologies grew even more polarized. Against this backdrop, the Labour government had to confront a range of long-term structural developments which were reducing the stock of national autonomy. Included in these were Britain's membership of the European Economic Community; the integration of British financial, industrial, and agricultural markets — indeed, the whole national economy — into international networks of interdependence; the erosion of national boundaries with rise of communications, technology, and multinational corporations; the increased demands made on the modern administrative state, and its declining capacity to satisfy them in a period of economic decline; the constraints imposed by the International Monetary Fund, the North Atlantic Treaty Organization and, not least, American military forces stationed in Britain; and, lastly, the growing sophistication of the 'corporate state' in which

> governments could not get their way without the agreement of the great producer groups who could bring the economy to a halt, and in which, in consequence, some important aspects of sovereignty now resided in those producer groups and not in the elected representatives of the people.[43]

These weaknesses were compounded by internal challenges. These varied from provocative amendments to government legislation by the House of Lords to the demands for Scottish and Welsh devolution; and from the assertiveness of third parties and the prospect of 'coalition governments' to a decline in Parliamentary authority as reflected in the need to resort to public referenda. The atmosphere of decaying and degraded government was encapsulated by Anthony King, writing in 1976.

> Men and women who have grievances . . . are far readier than a generation ago to take their grievances into the streets. Politically as well as economically, we in Britain can feel the ground shifting, ever so slightly, under our feet. Talk of the end of liberal democracy in Britain is, of course, premature. . . . Although no one has produced a plausible scenario for the collapse of the present British system of government, the fact that people are talking about the possibility at all is in itself significant, and certainly we seem likely in the mid or late 1970s to face the sort of 'crisis of the regime' that Britain has not known since 1832, possibly not since the seventeenth century.[44]

The specific problems of the Labour governments, therefore, were being extrapolated into a widespread anxiety about 'government' in the generic sense. British government appeared to be suffering from an intolerable overload of intractable problems, in which the challenge of full employment, for example, seemed as insuperable as a political settlement in Northern Ireland. Britain was seen to be becoming ungovernable.[45]

At the same time, despite the increasing external constraints on the British constitution, the system of government in relation to its traditional internal limitations appeared to be becoming progressively stronger and more centralized. Propelled by the severity of the problems with which it was confronted, the Labour government was placed in a position of having to maximize every available source of institutional power at a time when the government's authority was marginal and its failures manifest. That a government in such a besieged position could effectively mobilize the traditional machinery of the state and for the most part exercise its will upon Parliament was ostensibly a sign of great strength. Nevertheless, it was also regarded as the ultimate revelation of the British constitution's weakness in that it exposed in a dangerously explicit manner the administration's modern pre-eminence over Parliament and, therefore, over the central source of constitutional restraint and accountability within the system.

Such explicitness in the highly charged atmosphere of heightened public awareness of political arrangements stimulated a spirit of open enquiry into the British constitution. The inevitable effect of this new realism was to throw light into some of the dark areas of the constitution. The Westminster model's postulate of ministerial responsibility, civil service neutrality, and collective cabinet accountability, for example, were revealed not only as the misnomers they had always been, but as edifices which were becoming progressively less convincing as working constructions of government. Whether the seat of government was seen as being lodged in the 'corporate state', the ranks of the parties, the panoply of departmental powers, or the office of the Prime Minister, the conclusion was the same. Namely, that Parliamentary democracy was neither very Parliamentary nor particularly democratic. Yet its power was immense and it was being exercised to the full in Parliament's name. The constitution's fundamental precept of Parliamentary sovereignty was, as a result, fast becoming the constitution's fundamental problem.

Whatever the constitution had been — and it now appeared that it had never been much more than a basic trust in the sufficiency of self-imposed restraints by politically prudent, or else highly secretive, public servants — it now assumed an appearance of deficiencies and failures. It stood as a register of the inadequacies of collective inhibition, as a testament to the ephemeral meanings of Parliamentary supervision and accountability, and as a shroud shielding the genteel nostalgia for Victorian liberalism from the vulgar and colourless power of the modern state. The stark realism of the 1970s stripped away the comfortable securities of the 1950s and laid bare the problematic status of the many changes which the British system had accepted but hardly assimilated over the many years of its development.

There has always been a background rumble of disquiet over the British constitution's adaptation to the central developments of the twentieth century — a mass electorate, party politics, pressure groups, and the Whitehall machine of expanding government functions. Concern had wafted over the real substance of ministerial responsibility, cabinet government, civil service passivity, and Parliamentary accountability. Concern had not, however, given way to anxiety. While it was becoming evident that the Victorian system of democratic control had been overtaken by the modern administrative state, no alternative political theory or strategy of governmental control arose to take the place of the liberal presumptions in the Westminster model. Britain still 'adhered to the democratic doctrines enunciated by the late nineteenth-century liberals, but with flagging conviction'[46] and yet still with a faith that 'unanswered questions would resolve themselves'.[47] In the 1950s, 'the gap between Victorian theory and twentieth-century practice did no damage'. David Marquand continues:

> Ministers, civil servants, lawyers, journalists, back-bench MPs, even trade-unionists and business leaders continued to celebrate the Victorian constitution they had been taught to revere in their youth, oblivious of the fact that, in their daily lives, they adhered to a quite different constitution, which had grown up imperceptibly inside the skin of the old one. But the system worked: and the fact that it did not work as the textbooks said was of academic interest only.[48]

Even as late as the 1960s, when various gestures towards piecemeal and marginal reforms were made, the basic outlook was still that of assuming 'without really thinking about it, that our political system would remain essentially unchanged';[49] and that since 'everything had operated without fuss within an unwritten and flexible constitution',[50] everything would continue in much the same way.

In the corrosive atmosphere of the 1970s, these assumptions no longer held. Indeed, the British were placed in the unaccustomed position: they had seriously to question the constitution. The British constitution suddenly appeared to have stopped working and to be in a state of terminal decline. Whereas in the 1960s, 'there was almost a concern to avoid the problem of the British state', by the 1970s 'there was agreement that British politics had slipped beyond the explanatory grasp, and the control, of the established constitutional theory'.[51] In the ensuing hiatus of critical analysis, the normal cushioning effect of the constitution's network of abeyances was thrown into jeopardy.

Even senior politicians, elder statesmen, and high-ranking judges engaged in the new licentiousness of constitutional speculation. Lord Hailsham's indictment of British government as an 'elective dictatorship' acquired something of a cult status in the mid-1970s. The concentration of power in the hands of the executive formed by minority governments which were exercising an absolute Parliamentary sovereignty without adequate supervision, he said, led to one conclusion: the constitution was 'wearing out'.[52] Lord Hailsham's solution was a properly codified written constitution limiting Parliament 'both by law and by a system of checks and balances'.[53] His call for a bill of rights to be constitutionally entrenched and made applicable to Parliament was echoed by law lords Devlin and Scarman.

Lord Scarman went so far as to advocate a new constitutional settlement together with a supreme court to protect its provisions. He addressed himself to the international human rights movement and to the exposure of the 'unresolved difference between our legal system and our international obligations'.[54] Lord Scarman's solution was a set of new constitutional restraints 'designed to protect the individual citizen from instant legislation conceived in fear or prejudice and enacted in breach of human rights'.[55] Another law lord, Lord Denning, felt that a bill of rights was unnecessary because the custody of civil liberties could be left to common law and, in particular, to its mouthpiece, the judiciary. Favouring an enhanced role for judges, Denning proclaimed that 'the judges of England have always in the past been — and always will be — vigilant in guarding our freedom. Someone must be trusted. Let it be the judges.'[56]

Under normal conditions, judges and statesmen would be those most sensitive to the need for fundamental constitutional controversy to be deflected and defused. Indeed, their very credentials for being judges and statesmen would be closely linked to their skills in discreetly obscuring the gaps of basic unsettlement in the constitution. For them to join academics and commentators in drawing the constitution onto the sword and in predicting 'a generation's work of reform ahead of us, analogous to that between 1832 and 1870',[57] signified the depth of disarray in the constitution and the consequent alacrity with which previously obscured disjunctions within the constitution were being revealed. In the clarion call of two observers, 'constitutional fundamentals had been opened up with a vengeance'.[58]

Having had such basic constitutional issues brought to the surface of public controversy in the 1970s, it is appropriate to ask why such an apparently chronic condition of constitutional disintegration was not continued in the 1980s. Clearly this question begs many others; and it is true to say that the extent to which a crisis has existed in the British constitution during the 1980s is open to some dispute. It can be argued, for example, that the constitutional challenge of the 1970s has been maintained.

The record of the Thatcher government since 1979 supports the contention that the issue of the constitution is still prominent in British politics. The central government has restricted locally elected authorities in respect to expenditure control and rate-capping. It has abolished the entire tier of metropolitan councils, together with their Labour Party connections and policies. It has engaged in a drive against the unauthorized disclosure of embarrassing political information through the use of criminal prosecutions under Section 2 of the Official Secrets Act (cf. Sarah Tisdall in 1984, Clive Ponting 1985). It has enlarged police powers of arrest, search and seizure, and detention through the provisions of the Police and Criminal Evidence Act 1984. It has, through the successive reforms of trade union structures and practices, weakened unions by reducing their legal immunities, and has gone so far as to eliminate the right of workers at the Government Communications Headquarters (GCHQ) to join a union and to deprive the staff there of its legal rights under employment protection legislation. The Thatcher government has on these and many other issues given cause for concern over the scale of central power and the extent to which it has been used not only to emasculate centres of organized opposition in the community, but also to accommodate ever greater reserves of authority with which to control public resources and information.

Given these developments, it appears that governmental power has been as provocative and controversial a subject in the 1980s as it was in the 1970s. Certainly, the condemnations of the Thatcher government from the perspective of constitutional propriety have been just as severe as the assaults upon the Heath, Wilson, and Callaghan governments. Patrick McAuslan and John McEldowney, for example, perceive 'a crisis in the living constitution' because of

> the increasing use of governmental power and law for partisan ends, the increasingly aggressive manner in which this power is exercised, and the increasingly casual way in which the legal framework for and legal controls on the exercise of power are being treated. . . . Uses of power and law . . . seem to betray . . . a contempt for or at least an impatience with the principles of limited government and a belief that the rightness of the policies to be executed excuse or justify the methods whereby they are executed.[59]

Bearing in mind the stimulus to defensive forms of constitutional thought provided by the style and policies of the Thatcher government, it would appear at first sight that the constitution had retained its pivotal position in the arguments and emotions of British politics.

Yet, despite the provocation of the Thatcher governments and the heightened public consciousness of constitutional issues displayed in the period immediately prior to 1979, the 1980s have not been marked by the kind of political intensity which surrounded the constitution in the 1970s. It would be disingenuous to suggest that the decline of interest in the constitution has been due to Mrs Thatcher's 'lack of radical resolve in constitutional matters'[60] and the subsequent abandonment of several reforms from the political agenda. True, she has consistently opposed proportional representation, devolution, a reformed House of Lords, and a bill of rights out of a conservative impulse to leave well enough alone. It is known that 'whenever a written constitution or a bill of rights is mentioned to Mrs Thatcher, her eyes glaze [because] she is frankly bored by the subject'.[61] Nevertheless, as has been acknowledged above, the political radicalism of the Thatcher governments in the 1980s has necessarily had severe constitutional repercussions. Her governments have been every bit as constitutionally radical through their policies and behaviour as any administration avowedly dedicated to constitutional reform.

But much of the reason why Mrs Thatcher has been in a position to exercise the power to reach her political objectives has been because of the accommodating diminishment of concern for constitutional issues in the populace at large. Discomforted constitutional scholars have sought to expose the government's 'arrogance in the use of power'[62] and its 'brusque way with legal niceties'[63] in order to draw attention to governmental practices which 'live very uneasily' with society's expectations of 'openness, democracy and public accountability'.[64] The public temper, however, has proved to be far less susceptible than before to anxieties over governmental legitimacy, or to appeals for constitutional renovation. Even when faced with direct evidence of arbitrary government and abuse of power, 'we British', as Tam Dalyell put it, 'nowadays too often simply shrug our shoulders at wrongdoing in public life'.[65] He concludes his book, *Misrule*, on what he regards as the 'predatory, authoritarian and dishonest trends in government'[66] with the comment that 'cynicism at the top has bred a cynicism to match it among the British people, which now expects its politicians to be untruthful as a matter of course'.[67]

A number of factors lay behind this decline in the prominence of constitutional change and reform. A central reason was the Thatcher governments' substantial working majorities in the House of Commons. Although the Conservative party won the 1979, 1983, and 1987 elections by only a plurality of 43.9, 42.4 and 42.3 per cent of the national vote respectively, the Thatcher administrations proceeded on the assumption of a full, robust mandate from the electorate. The zeal of the government, combined with the ineffectualness of a demoralized and divided opposition, produced an old-fashioned governing party on the lines envisaged by the Westminster model — a majority party emancipated from the need to rely upon Parliamentary pacts or to give consideration to constitutional reform.

Another related factor was the absence of a breakthrough by either of the two main third parties, the Liberal and Social Democratic parties, which, at the beginning of the 1980s, had threatened to produce a multi-party system, but which after the 1987 election appeared to be relegated to the margins of British politics. With the decline of these parties, both standard bearers of constitutional reform, the Thatcher administrations have assumed an additional implicit mandate not to concern themselves very much with matters of constitutional innovation.

A final factor has been the recovery of the British economy. The economic depressions of the 1930s and 1970s coincided with periods of profound constitutional introspection and calls for change. The revival of Britain's economy during the 1980s has been sufficient to orient minds away from the fundamental structures of government and back to the normal fare of parties and policies, and the competitive struggle for the prize of Parliamentary sovereignty.

What the 1980s have witnessed has been a reaffirmation of the old notion of a 'political constitution' in which constitutional norms are transposed to points of political prudence, and fundamental laws are reduced to ramifications of the electoral sanction. Government authority and individual protection have become as firmly lodged in the power politics of the House of Commons as they ever were in the past. Calls for a written constitution, an entrenched bill of rights, and an assertive judiciary to limit government within set boundaries have declined markedly. They had always been eschewed by the Labour governments of the 1970s partly because of their status as governments, but also because they had interpreted the calls for a constitutional restructuring by the legal *prominenti* as attempts to use judicial means to frustrate their socialist programme which would always be dependent upon the instrument of the state. Even in opposition, Labour has remained suspicious of the constitutional strategy of government restraint.

Such suspicions have not been without some foundation. Professor J.A.G. Griffith, for example, has revealed the similarity in the privileged social background of senior judges and in the personal political prejudices which are brought to bear in their legal judgements. According to Griffith, judges normally interpret the public interest in terms of law and order, of police powers, of property rights in preference to human rights or civil liberties, and of the interests of the state over rights of individuals in areas of national security. Griffith concludes by noting the close congruence of the prevailing political persuasions of the judges with views strongly associated with the Conservative Party.[68] Those who wish to deny such an affinity have not been helped by Lord Hailsham who, when he was afforded a position (i.e., Lord Chancellor) to do something about the 'elective dictatorship' he had so eloquently admonished in the 1970s, suddenly lost his resolve. Alan Watkins observed the transformation.

Happily, he was in Opposition when he coined his phrase and made his orations. In Government we see a changed Quintin displayed before our wondering eyes. From time to time he pops up in the Lords to declare that, while his own deeply held views have not changed, no, not by one iota, nevertheless . . . practical difficulties . . . time is not ripe. . . . much work to be done. Indeed, Lord Hailsham's woebegone performance over the bill of rights has confirmed [that he is] . . . not the man to get things done when the going is rough.[69]

The affirmed statism of the Conservative and Labour parties demonstrates yet again the absence of a unifying political faith in the content, authority, and agency of a politically neutral constitution which would allow British politics to be safely accommodated within a standard medium of constitutional principle.

Because the 'law has been increasingly used by government to regulate relationships in which conflict is inherent'[70] (e.g., trade-union powers, centre-local relations, discrimination practices); and because judges and courts have been called on to apply the law in such politically charged conditions, the consequence has been a greatly enlarged public suspicion of both the law and the judiciary. During the miners' strike (1984–5), for example, it 'appeared that the government was using or relying on the police and the courts to put down opposition and to enable the government to implement its policy'.[71] This has been a common complaint in the 1980s. The government has been accused of 'using the police not to defend the law, but as a means of implementing Tory policy' aided and abetted by a 'compliant judiciary'.[72] The distinctions between policy and law are, of course, extremely fine and dependent, ultimately, upon a sense of perception and discrimination, which is not a facility easily exercised in acrimonious political conditions.

As a result, it is commonly thought that the judiciary's impartiality has been impugned and its independence compromised by its new role. It is true that the courts have in many ways continued to develop the group of legal protections against public authorities which were first cultivated in the 1970s and which were based upon natural justice grounds like 'reasonableness', 'procedural fairness', 'decision-making propriety', and 'legitimate expectation'.[73] However, it is also true that highly publicized cases involving such subjects as trade-union powers, the right to demonstrate, or the public-interest claim of unauthorized disclosure of information by civil servants have led to numerous accusations of 'Tory judges' working hand in glove with a manipulative executive to give judicial sanction to government demands.

This alleged politicization of the courts has led not only to greater instances of deliberate law-breaking by dissident groups in society and to a decline in the public's belief in the judiciary's independence, but, more significantly, to a heightened resistance to any prospect of an acceptably superior level of constitutional law being continuously revealed by judicial construction. One of the casualties of the judiciary's increased prominence, therefore, has been its reputation for impartiality and, with it, the idea that courts and a newly written constitution could be anything other than politically motivated.

The net effect of these changes has been a return to the old pattern of constitutional abeyances. No other conclusion can support the weight of indifference now shown towards constitutional issues or the pressure of resistance to converting political issues into constitutional controversy. This is not to say that the opportunities for constitutional debate have been absent in the 1980s. Quite the opposite, as the following three cases will bear witness.

The intelligence services have been the subject of a variety of articulated concern over the misuse, and even abuse, of their powers.[74] For example, *The Times* recorded in July 1984 that MI5 had received unprecedented 'public exposure of its . . . dirty linen'[75] with the widespread allegations tht MI5 officers had attempted to destabilize the Labour government in 1974–5. Despite such accusations, Mrs Thatcher announced that there would be no independent inquiry; internal MI5 investigations, she said, had already revealed the allegations to be false. She was following Harold Wilson's prescription for Prime Ministers when asked questions about security matters. In the one-page chapter on national security in his book *The Governance of Britain*, Wilson reported that Prime Ministerial answers to national security questions should be such that they 'may be regarded as uniformly uninformative'.[76]

One rather minimal change has been government acknowledgement that the security services actually exist, although they have yet to be given full official recognition. With more information on the security services becoming available to the public, together with calls for reforms in the supervision and accountability of such agencies and with demands for the repeal of the Official Secrets Act, it might be thought that open government and the control of the intelligence community would be live constitutional issues. But despite the stimulus, the public reaction has been insubstantial. Edward Shils's sagacious observation that British government was an organization run by public men as a private affair still seems apposite.[77]

In the face of the most lurid allegations of failure and mismanagement, and the most desperate press demands for a freedom of information act, the Thatcher government took a full nine years before it felt constrained to present (in July 1988) its first serious proposal for reform. Even then, it contained no freedom of information provision and no proposals for any structure of Parliamentary accountability by either a set of Privy Councillors or a select intelligence committee. It did, however, contain a specific provision affirming that ministerial disclosures by past or present intelligence officers would be a criminal offence. The consequence of the government's plan, should it be passed into law, was thought by *The Economist* to have very little effect on the way Whitehall works; government would 'still be conducted on the presumption that everything should be kept secret unless it has to be published'.[78]

Another opportunity for constitutional controversy was provided in 1984 by Mrs Thatcher's peremptory decision, as Minister for the Civil Service, to withdraw from the employees of the Government Communications Headquarters at Cheltenham (GCHQ) their right to be members of a trade union.[79] The courts were prepared to review the legality of this decision on the grounds that it had been made without proper prior consultation with the civil servants' union representatives. The government initially lost the legal argument because it was shown to have contravened the legitimate expectations of the employees in unfairly altering their terms of service without consultation. The minister then resorted to crown prerogative and based the defence of her actions on national security grounds. Although the law lords controversially declared the case to be justiceable despite the presentation of prerogative powers, they unanimously found in favour of the minister.[80]

The judiciary's stipulation of correct and fair procedures in such industrial action were swept aside by the trump card of national security, which nullified any rights of consultation. The Prime Minister's drastic change in working practices at GCHQ represented, at the very least, a denial of basic trade-union rights and yet, apart from some spasmodic resistance and a number of demonstrations organized by the Trades Union Congress, the government's action provoked conspicuously little public outcry.

Just as remarkable for the public quiescence it engendered was the issue of the community charge in 1988. During a prolonged struggle in the House of Commons, a group of thirty-five Tory rebels, led by Michael Mates and supported by six former ministers, had tried unsuccessfully to amend the bill to replace the projected flat-rate poll tax with a graduated tax linked to people's ability to pay the charge. The only remaining opportunity to challenge the government's flagship legislation for local government lay in the House of Lords. The opposition forces mobilized around an amendment proposed by Lord Chelwood, which simply requested the House of Commons to take 'a second look' at the proposed structure of the community charge. It was clear that the intention of this invitation to reappraise the bill was to afford the House of Commons the opportunity of unpacking the flat-rate charge.

Such a modification was clearly against the government's interests; the very severity of the community charge was seen as integral to the solution of local authority overspending.[81] The Prime Minister personally lobbied Conservative peers, arguing the importance of preventing any major amendments to the legislation. Lord Chelwood's amendment in particular was seen as a wrecking amendment and the one proposal which the government had to defeat to ensure the progress of the bill. Until the day of the vote, it was generally thought that the margin between government supporters and opponents would be extremely narrow. In the event, the government defeated the amendment by 317 to 183 votes.

The main reason for such an emphatic victory was that the Tory whips had mobilized large numbers of those Conservative peers who rarely attended the chamber, but who could be relied upon to make the trip to Westminster in a crisis. The availability of such backwoodsman reservists was not a matter of wide public knowledge, but it became so on May 22, 1988, when the normal level of Conservative peers in the House of Lords on a working day (i.e., 120–170) was suddenly inflated to 277 in the biggest voting turnout since the 1971 vote on Britain's entry to the European Economic Community. The additional forces, together with the votes of 40 unaffiliated 'cross-benchers', were enough to convert what in normal conditions would have been a threateningly high level of opposition into a mere gesture of insignificant complaint.[82] Despite the spectacle of the House of Lords having its own constitutional anomalies and anachronisms exploited to the full by a government in the very act of securing passage of what was itself a most profound constitutional change, the episode prompted barely a modicum of critical outcry.

The contrast between the constitutional storms of the 1970s and the drizzle of the 1980s could hardly be more notable, or more illustrative of a fundamental characteristic of British politics. The 1970s opened up many of the gaping holes of unsettlement within the British constitution to the corrosive forces of public scrutiny, political debate, and drives for reform. What had been so amply concealed in the 1950s had become patently obvious in the stark explicitness of the 1970s. It had suddenly become crystal clear, for example, that the British 'no longer had Cabinet government';[83] that Britain lacked 'a clear, popularly accepted doctrine of representative government';[84] and that the 'notion of the absolute sovereignty of Parliament was a formalism expressive of a society in which authority flowed easily and unquestionably from government to people'.[85] It was a time when Keith Middlemas was hailed as the new Bagehot for his efforts at removing the constitutional superstructure of British politics and exposing the corporate bias which lay at the heart of government,[86] and when the Gladstone Professor of Government and Public Administration at Oxford denounced the party system as 'inimical' because in Britain's two-party structure a party did not have to 'earn its Parliamentary majority' so much as have it presented 'as the uncovenanted prize in an archaic lottery'.[87]

This brutal denuding of the forms and fictions of the British system would appear to be so antithetical to the spirit required for constitutional abeyances that it might be thought that they had suffered irreparable damage in the 1970s. But this had hardly been the case. The 1980s have been marked by a compulsive movement back to the safety of constitutional neglect and to the digressive and distractive qualities of the 'political constitution' — geared as it is to the clarity of partisan competition and to the alternation of government as the comprehensive solution to any problems concerning the content, distribution, and use of state power. British politicians in the 1980s have shown yet again that they prefer working within a structure of constitutional abeyances which keeps the deeply disruptive issues of the structure and operation of the constitution mercifully at bay, thus allowing the immediate objectives of the party to be fought for without constant recourse to constitutional principles. Much of what brings politicians and parties together in the good fight is a reciprocal commitment to keep the issue of the constitution permanently defused — a fact which explains many conventions and political practices.

For example, there are the insulating properties of Parliamentary privilege which can keep the relationship between the representative and the represented lodged satisfactorily in ambiguity. There is the elusive conceptual device of the government front bench acting not in their own names, but on behalf of the anonymity of the crown. And there is the convention that socially controversial measures (e.g., abortion and capital punishment) will be decided by free votes in the House of Commons, through which parties can not only elude political responsibility for the fate of such measures, but, more importantly, prevent them from becoming party issues and from compromizing the essential imprecision surrounding such integral formalities of party government as public choice, the electoral mandate and party responsibility. The operating principle is the same in all three cases, namely, reciprocal protection.

In protecting one another, politicians protect the constitution's abeyances at the same time. It is noteworthy, for example, that even at the height of the miners' strike in July 1984 a Labour MP, Martin Flannery, was suspended from the House of Commons for refusing to withdraw a reference to 'tame Tory judges'.[88] It was against the rules of the House to have the impartiality and independence of the judiciary impugned in such a way — even if that impartiality and independence was being called into doubt by the judges' behaviour at the time.

What is important to note is that the preservation and cultivation of abeyances are motivated not out of any self-denying sense of collective obligation, but out of a sophisticated grasp of self-interest. Politicians are well aware that the programmes of their respective parties can be achieved within the structure of the constitution's abeyances. Indeed, most politicians proceed on the assumption that their party platform can *only* be secured by keeping constitutional issues in a state of dormant suspension. Constitutional scholars like Lord Crowther Hunt may relish 'the exciting prospect of a real Pandora's box of constitutional issues and crises if the Labour Party perseveres with its abolition proposals',[89] but astute politicians see such a prospect as yet another occasion on which to keep Pandora's box firmly shut.

In this spirit, the Labour Party's National Executive Committee has recently dropped the party's commitment to abolish the House of Lords. It has seen fit to conform to Edward VII's style of matrimonial management rather than to that of Edward VIII. In other words, while Edward VII's succession of mistresses were maintained within an agreeable swathe of ambiguity in accord with court protocol, Edward VIII and Mrs Simpson's confrontational effort to open their particular Pandora's box was not appreciated at all. Ultimately, it brought down upon them that special opprobrium reserved by the public when it is forced into the unaccustomed position of having a profound moral and constitutional issue thrust discomfortingly upon it.

The 1980s have revealed the advanced British facility for sustaining constitutional abeyances. Even after the severe disruption of the 1970s and the continued pleas from some constitutional scholars for the 'contradictions involved in the various strands of traditional constitutional theory . . . to be drawn out and exposed',[90] the periods of the Thatcher governments have been characterized far more by quiescence in constitutional ambiguity than by any drive for constitutional clarification or reform. Despite the efforts of the recent Charter 88 campaign for a bill of rights, the 1980s have witnessed a re-emergence of the British political temper described by Graeme Moodie in the 1960s as an attitude that 'encourages forbearance (or possibly indolence) in the use of, and opposition to, power and privilege of all kinds'.[91]

This temperament can live with disjunctions and anomalies. It can regard with equanimity the unsettled and incomplete nature of the British constitution as a euphemism, and as an opportunity, for 'growth'. A positive value is accordingly placed on mutability and change and, ultimately, upon ambiguity and equivocation. The British constitution remains constructively vacuous in that it draws people together in response to the potential instability, and even danger, of attempting to elicit *the* constitution from what is now an acceptable melange of coexisting *constitutions*. Any major departure from this collective amnesia of contented disarray is dangerous because, in its absence, there would be nothing on which to fasten in the ensuing hiatus. Apart from the absence of a written document that would provide the constitution with at least a tangible form, the breakdown of abeyances would mark a breakdown in the social consensus; and the subsequent sectional demands for a clarified constitution might well represent the prelude to a civil war as they were in the seventeenth century.

Instead of being a derivative of some concrete social homogeneity, the British constitution approximates far more to a set of sustained improvisations to keep the constitution's gaps off the political agenda. Instead of Arthur Balfour's dictum that the British are so 'fundamentally at one that we can afford to bicker', the real position is that we are so fundamentally at one with knowing our potential for division that we can only afford to bicker. The British are particularly adept at evading constitutional crises when the opportunity for them is so prodigious, and when the social and political divisions are sufficiently deep to have conflicting conceptions of the rule of law and of constitutional government. The British constitution's silences and unwritten nature are a sign of an instinctive, and even fearful, acceptance of genuine indeterminancy, not an effortless projection of an impregnable political solidarity. It is kept safely in a condition of nebulous intimation by the very politicians and statesmen who work successfully *in* it and, thereby, *with* it.

The British constitution therefore only remains workable by way of, and at the level of, condoned obscurities. Characterizations of the British political system such as 'parliamentary sovereignty', 'cabinet government', 'constitutional monarchy', and 'the rule of law' are in effect simply the euphemisms for constitutional abeyances. 'Parliamentary sovereignty', for example, may sound as though the sources, magnitude, location, and usage of ultimate power have been thoroughly resolved. In reality, the Glorious Revolution simply transferred many of the old sources of constitutional friction into a revised state of imprecision, where they continue to be felt today and where their many ramifications have yet to be worked out three hundred years later. The British affinity for constitutional silences has not been a product of the constitution's basic settlement, but of its basic lack of settlement. After centuries of adapting the constitution without unpacking it, the British way is to look after politicians and to let the constitution look after itself.

History may well explain how we have come to possess the kind of constitutional arrangements we have at our disposal. What it cannot so easily explain is how such arrangements function and sustain themselves. It is not enough to impute a simple nexus between constitutional meaning and a social solidarity that is at once the historic cause and effect of the British constitution. As the 1970s displayed so graphically, the potential for civil strife, political polarization, and profound scepticism smoulders beneath an apparently tranquil British constitution. The social homogeneity which does exist, therefore, is not one that simply converts into a positive constitutional unanimity, but one that under normal conditions successfully manages the manifest blind spots of the constitution.

This induced myopia is accomplished through a host of preventative strategies. Some are consciously orchestrated while others are unconsciously made. The net effect is to close down constitutional arguments by holding the gaping holes of constitutional unsettlement in a state of indeterminate suspension to the basic satisfaction of opposing interests and parties, who often agree on little else other than maintaining fundamental constitutional questions in abeyance and keeping the explosive properties of the constitution away from the sparks of political conflict. The social attitudes which sustain the darkness of constitutional abeyances might well be contrary to the customarily evoked spirit and logic of constitutional law, but they are nevertheless integral to the British approximation to a constitutional order.

The British propensity for obscurantism appears to be the archetypal case of constitutional abeyances. As has already been acknowledged, however, the American system possesses its own comparable, though markedly different, techniques of constitutional evasion. The American comparison in this context is highly significant, for it demonstrates that there is more than one way to preserve constitutional abeyances, and more than one type of political culture with the necessary sophistication to work successfully within the bounds of measured obscurity. The American case shows that while the attitudes required for the cultivation and preservation of abeyances are similar in substance to those in the British case, they are channelled in different ways and expressed through different forms — albeit with similar consequences.

In a country which possesses a written constitution and, therefore, a constitution with a tangibly material form and the promise of an accessible set of objectified meanings, the United States seems at first sight to have a form of government which can be readily and precisely determined. This documentary bequest — together with its transformation into the nation's central 'symbol of political maturity'[92] and into the repository of ultimate political sovereignty, combined with the provision of an authorized mouthpiece in the form of the Supreme Court — has engendered a 'cult of constitutional worship' and 'the removal of high policy to the realm of adjudication'.[93] The centrality of the constitution in American life has brought constitutional law directly into the field of politics and vice versa for, as Alexis de Tocqueville observed, 'scarcely any question arises in the United States which does not become, sooner or later, a subject of judicial debate'.[94]

Given that there is no shortage of a desire amongst political interests for the imprimatur of constitutional legitimacy, American politics is usually cast in the guise of a competitive scramble for constitutional truth, a scramble in which no constitutional stones are left unturned and no gaps remain unfilled in the search for the constitutional exactitude. This imagery is supported by the Supreme Court, which seems to provide answers with sufficient definitiveness and finality for Chief Justice Charles Evans Hughes to have once claimed that 'we live under a constitution, but the constitution is what the Supreme Court says it is'.[95] As a result, the abiding impression of the American system is of a thoroughly uninhibited movement to acquire hard definitions and reasoned deductions from an existent constitution — leading to a tradition of comprehensive constitutional speculation and to a corresponding accumulation of judicial pronouncements couched as derivatives of the original document.

In Britain, there is no happy medium between politics and the constitution. The passage from political conflict to constitutional dispute requires a quantum leap, and one usually occasioned by a critical situation in which interests gravitate towards widely divergent constitutional doctrines and concepts in a highly charged political atmosphere. In the United States, by contrast, the political dimension is permanently fused into the constitutional dimension. Americans are accustomed to thinking and arguing in constitutional terms. They are encouraged by a voluminous literature to give very careful consideration to the structure, dynamics and principles of the constitution and the ways by which they can be determined. Americans are continually surrounded not only by deep constitutional questions over legal rights, public authority, individual liberties, and institutional demarcation, but also by analytical questions concerning the nature of constitutional interpretation — i.e., what judges are doing when they make their decisions, how they arrive at their choices, how constitutions should be interpreted, whether the nature of the constitution changes over time.

Americans are used to taking on the constitution for themselves and to exercising their minds upon it. They interpret it for themselves and many are in decision-making positions to translate their interpretative opinions into operational fact. This is all part of the comfortable, familiar interplay between law and politics in the United States. The lack of a tradition of legal mystique has allowed the constitution to be seen as widely accessible to the populace and, at the same time, has given the final judicial arbiters of the constitution a social prominence unheard of in Britain. In Philip Allott's words,

> Law is evidently and necessarily the rock on which the American nation is built. . . . The American people and all their institutions are engaged in the endless process of making the American nation — and the judges are participating, directly and explicitly and actively, in that process.[96]

In Britain, the law lords are almost entirely anonymous. In the United

States, Supreme Court justices are appointed in a blaze of presidential and senatorial publicity. Their personal decisions are recorded and appraised in the press. Their votes are tabulated. Their legal philosophies are sorted into categories approximating to party labels. Their function as judges is even viewed as a political process in its own right.[97] Most significantly, the Supreme Court provides a continuous stream of authoritative judgements on what the constitution consists of. In doing so, the justices perpetuate the idea that any aspect of the American constitution has the potential to be ascertained at any time. The Supreme Court both responds to and stimulates the political demands for constitutional sanction by engaging in successive exercises of constitutional definition. In effect, the Supreme Court expresses the system's craving for constitutional elucidation and, in doing so, radiates the image of a political culture content with the prospect of full constitutional explicitness.

In British terms, the level of constitutional controversy and adjudication in the United States would be tantamount to a state of permanent constitutional crisis. Yet, where the United States is concerned, such a condition of permanent crisis is the same as no crisis at all. As the case of the American presidency and executive prerogative showed in Chapter 3, the prevailing image of constitutional exactitude being ruthlessly and incessantly extracted through documentary interpretation is far from accurate. In many respects, the emphasis is on constitutional circumvention, evasion, and equivocation. While the American system is seen as both providing and depending upon the availability of assured and final constitutional arbitration, the actual performance of the Supreme Court is one generally geared to turning cases and decisions away.

Only a tiny fraction of constitutional disputes are judged by the Supreme Court. This is partly because of the huge number of contested cases at any time, and partly because the Court operates a highly restrictive set of self-limiting conventions concerning which cases are justiceable and how adjudications should be conducted.[98] A group of these conventions is known as the 'Ashwander rules'; included in these rules is the prescription that the Court will not determine any constitutional questions 'unless they are absolutely necessary to a decision' and that in the case of an act of Congress, it is a 'cardinal principle that this Court will first ascertain whether a construction of the statute is fairly possible by which the question may be avoided'.[99]

The Court has also used the technique of classifying some particularly difficult constitutional questions as 'political questions'.[100] This device is similar to that used by gardeners to distinguish weeds from flowers: weeds are flowers in the wrong place. Likewise, political questions are constitutional questions, but raised in the wrong place or at the wrong time (see pp. 77–8). By designating some issues as political questions, the Court has been able to defer decisions back to the more explicitly political branches of government for resolution by means that do not involve formal constitutional pronouncements. In these cases, the Court is not stating that the constitution has nothing to say on such issues, only that the judiciary, which is entrusted with the 'province and duty . . . to say what the law is',[101] is declining to do so for political reasons.

These self-imposed and well-known limitations, however, are probably not as important as the implicit nature of the judicial pronouncements given by the Supreme Court when it does choose to decide the constitutionality of a case. It is noticeable that in its use of language, the Court very rarely establishes the meaning of the constitution in a direct and positive manner. It only ever *infers* what the constitution is by reference to the legislation or action under review. Customarily the Court works within the framework of what is in dispute and relates that to the constitution in order to determine whether it is in accord with the constitution. The effect of this linguistic convention is that the Court will say that a challenged statute or action is either in line or out of line with the constitution.

Decisions are given as to what is constitutional, rather than as to what the constitution is. Instead of using the constitution as the active and originating frame of reference which is then swept through the areas of disputed constitutionality in an evaluative manner, the constitution remains, in the hands of the Court, a dim and distant standard of adjudication. In this standard, the constitutionality of positions is ascertained by the degree to which they are thought to coincide with the constitution — or more likely with patterns of previous judgements — rather than the extent to which they represent or embody the essence of constitutional truth. This is a small and subtle distinction, but a very powerful one. It means that although constitutional cases in the United States are motivated by the desire for constitutional veracity and that the Supreme Court is positioned to provide that final service, there is gloom at the very moment of enlightenment. Cases are not really used to illuminate the constitution. The Supreme Court will often say what the constitution is not, but when it comes to what the constitution actually is, then the Court's practice is to resort to equivocal imputation by which the constitution is alluded to as a point of comparison, but never revealed as an objective entity — despite the fact that the Court's role and authority are centred on the ultimate belief in the constitution's independent existence.

The Supreme Court's use of judicial review, therefore, is significant for what it does *not* provide. The Court does not assert, for example, that the constitution contains basic inconsistencies and even contradictions, or that it possesses dark voids of unsettled meaning, or that the lines of demarcation between constitutions or levels government can never be ascertained, or that there is no prospect of final answers. Litigants would not, and do not, ask the Supreme Court to unpack the constitution and to expose its many anomalies and ambiguities. This is partly because it would not be in their interests to do so as they would be refused a hearing. But it is also because it would not be in the interests of the Court; any radical attempt to erode the constitution's vital ambiguities would undermine the Court's conventions of defining constitutional dispute and limiting constitutional declaration, and its entire prerogative of judicial review. The Supreme Court is well aware that its function and powers lie in the gaps of the constitution and in the crevices of the public's political consciousness.

As the handmaiden of the constitution, therefore, the Supreme Court is traditionally a most zealous guardian of the document's modesty. The Court has a reputation for clarifying the constitution, but its chief contribution, and the one for which it is most valued, is to answer constitutional questions while preserving the constitution's imprecision. In this way, the Court protects the constitution by continually offering hope to its many supplicants. By giving only a few and usually narrow judgements containing only partial and provisional answers, the Court keeps the constitution in the public eye, but safely in the dark. The Supreme Court's use of judicial review keeps litigants coming. It provides just enough answers to satisfy the belief that the constitution is accessible, but, in doing so, the Court often turns questions back with renewed forms of ambiguity that keep the constitutional options open for later and provides the prospect of altered constructions in the future to disappointed parties.

The Court's ability to work so creatively with ambiguity at the font of constitutional interpretation — together with its traditional rebuttal of *stare decisis* and its practice of concurring and dissenting opinions — means that it has almost invariably been the chief agent for managing constitutional abeyances in the American system. It is true that most people most of the time live and work in a limbo of an unwritten constitution made up of customs, conventions, and traditional practices which are not palpably unconstitutional. But in a political culture which is as permeated as the United States is with the idea of an ultimate and available constitutional reality, there is a correspondingly greater drive to resort to constitutional politics and to its fundamentalist appeal of the heaven of constitutionality and the hell of unconstitutionality.

The American judiciary's position as the formal arbiter of the constitution may in part account for some of the ferocity of the search for constitutional sanction. What is certain, however, is that it is the courts which draw the fire of the combatants and which formulate a succession of partial truces, which usually manage to prevent profound constitutional disjunctions from being churned up into serious political disorder. In contrast to the British system, therefore, where constitutional abeyances are generally protected by an unwritten code of instinctive and self-interested constitutional somnolence, the American system seems deliriously restless over its constitution but with a specialist judiciary to stabilize the fever and keep the furies of constitutional disarray at bay.

In order to perform its role adequately, the Supreme Court must have the skill to make decisions in contested cases in a way that generates sufficient satisfaction. Failure to do so disturbs the populace's general acquiescence over judicial power. The Court, in effect, must have the sensitivity to draw on the public's ability to be satisfied with judicial decisions in a society strongly oriented to the principles of popular sovereignty and democratic consent. It must strike a balance between avoiding explicitly anti-majoritarian rulings which could 'animate a public sentiment that it has but a gossamer claim to legitimacy in a democratic society',[102] while avoiding the disdain which the justices would inevitably attract should they 'abandon their role as educators and supervisors of the national conscience'.[103] The Court, therefore, is expected to ensure that the constitution remains true to itself, but in the knowledge that both its position to decide constitutional questions and the decisions themselves are ultimately dependent upon consent, or at least upon the absence of severe dissent.

'Analytically, supreme judicial autonomy is not easily reconciled with any theory of political democracy'.[104] In practice, the Court more often than not manages to steer a course around and away from those political issues and constitutional doctrines which would provoke sustained public outcry. While the Court is well aware of the value and importance of constitutional abeyances in general, it is particularly conscious of the constitutional abeyance which protects it from the smouldering and unresolving tension between democratic authority and judicial supremacy. The Court has to guard this abeyance with special care; it is commonly observed, for instance, never to 'depart drastically from the policy of the lawmaking majority in the long run'.[105] In the short run, however, when the Court appears to drop its customary penchant for creative ambiguity and departs from the general direction and pace of current public policy, it attracts a notoriety which threatens the equanimity surrounding the constitution's abeyances and, in particular, that abeyance which supports the constitution's own position.

The controversy over the Warren Court (1953–69) and its legal bequest can be seen and understood very much in the light of disrupted abeyances. The decisions of the Warren Court radically transformed the nature of American constitutional law. By venturing into sensitive areas previously avoided by the courts (e.g., racial discrimination, rights of criminal defendants, legislative re-apportionment, church and state relations), the Warren Court pronounced an array of state statutes and practices to be unconstitutional. In a succession of cases, the Court intruded into previously untouched fields of state autonomy and began a process of intense and prolonged federal supervision of required reforms to desegregate public schools, to uphold the voting rights of racial minorities, to protect the rights of accused persons in state court procedures, to regulate state police powers, to correct the malapportionment of voting districts, and to maintain the barriers between church and state by preventing compulsory prayer or bible readings in state schools. The Warren Court's liberal use of the Fourteenth Amendment greatly accelerated the process towards a nationalization of American civil liberties and the construction of a huge infrastructure of case law and administration to implement what has been widely termed a 'second bill of rights'.[106]

Not surprisingly, this degree of judicial activism was greeted in many quarters with intense political opposition, which in some cases spilled over into defiance of court orders and even violent resistance. The call for Earl Warren to be impeached became a clarion cry of political mobilization, especially in the conservative southern region of the country. In becoming the chief agent for social change, the Warren Court acquired a prominence which induced considerable anxiety amongst the legal profession. Constitutional lawyers not only expressed doubts over the magnitude, merits, and motivations of the Court's legal arguments, but were concerned that the Court was exploiting its privileged position with such alacrity that it risked placing an excessive strain upon the levels of public tolerance for the anomaly of judge-made law.[107]

The immediate problem of the Warren Court was thought to have been resolved by the onset of the Burger Court and the dissipation of the Court's liberal-activist majority into a 'less cohesive, more cautious group of justices without any dominant philosophy of constitutional interpretation'.[108] While the pace of the Court generally slowed down, its basic direction remained much the same as it sought to consolidate and to refine the bold movements of the Warren Court.[109] On occasion it showed an audacity equal to anything produced in the Warren years, such as the dramatic decision in *Roe v. Wade* (1973) to deprive states of the choice of making abortion a criminal offence.[110] The controversy surrounding the Supreme Court, therefore, persisted throughout the 1970s and into the 1980s when President Reagan began a campaign to satisfy right-wing demands for the Court decisions to be reversed, by a deliberate White House policy of partisan judicial appointments.

The circumstances surrounding Reagan's unsuccessful appointment of Judge Robert Bork in 1987 were particularly illustrative of the strains and tensions connected with the Supreme Court. The appointment was made against a background of intense debate over the Supreme Court's behaviour in interpreting the constitution. The debate was a renewal of a familiar controversy over the Court, namely, the dispute between those who claim that the Court should seek to arrive at its decisions through the employment of neutral and consistent principles of constitutional adjudication, and those who stress the need for law to be accommodated to the changing requirements of the community. The former have traditionally deferred to the idea of the constitution as an objective and fundamental entity whose principles have to be impartially adhered to in order to retain both the document's and the Supreme Court's legitimacy.[111] The latter have sought to evoke the spirit rather than merely the letter of the constitution and to conjoin the conditions of modern society with a commitment to the law as a vehicle for social justice and individual rights.[112]

The Warren Court had stood accused by a large segment of the legal and academic community as erring so much on the side of social reform that the judges stood indicted for 'erratic subjectivity of judgement, for analytical laxness, for what amounts to intellectual incoherence in many opinions, and for imagining too much history'.[113] Critics warned that the Court's rush to ensure that the constitution was a 'living' document threatened not only to make its judgements purely a matter of policy consideration and social advantage, but to elevate the Court itself into a precarious state of reckless judicial supremacy. These conflicting arguments over the Supreme Court, which stretched back to the Progressive era and to the jurisprudence of Oliver Wendell Holmes, Benjamin Cardozo, and Louis Brandeis, were projected into the 1980s by the continuation and elaboration of the Warren Court's original judgements over the previous twenty years.

On one side of the debate were writers like Arthur S. Miller, who still defended judicial activism as 'necessary and desirable' as long as it 'furthered the attainment of human dignity'[114] by allowing the terms and language of the constitution to be understood and accepted as intrinsically mutable properties. His position was not dissimilar to the subtle scholarship of Ronald Dworkin, who sought to place adjudication at the focal point of law. Dworkin's assertion was that all legal judgement is political by its very nature because adjudication is impossible without moral and political presuppositions. This did not mean that interpretation was merely a matter of opinion or of policy priorities. It meant that judges should conform to that inner coherence of law provided by the prevailing beliefs and practices that embodied a political community. Dworkin's fusion of legal rules and political morality afforded a circumscribed and uninventive role to judges, but an important role, nonetheless, by which the actuality of community values could successively inform the substance of laws.[115]

Pitted against these positions was a formidable array of scholars and publicists who objected to what they saw as the modern phenomenon of the Supreme Court departing from the constitution. According to

Christopher Wolfe, for example, 'the traditional understanding of constitutional interpretation and judicial review was rooted in fidelity to the constitution [and] its original intention derived from a fair reading of the document', while the modern approach was 'characterized by its tendency to seek freedom from the constitution and that intention'.[116] Walter Berns took exception to the recently claimed prerogative of the Supreme Court to create rights such as the right to privacy which encompassed a woman's decision to terminate a pregnancy. Such rights were not written into the constitution, but fabricated by the Court as part of the document. 'In this view', according to Berns, 'the job of the Supreme Court is not to expound the meaning of the constitution but to provide it with meaning'.[117] Berns accused the Court of deforming the constitution by employing legal interpretations ill-adapted to the ends pursued by the justices. As a result, the Fourteenth Amendment had been transformed from 'the embodiment of fundamental and clearly articulated principles of government' into a 'collection of hopelessly vague and essentially meaningless words and phrases inviting judicial construction'.[118] Both Wolfe and Berns typify the deep sense of disquiet within the American legal and political community over what was claimed to be judicially induced departures from the constitution and over the corresponding need to recover the original meaning of the text and the original intentions of the Founding Fathers.

The jurisprudential debate was blown up into a full public controversy by the intervention of Attorney-General Edwin Meese, who openly admonished the Supreme Court for 'pouring new meaning into old words', thereby creating 'new powers and new rights totally at odds with the logic of [the] constitution'.[119] Meese's solution was to de-politicize the law by encouraging the Court to adhere to the original text and intentions of the Founding Fathers. The issue was joined by no less a figure than a member of the Supreme Court itself. Justice William Brennan accused the Attorney-General of arrogance and dismissed the buzz word of 'original intent' as an empty phrase; there were innumerable problems associated with identifying the intentions of the Founders and of those who ratified the constitution, to say nothing of whether the Founders ever intended their intentions to condition future interpretations. More generally, Mr Meese's political opponents insisted that 'original intent' was a device to limit the judiciary and increase the discretion of the national and state governments, particularly in the field of legally guaranteed rights. His legal opponents objected to the 'original intent' concept on the grounds that it was a disguised attempt to establish a form of Benthamite positivism in which judgement becomes a mechanical exercise of extracting neutral plain meanings that commanded general assent.[120] This legal debate, along with Congress's consideration of a profusion of bills seeking to curb the jurisdiction of

The silence of constitutions

the Supreme Court and President Reagan's attempts to appoint as many 'ideologically sound' judges as possible to the federal judiciary, was the context in which Judge Robert Bork was selected to replace Justice Lewis Powell, who had been the figure holding the balance between the conservative and liberal wings of the Supreme Court.

Bork's nomination provoked a bitter political debate. He was seen as an ultra-conservative who embraced the concept of original intent and the idea that the constitution contained fixed neutral principles. Earlier Bork had made it clear that the constitution contained nothing other than what the Founders had written and that therefore when the Supreme Court made its decisions in such areas as abortion, legislative apportionment, capital punishment, and affirmative action, it was merely gratuitously injecting its own moral precepts into the constitution. With these views, Bork was widely regarded as a highly controversial appointment; he was thought to possess a philosophy which would lead him to advocate a reversal of previous Supreme Court decisions and it was feared that he would secure such reversals by altering the balance of the Court.

Right-wing pressure groups mobilized a pro-Bork campaign in the Senate, which was to vote on his nomination. They were intent on exploiting the opportunity for, as they saw it, a conservative victory over the unrepresentative judicial barriers which had permitted liberal forces to frustrate common opinion for so long. Bork was viewed as the linchpin which would finally secure the Supreme Court for what conservatives saw as the American mainstream. At the same time, scholars and politicians warned of the dangers of a Bork seat on the Supreme Court. Ronald Dworkin called him a 'constitutional radical' who rejected 'the view that the Supreme Court must test its interpretations of the constitution against the principles latent in its own past decisions as well as other aspects of the nation's constitutional history'.[121]

In light of the debate, it became difficult for the Reagan administration to subdue suspicions that Bork's selection was part of a politically and ideologically motivated plan designed to establish the Supreme Court within a conservative orthodoxy for the next generation. What were seen as the politically charged intentions of the Reagan administration produced a correspondingly zealous political assault on the appointment. In this pre-election year, the opposition was boosted by party-political dissatisfaction with the administration's policies and principles. But the crucial factor in defeating the Bork nomination was the underlying public disapproval of Reagan's efforts to bring the Supreme Court directly into the political arena. The president's opponents took full advantage of this impropriety and were able to withstand the White House's formidable lobbying campaign in support of the appointee. In the end, the appointment of Robert Bork was rejected by the Senate on October 23 1987 by 58 votes to 42.[122]

What the debate over the Supreme Court in the 1980s shows is that however much of the controversy surrounding the Court was derived from the judiciary jeopardizing the encoded ambiguity of various constitutional abeyances, the most important of all the abeyances in the American system remains the one governing the Court's own position to preserve, protect, and defend all the others. The appointment of Judge Bork exemplified that protocol of obfuscation which underlies the Court's whole position. Just as presidents may make politically motivated appointments to the Supreme Court, and their opponents may make politically motivated objections to such appointments, the 'pros' and 'cons' have to be argued out in terms of legal or personal competence rather than on political or ideological grounds.[123] Well-aware that de Tocqueville's dictum works in reverse and that there is scarcely a judicial question which does not become a matter of political debate, the proponents and opponents of Supreme Court appointees go to great verbal lengths to disguise their political persuasions in euphemisms and circumlocutions. An integral part of the politics of Supreme Court appointments is that they should not be seen as political at all. On the contrary, the debates surrounding such appointees should assume something of the elevated and detached character of the Court itself and of its solemn function of constitutional adjudication. For the most part, such conventions are zealously adhered to. In the case of Robert Bork, it is true that for much of the time the customary indirection was employed. While the White House stressed that Bork was a gifted legal scholar, Senate opponents like Senator J. Bennett Johnston said that Bork 'missed the spirit of the constitution'.[124] Nevertheless, Bork was such a controversial candidate that the devices of political concealment became conspicuously strained.

Bork became a double victim. He was first of all a victim of his own philosophy, which had led him to publicly oppose various specific decisions previously made by the Supreme Court, and to adopt a generalized approach to the Supreme Court's legal role. Bork's advocacy of the jurisprudence of 'original intent' was a radical strategy designed to negate the history of constitutional development by substituting it with a static history of constitutional fundamentalism. This was iconoclasm in the name of preservation. No amount of prevarication or equivocation by Bork and his supporters could disguise the fact that the Court's position in American society was being put in question. As a result, Bork was secondly a victim of the publicity which his own appointment had helped to generate. Publicity, and particularly adverse publicity, in these circumstances when the objective is the emergence, rather than the mere selection, of a Supreme Court justice amounted to the kiss of death. Bork's rejection was symptomatic of that pattern of attitudes which has sustained the Supreme Court's anomalous position in the American republic — namely, the public's assimilation of the Court as a political institution on the understanding that it does not appear to be one, behave like one, or be treated as one.

The two examples of the United States and the United Kingdom serve to underline the commonality between two ostensibly different systems. The United States appears to be the living embodiment of constitutionalism: its political ideals and practices revolve around a constitution whose meanings are regarded as ascertainable and binding in character. In reality, the constitution is replete with anomalies, gaps, and areas of utter unsettlement which, even after two hundred years of adjudication, remain as unsettled as ever. Judicial consistency is unknown, final authoritative judgements are unavailable. It is not simply that the constitution is seen as possessing 'inevitably indeterminate categories and phrases';[125] it is that the constitution is seen as *needing* to possess and sustain a strategic element of indeterminancy which can satisfy a sufficiently high level of popular acquiescence to render the constitution politically viable.

Despite the prodigious degree of constitutional litigation in the United States and the sophisticated grasp of constitutional language and concepts amongst competing American interests, the fact remains that the Supreme Court combines a gargantuan claim to be the ultimate determinant of all constitutional controversies with a fundamental inhibition which has made judicial review an indispensable 'aspect of the practical process of governing a nation [and] an integral part of the art of politics'.[126] In its position of affirming the centrality of constitutional truth to the normal conduct of American politics, the Supreme Court almost invariably acts in such a way as to avoid answering the questions put to it.

The British system, by contrast, operates with very little of the American infrastructure of constitutional speculation and concern. 'The language of constitutional debate is somewhat alien'[127] to the British. observers are struck by the 'failure of politicians and civil servants to think constitutionally'[128] and by the similar failure on the part of those who wish to challenge the politicians. Of course, much of this dearth of constitutional argument has been caused by the British propensity for Parliamentary sovereignty. But it also owes its origins to the British tradition of reciprocal self-restraint. The lack of any materially identifiable constitution has given the British and, in particular, British governments enormous scope for irresponsibility and excess. It has likewise engendered a corresponding appreciation of the value and importance of political responsibility and self-restraint in such a potentially licentious context. The disposition of the British system, therefore, is ultimately comparable to that of the American system.

The American constitution is comparable to a room covered with a dust sheet. The outline of the furniture is visible but not precisely determinable. The sheet only approximates the underlying forms. In spite of the tantalizing proximity of the hidden objects and the availability of an official (i.e., the Supreme Court) who has the authority to remove the covers, Americans are ultimately loath to have them drawn back. The official responds to this inner caution by only rarely agreeing to indulge the nervous excitement of revelation — and only then to the extent of disturbing very little of the concealing sheet.

Americans are conspicuously satisfied by the official's reluctance to draw back the sheet. Judging by the nature of many of the official decisions, Americans even seem noticeably content with the official laying additional covers down. The British constitution, on the other hand, is comparable to an empty room covered with a dust sheet. There appear to be no pre-existing objects to which the sheet conforms. On the contrary, the sheet appears to take the shape of whatever forces the occupants of the room care to exert upon it. And yet, despite the fact that nothing seems to be concealed beneath the sheet, the British practice is to depend upon one another in not exposing the room and in leaving the possible holes in the floorboards and the hazardous foundations safely concealed.

In both countries, normal politics is conditioned by the inbred expectation that deep institutional disjunctions or fundamental constitutional anomalies will remain covered up and held in abeyance. While the Supreme Court effectively acts as a final guardian for American abeyances, British abeyances are rooted in the same general reticence which sustains an institution like the Court. It is not entirely impossible, but it is wholly unlikely, that British courts could perform the same function. This is mainly because the British judiciary is not thought to be sufficiently skilful or astute in handling profound constitutional issues in ways that would preserve the constitution's abeyances.

In the celebrated official secrets trial of Clive Ponting in 1985, for example, the judge effectively undermined the prosecution's position by blatantly supporting the crown's case. In his summing up, when Mr Justice McCowan all but directed the jury to return a verdict of guilty, he openly endorsed the prosecution's assertion that 'the interest of the state' meant 'the policies laid down for it by the recognised organs of government and authority'.[129] As it happened, the assertion was probably valid in constitutional content. But what made it provocative was that such presumptions are usually shrouded in obscurity and ambiguity. Justice McCowan's indigestible lesson on the British constitution aggravated the jury, which later found Mr Ponting not guilty in the face of overwhelming evidence against him. The government was thought to have placed much of the blame for the debacle upon the judge, whose heavy-handed candour was quite contrary to the customary evasiveness of the British constitution.[130]

The silence of constitutions

British governments prefer to work in the twilight world of abstruse crown prerogative and discreet indirection and, as such, they are unlikely ever to risk the delicate circumventions around the areas of deep constitutional unsettlement in the public arena of courtrooms and judicial pronouncements. This means that although the British constitution's abeyances are more directly dependent upon implicit and self-restraining agreements amongst politicians and governments than they are upon judges, the abeyances in both systems are ultimately attributable to each society's ability to contrive ways of coping with constitutional gaps without resorting to the precipitous strategy of trying to fill them.

The roots of this ability are not easy to trace. They may lie in the effects of traumatic historical experiences (e.g., civil wars) which are preserved through institutional traditions and arrangements. They may, on the other hand, come more from social-psychological influences, whereby individuals and groups learn how to suppress divisive controversies for the sake of the benefits to be accrued from the larger group. Whatever the reason, it is plain that in two such normally inquisitive and critically introspective countries as the United States and the United Kingdom, there exists an extraordinary degree of indeterminancy over the machinery and fundamental principles of government. The explanation for this apparent lapse is that such indeterminancy is managed and cultivated by what have become — irrespective of their origins — traditional techniques for retaining constitutional incoherence in abeyance. The importance of history in the British and American constitutions, therefore, lies not so much in its being the generative process of the constitution's substantive development or, in the British case, the equivalence of constitutional documentation, but in its conditioning of those social attitudes capable of sustaining abeyances.

The United States and the United Kingdom are reputedly two of the most settled systems of government in existence. Yet under closer inspection it is evident that they contain vast tracts of constitutional unsettlement. What is 'settled' are the strategies and disciplines required for maintaining political stability and national security in conjunction with political conflict without disturbing the fundamental disjunctions within both constitutions. The methods differ, but the Americans and the British operate on the same assumption that it is needless, and even dangerous, to allow political divisions to become actively aligned with constitutional disjunctions. The great majority of other countries, particularly outside the western tradition, are not only more obviously unsettled in their constitutional systems, but are more explicitly unsettled in their attitudes towards them. Very often, the only way in which political stability is maintained in these circumstances is for an artificial set of settling attitudes to be externally imposed upon the populace through authoritarian techniques of force and fear.

In this way, the theory of abeyances divides governments into two basic types: those like the United States and the United Kingdom, that can be designated as 'settled unsettlements'; and those that can be classified as 'unsettled unsettlements'. In other words, all governmental systems are basically unfinished and unsettled entities. Those like the American and British systems are different only in so far as they have cultivated a settled and self-sustaining adherence to working with the indigenous anomalies of their own constitutions, in such a way as to evoke a belief in the efficacy of neglect and an expectation that should such a virtue ever be abused then those responsible would reap the political penalities commensurate with a breach of trust.

Evidently, abeyances do not help in clarifying the meaning that can be attached to the term constitutionalism. In many respects, the theory of abeyances seems to fly in the face of what is normally understood by constitutionalism. First, while constitutions are usually associated with the rule of law and therefore with the properties of legal precision, ascertainable rights, and determinable powers, the feature of abeyances gives emphasis to those elements of a constitution which are not reducible to demarcated rules. Secondly, constitutional development usually evokes a process of accumulated refinement of constitutional definition, by which the initial gaps in the constitution are successively reduced. But the theory of abeyances correlates constitutional development with the maintenance of gaps for strategic purposes. Thirdly, the social consensus which is so often seen as an indispensable foundation to a constitutional order is a consensus in which negative factors like negligence, ambiguity, fear of dissensus, and a resolve to exclude fundamental constitutional issues from the political agenda are just as important as any of those explicitly positive factors, concerning solid allegiances to solid ideals, that normally serve to characterize the meaning of consensus. Finally, the ideals traditionally associated with constitutionalism have normally been viewed as being dependent either upon defined government restrictions, or upon crafted institutional dynamics. The theory of abeyances, however, brings to light a deeper set of guarantees that keeps liberties intact and governments in their place through an unwritten code of deterrence, by which the volatile properties of constitutional unsettlements are kept safely buried to the mutual satisfaction of conflicting political interests.

In these varied senses, constitutional abeyances are nothing if not awkward, and even perverse, political phenomena. They do not readily conform to either the traditional constructions of constitutionalism, or to the positivistic habits of political scientists who seek to describe constitutions by marrying hard information to ascertainable entities. Abeyances seem to contrive a topsy-turvy world, in which gaps of unsettlement are not signs of constitutional weakness so much as marks of potential strength; where 'living constitutions' are characterized by static abeyances; and where constitutional values are served by way of constitutional incoherence, rather than in spite of it.

Abeyances indisputably make any stock definition of constitutions far more difficult and, ultimately, more equivocal in nature. Viewed through the prism of abeyances, what once ranked as a constitutional order becomes significantly more porous, and can no longer be so easily confined to certain parts of the world (e.g., Western Europe and North America) during a certain period of time (i.e., the nineteenth and twentieth centuries). It may well be that under closer scrutiny, some western liberal democracies will be shown as lacking the social skills to accommodate their areas of constitutional unsettlement without recourse to less-than-constitutional methods of control.

At the same time, however, it may be possible to locate that characteristic complicity in servicing unsettlement by perpetuating it in other political traditions, in other regions of the world, during other periods of history. The study of the seventeenth-century Stuart constitution in Chapter 2, for example, bears witness to the fact that the social attitudes and political sophistication required for a vibrant constitutional order are not exclusive to the era of liberal democratic systems and ideas. The uncertainty and imprecision of assimilating the phenomenon of abeyances within our ideas of constitutional practice does seem to be an intolerable imposition. But it is the price to be paid for an improved understanding of what constitutions mean and of why constitutions look like exercises in settlement and definition when in reality they are devices for evasion and deferment.

Notes

Preface

1 M. Oakeshott, 'Political education', in M. Oakeshott, *Rationalism in Politics and Other Essays*, London: Methuen, 1962, p. 128.

Chapter 1: The concept and practice of constitutional abeyances

1 See H. Finer, *Theory and Practice of Modern Government*, rev. edn, London: Methuen, 1949, pp. 116-38; L. Wolf-Phillips (ed.) *Constitutions of Modern States: Selected Texts*, London: Pall Mall, 1968, pp. xi-xii; K.C. Wheare, *Modern Constitutions*, 2nd edn, London: Oxford University Press, 1966, pp. 14-15; G. Marshall and G.C. Moodie, *Some Problems of the Constitution*, 3rd edn, London: Hutchinson, 1964, pp. 11-27; E.C.S. Wade and C.G. Phillips, *Constitutional and Administrative Law*, 9th edn, London: Longman, 1977, pp. 2-5; M. Curtis, *Comparative Government and Politics: An Introductory Essay in Political Science*, New York: Harper & Row, 1968, pp. 71-4; P. Bromhead, *Britain's Developing Constitution*, London: George Allen & Unwin, 1974, pp. 13-19; J. Harvey and L. Bather, *The British Constitution*, London: Macmillan, 1964, pp. 503-16.
2 M. Shaw, *Anglo-American Democracy*, London: Routledge & Kegan Paul, 1968, p. 13.
3 G.C. Moodie, *The Government of Great Britain*, London: Methuen, 1964, pp. 1-2.
4 R.M. Punnett, *British Government and Politics*, 3rd edn, London: Heinemann, 1976, p. 159.
5 R. Rose, *Politics in England Today: An Interpretation*, London: Faber & Faber, 1974, p. 66.
6 A. de Tocqueville, quoted in Marshall and Moodie, *Some Problems of the Constitution*, 3rd edn, p. 20.
7 I. Jennings, *The Law and the Constitution*, 5th edn, London: University of London, 1967, p. 36.
8 Wheare, *Modern Constitutions*, 2nd edn, p. 9.
9 Bromhead, *Britain's Developing Constitution*, p. 1.

10 A.H. Birch, *The British System of Government*, London: George Allen & Unwin, 1967, p. 29.
11 Wolf-Phillips (ed.) *Constitutions of Modern States*, p. xi.
12 S.E. Finer, *Comparative Government*, Harmondsworth: Penguin, 1974, p. 146.
13 A.V. Dicey, *Introduction to the Study of the Law of the Constitution*, 10th edn, London: Macmillan, 1960, pp. 24–30, 417–38; O. Hood Phillips and P. Jackson, *Constitutional and Administrative Law*, 6th edn, London: Sweet and Maxwell, 1978, pp. 113–19; Wade and Phillips, *Constitutional and Administrative Law*, 9th edn, pp. 107–19; Marshall and Moodie, *Some Problems of the Constitution*, 3rd edn, pp. 28–46; Jennings, *The Law and the Constitution*, 5th edn, pp. 80–136; Harvey and Bather, *The British Constitution*, pp. 196–205, 232–35, 506–7, 513–16; Nevil Johnson, *In Search of the Constitution: Reflections on State and Society in Britain*, London: Pergamon, 1977, pp. 25–41.
14 Finer, *Theory and Practice of Modern Government*, rev edn, p. 118.
15 Jennings, *The Law and the Constitution*, 5th edn, p. 71.
16 Wheare, *Modern Constitutions*, 2nd edn, p. 14.
17 Dicey, *Introduction to the study of the Law of the Constitution*, 10th edn, pp. 28–9. This point is reiterated by W. B. Munro, who refers to the existence of an unwritten constitution.

> It fills the statutes-at-large, the law reports, the printed laws of the individual commonwealths, and constitutional treatises to the extent of a million pages or more. This unwritten constitution is made up of federal and state enactments, judicial decisions, usages, doctrines, precedents, official opinions, and points of view which have profoundly altered the implications of the original instrument . . . So great has this divergence become at the present day that no one can obtain even a silhouette of the American political system if he confines his study to the nation's fundamental law as it left the hands of the architect. (*Makers of the Unwritten Constitution*, New York: Macmillan, 1930, p. 1).

To a large extent the American constitution's dependence upon convention and usage is a self-evident condition as the logical alternative would be 'to prohibit adaptation based on custom [which] would require several hundred amendments to the constitution and a willingness to keep it in a perpetual state of agitation and flux', according to L. Fisher, *Constitutional Conflicts between Congress and the President*, Princeton: Princeton University Press, 1985, p. 27. For a representative study of the fluidity of relationships between units of government based upon changing requirements, pragmatic adjustment and evolving custom, see M.D. Reagan, *The New Federalism*, New York: Oxford University Press, 1972. For an illustrative portrayal of the constitution's internal mutability behind an edifice of apparent constancy, see A.S. Miller 'A new constitution — without amendment', in A.S. Miller (ed.) *Toward Increased Judicial Activism:*

Notes

    The Political Role of the Supreme Court, Westport: Greenwood, 1982, pp. 175–92. For a persuasive assertion of the existence of an entrenched yet informal system of government based on traditional attitudes to authority, see D.K. Price, *America's Unwritten Constitution: Science, Religion and Political Responsibility*, Cambridge: Harvard University Press, 1985.

18 J. Blondel, *An Introduction to Comparative Government*, London: Weidenfeld & Nicolson, 1969, p. 276.

19 Wolf-Phillips (ed.) *Constitutions of Modern States*, p. xii.

20 C.J. Friedrich, 'Constitutions and constitutionalism', in D.L. Sils (ed.) *The International Encyclopaedia of Social Science*, vol. 3, New York: Crowell Collier & Macmillan, 1968, p. 318.

21 See Jennings, *The Law and the Constitution*, 5th edn, pp. 80–7, 101–3, 106–9, 115–21, 134–6. See also Marshall, 'What are constitutional conventions?' *Parliamentary Affairs*, vol. 38, no. 1 (1985), pp. 33–9; Wade and Phillips, *Constitutional and Administrative Law*, 9th edn, pp. 16–17, 19–26; Phillips and Jackson, *Constitutional and Administrative Law*, 6th edn, pp. 104–13; H. Street and R. Brazier (eds) *Constitutional and Administrative Law*, 5th edn, Harmondsworth: Penguin, 1985, pp. 40–60.

22 Finer, *Theory and Practice of Modern Government*, rev. edn, p. 118.

23 Friedrich, 'Constitutions and constitutionalism', p. 118.

24 Wheare, *Modern Constitutions*, 2nd edn, p. 15.

25 See Wolf-Phillips, *Constitutions of Modern States*, pp. xiii–xxvi; Blondel, *An Introduction to Comparative Government*, pp. 265–81; Karl Loewenstein, 'Reflections on the value of constitutions in our revolutionary age', in H. Eckstein and D.E. Apter (eds) *Comparative Politics: A Reader*, New York: Free Press, 1963, pp. 149–63.

26 Quoted in I. Gilmour, *Inside Right: Conservatism, Policies and the People*, London: Quartet, 1978, p. 198.

27 See Baron de Montesquieu, *The Spirit of the Laws*, trans. by T. Nugent, New York: Hafner, 1940, pp. 1–7; R. Aron, *Main Currents in Sociological Thought I*, trans. R. Howard and H. Weaver, Harmondsworth: Penguin, 1968, pp. 47–62.

Chapter 2: Constitutional abeyances and crisis conditions: the early Stuart constitution

1 The accounts of the Stuart constitution used in this study were drawn from the following sources: J.P. Kenyon, *The Stuart Constitution: Documents and Commentary*, Cambridge: Cambridge University Press, 1966; M.A. Judson, *The Crisis of the Constitution: An Essay in Constitutional and Political Thought in England, 1603–1645*, New Brunswick: Rutgers University Press, 1949; S.G. Gardiner, *The Constitutional Documents of the Puritan Revolution, 1625–1660*, 3rd edn, Oxford: Clarendon, 1906; F.W. Maitland, *The Constitutional History of England*, Cambridge: Cambridge University Press, 1931, pp. 251–75; T.P. Taswell-Langmead, *English Constitutional History:*

From the Teutonic Conquest to the Present Time, 10th edn, rev. and enlarged by T.F.T. Plucknett, London: Sweet & Maxwell, 1946, pp. 368–440; D.L. Keir, *The Constitutional History of Modern Britain since 1485*, London: Adam and Charles Black, 1964, pp. 154–208; C.R. Lovell, *English Constitutional and Legal History: A Survey*, New York: Oxford University Press, 1962, pp. 282–336; S.B. Chrimes, *English Constitutional History*, 4th edn, London: Oxford University Press, 1967, pp. 102–20; F.D. Wormuth, *The Royal Prerogative, 1603–1649*, Ithaca: Cornell University Press, 1939; Wormuth, *The Origins of Modern Constitutionalism*, New York: Harper & Row, pp. 43–58; G.E. Aylmer, *The Struggle for the Constitution: England in the Seventeenth Century*, 4th edn, London: Blandford, 1975, pp. 11–105; C. Hill, *The Century of Revolution, 1603–1714*, London: Abacus, 1978, pp. 47–72; C.H. McIlwain, *Constitutionalism: Ancient and Modern*, rev. edn, Ithaca: Cornell University Press, 1947, pp. 93–122; A. Sharp, *Political Ideas of the English Civil Wars, 1641–1649*, London: Longman, 1983, pp. 6–13; J.P. Sommerville, *Politics and Ideology in England, 1603–1640*, London: Longman, 1986; R.W.K. Hinton, 'English constitutional theories from Sir John Fortesque to Sir John Eliot', *English Historical Review*, no. 296 (1960), pp. 410–25; M. Hawkins, 'The government — its role and aims', in C. Russell (ed.) *The Origins of the English Civil War*, London: Macmillan, 1973, pp. 35–65; H. Hulme, 'Charles I and the constitution', in W.A. Aiken and B.D. Henning (eds) *Conflict in Stuart England*, London: Jonathan Cape, 1960, pp. 87–128.

2 Judson, *The Crisis of the Constitution*, p. 53.

3 C. Russell, 'Parliamentary history in perspective, 1604–1629', *History*, vol. 61 (1976), pp. 1–27; Russell, 'The nature of Parliament in early Stuart England', in H. Tomlinson (ed.) *Before the English Civil War: Essays on Early Stuart Politics and Government*, London: Macmillan, 1983, pp. 123–50; Russell, 'Parliament and the King's finances', in Russell (ed.) *The Origins of the English Civil War*, pp. 91–116; R.W.K. Hinton, 'The decline of Parliamentary government under Elizabeth I and the early Stuarts', *Cambridge Historical Review*, vol. 37 (1957), pp. 116–32; Judson, *The Crisis of the Constitution*, pp. 68–106; Kenyon, *The Stuart Constitution*, pp. 24–89; A.G.R. Smith, 'Constitutional ideas and Parliamentary developments in England, 1603–1625' in A.G.R. Smith (ed.) *The Reign of James VI and I*, London: Macmillan, 1973, pp. 160–76; Taswell-Langmead, *English Constitutional History*, pp. 368–405.

4 Judson, *The Constitutional Crisis*, p. 24.

5 Judson, *The Constitutional Crisis*, p. 158.

6 Aylmer, *The Struggle for the Constitution*, p. 35.

7 'James Whitelocke's speech on impositions (House of Commons, 29 June, 1610)', in Kenyon (ed) *The Stuart Constitution*, p. 70.

8 See J.G.A. Pocock, *The Ancient Constitution and the Feudal Law: A Study of English Historical Thought in the Seventeenth Century*, New York: Norton, 1967, pp. 30–69; Sommerville, *Politics and Ideology in*

England, 1603-1640, pp. 86-114; Wormuth, *The Royal Prerogative, 1603-1649*, pp. 47-68; Kenyon, *The Stuart Constitution*, pp. 90-116; Hill, 'Sir Edward Coke — myth-maker', in Hill, *Intellectual Origins of the English Revolution*, Oxford: Clarendon, 1965, pp. 225-65.

9 W.J. Jones, *Politics and the Bench: The Judges and the Origins of the English Civil War*, London: George Allen & Unwin, 1971, p. 15.
10 W.J. Jones, 'The crown and the courts in England, 1603-1625' in Smith (ed.) *The Reign of James VI and I*, pp. 182-3.
11 Quoted in C.V. Wedgwood, *The King's Peace, 1637-1641* Harmondsworth: Penguin, 1983, p. 135.
12 Judson, *The Crisis of the Constitution*, p. 7.
13 Wormuth, *The Royal Prerogative, 1603-1649*, pp. 47-8.
14 Kenyon, *The Stuart Constitution*, pp. 10, 9, 11.
15 Hawkins, 'The government: its role and aims', pp. 38, 41.
16 Wormuth, *The Royal Prerogative, 1603-1649*, p. 48.
17 Hawkins, 'The government: its role and aims', p. 42.
18 See Wormuth, *The Royal Prerogative, 1603-1649*, pp. 69-107; Sommerville, *Politics and Ideology in England, 1603-1640*, pp. 9-56; Kenyon, *The Stuart Constitution*, pp. 7-23.
19 Kenyon, *The Stuart Constitution*, pp. 12-13.
20 M. Ashley, *England in the Seventeenth Century*, 3rd edn, Harmondsworth: Penguin, 1961, p. 10.
21 'The King's speech at the opening of Parliament (19 February, 1624)', in Kenyon, *The Stuart Constitution*, p. 48.
22 Kenyon, *The Stuart Constitution*, p. 8.
23 Hulme, 'Charles I and the constitution', p. 93.
24 Judson, *The Crisis of the Constitution*, p. 20.
25 Kenyon, *Stuart England*, Harmondsworth: Penguin, 1978, p. 94.
26 Impositions was the name given to those customs duties levied over and above the traditional, yet statutory, tonnage and poundage rates by James I. He based these exactions upon his prerogative right to regulate trade and to provide for the general benefit of the people. Financially pressed monarchs had been barred from direct taxation by specific statutes and by a general constitutional sanction against infringing upon the liberty of subjects by way of taxation or legislation without their consent. The position of custom duties was more ambiguous. In 1557, Queen Mary began the practice of setting additional duties on selected goods (cloth exports) in excess of those that she was statutorily entitled to through tonnage and poundage. Queen Elizabeth extended it to sweet wine imports and King James I to an import duty on currants. His action was pronounced a legitimate exercise of his prerogative power in *Bate's Case* (1606) and in 1608 a new *Book of Rates* was issued imposing heavy duties upon almost all mercantile commodities.

It was these duties that became known as the 'impositions'. They aroused great controversy because of (i) their scale; (ii) their evident function in raising revenue rather than regulating trade; (iii) their value in generating more income than that statutorily granted by Parliament;

(iv) their appearance of being an attack upon property and one that could be perpetually extended; and (v) their capacity to make the crown more self-sufficient and autonomous. The accession of a new king, therefore, provided the opportunity for Parliament to review the whole position of customs before any resumption of the tonnage and poundage powers were released to Charles I.

The impositions had been a source of contention in the Parliaments of 1610 and 1624. They were to become so again with increasing severity in the Parliaments of Charles I. Many of those who had queried impositions since 1608 believed that tonnage and poundage had been the original root of these additional sources of extra-Parliamentary supply and that they should be made to conform to those roots by Parliamentary approval. Charles, for his part, wanted the formal Parliamentary grant of tonnage and poundage, but he made it clear that he would not only continue to collect it pending Parliamentary approval, but that the impositions did not require Parliamentary authority as they rested upon legal precedent and upon his prerogative rights.

27 See B. Manning, *The English People and the English Revolution, 1640–1649*, London: Heinemann, 1976, pp. 21–45, 99–111, 163–227; L. Stone, *The Causes of the English Revolution, 1529–1642*, London: Routledge & Kegan Paul, 1972, pp. 26–146; A. Fletcher, *The Outbreak of the English Civil War*, London: Edward Arnold, 1981, pp. 1–227; Hill, *The Century of Revolution, 1603–1714*, pp. 19–102; Wedgwood, *The King's Peace, 1637–1641*, pp. 173–486; J. Morrill, 'What was the English revolution?', *History Today*, March 1984, pp. 11–16; B. Manning, 'What was the English revolution?', *History Today*, March 1984, pp. 18–21; D. Underdown, 'What was the English revolution?', *History Today*, March 1984, pp. 22–25.
28 Quoted in Kenyon, *The Stuart Constitution*, p. 101.
29 Gardiner, *The Constitutional Documents*, p. xx.
30 Hulme, 'Charles I and the constitution', p. 100.
31 Hulme, 'Charles I and the constitution', p. 101.
32 Aylmer, *The Struggle for the Constitution*, p. 75.
33 Jones, *Politics and the Bench*, p. 75.
34 G.R. Elton quoted in Sommerville, *Politics and Ideology in England, 1603–1640*, p. 166.
35 Judson, *The Crisis of the Constitution*, p. 116.
36 Hulme, 'Charles I and the Constitution', pp. 100–1
37 Hill, *The Century of Revolution, 1603–1714*, pp. 62–4.
38 Jones, *Politics and the Bench*, p. 73.
39 Stone, *The Causes of the English Revolution, 1529–1642*, p. 93. See also R. Ashton, *The English Civil War: Conservatism and Revolution, 1603–1649*, London: Weidenfeld & Nicolson, 1978, pp. 3–21, 39–42, 124–6, 156, 179–85, 347–52; Hill, 'The Norman yoke', in Hill, *Puritanism and Revolution: Studies in Interpretation of the English Revolution of the 17th Century*, London: Panther, 1968, pp. 58–125.
40 McIlwain, *Constitutionalism: Ancient and Modern*, p. 127.

Notes

41 'Protestation of the House of Commons (2 March 1629)', in Gardiner, *Constitutional Documents*, p. 83.
42 'The King's declaration showing the causes of the late dissolution (10 March, 1629)', in Gardiner, *Constitutional Documents*, p. 98.
43 'A proclamation for suppressing of false rumours touching Parliaments (27 March, 1629)', in Kenyon, *The Stuart Constitution*, p. 85.
44 'A proclamation for suppressing of false rumours', p. 86.
45 See Wedgwood, *The King's Peace, 1637–1641*, pp. 21–170; P. Gregg, *King Charles I*, London: J.M. Dent, 1981, pp. 201–84; K. Sharpe, 'The personal rule of Charles I', in Tomlinson (ed) *Before the Engish Civil War*, pp. 53–78.
46 McIlwain, *Constitutionalism: Ancient and Modern*, p. 127.
47 Judson, *The Crisis of the Constitution*, p. 20.
48 Kenyon, *The Stuart Constitution*, p. 7.
49 Judson, *The Crisis of the Constitution*, p. 150.
50 Sommerville, *Politics and Ideology in England, 1603–1640*, p. 165.
51 G.H. Sabine and T.L. Thorson, *A History of Political Theory*, 4th edn, Hinsdale: Dryden, 1973, p. 404.
52 The unexpected and unintended nature of the breakdown is a common historical theme. 'Fewer men feared or anticipated, let alone sought, civil war in the 1620s or 1630s than had done so in the 1580s and 1590s . . . . There was much outspoken criticism of royal policies, but no unity of criticism . . . . No change of political institutions and no change in the constitution was envisaged . . . . Civil war itself broke out . . . to the dismay and bewilderment of almost everyone'. J. Morrill, 'The Stuarts (1603–1688)', in K.O. Morgan (ed.) *The Sphere Illustrated History of Britain, 1485–1789*, London: Sphere Books, 1985, pp. 91, 99, 100, 103. 'When war came there were some who were able to articulate the principles and convictions for which they fought. Yet even they, let alone the many who found it impossible to attach themselves steadfastly to one side or the other, had not sought war. This was a war that nobody wanted, a war that left men bewildered . . . as it broke out in fits and starts all over England in the summer of 1642', Fletcher, *The Outbreak of the English Civil War*.
53 Manning, 'The nobles, the people, and the constitution', *Past and Present*, vol. 9, 1956, p. 54.
54 Stone, *The Causes of the English Revolution, 1529–1642*, p. 94.
55 'The King's speech at the opening of Parliament (19 February 1624)', in Kenyon, *The Stuart Constitution*, p. 49.
56 For example: 'While planes sometimes crash because of metal fatigue or mechanical failure, they also sometimes crash because of pilot error. The causes of the English Civil War are too complex to be explained in terms of such a simple metaphor, but it does seem that the English Civil War was more the consequence of pilot error than of mechanical failure. When, with the wisdom of hindsight, contemporaries looked back at the cause of the Great Rebellion they very rarely went back before the accession of Charles I in 1625. They

were probably right.' Morrill, 'The Stuarts (1603–1688)', in Morgan (ed.) *The Sphere Illustrated History of Britain, 1485–1789*, p. 93. See also C. Carleton, 'Three British revolutions and the personality of kingship', in J.G.A. Pocock (ed.) *Three British Revolutions, 1641, 1688, 1776*, Princeton: Princeton University Press, 1980), pp. 184–95.
57 Judson, *The Crisis of the Constitution*, p. 76.
58 Quoted in Judson, *The Crisis of the Constitution*, pp. 31–2.
59 Quoted in Sommerville, *Politics and Ideology in England, 1603–1640*, p. 171.

Chapter 3: Constitutional abeyances and crisis conditions: the imperial presidency

1 See P. Gay, *The Enlightenment: An Interpretation, Volume II: The Science of Freedom*, London: Weidenfeld & Nicolson, 1970, pp. 555–68; Gay, 'The Applied Enlightenment?', in E.M. Adams (ed.) *The Idea of America: A Reassessment of the American Experience*, Cambridge, Mass: Ballinger, 1977, pp. 11–37; H.S. Commager, *The Empire of Reason: How Europe Imagined and America Realized the Enlightenment*, London: Weidenfeld & Nicolson, 1978, pp. 198–235; A.J. Beitzinger, *A History of American Political Thought*, New York: Dodd, Mead & Co., 1982, pp. 202–44; R.D. Mosier, *The American Temper: Patterns of Our Intellectual Heritage*, Berkeley: University of California Press, 1952, pp. 85–155; A. Koch (ed.) *The American Enlightenment: The Shaping of the American Experience and a Free Society*, New York: Braziller, 1965, pp. 19–48; D. Adair, ' "That politics may be reduced to a science": David Hume, James Madison, and the Tenth Federalist', *The Huntington Library Quarterly*, vol. 20. no. 4 (1957), pp. 343–60.
2 M.J.C. Vile, *Constitutionalism and the Separation of Powers*, Oxford: Clarendon, 1967, p. 110.
3 A. Ranney, ' "The divine science": political engineering in American culture', *The American Political Science Review*, vol. 70, no. 1 (1976), p. 140.
4 W. Lippmann, *A Preface to Politics*, Ann Arbor: University of Michigan Press, 1962, p. 16.
5 See for example R. Hofstadter, *The American Political Tradition*, London: Jonathan Cape, 1967, pp. 8–9; Mosier, *The American Temper*, pp. 97–133; H.S. Commager, *The American Mind: An Interpretation of American Thought and Character since the 1880s*, New York: Bantam, 1970, pp. 317–21; Lippmann, *A Preface to Politics*, pp. 15–17; W. Wilson, *Constitutional Government in the United States*, New York: Columbia University Press, 1908, pp. 54–7; M. Landau, 'On the use of metaphor in political analysis', in M. Landau (ed.) *Political Theory and Political Science: Studies in the Methodology of Political Inquiry*, Hassocks: Harvester, 1979, pp. 78–121; H. Wheeler, 'Constitutionalism', in F.I. Greenstein and N.W. Polsby (eds) *Handbook of Political Science, Volume 5: Governmental*

Institutions and Processes, Reading, Mass.: Addison-Wesley, 1975, pp. 6, 38–41, 76–8.
6 J.M. Burns, *The Deadlock of Democracy Four-party Politics in America*, London: John Calder, 1963, p. 6.
7 K. Phillips, 'Our obsolete system', *Newsweek*, 28 April 1973.
8 D.J. Boorstin, *The Genius of American Politics*, Chicago: University of Chicago Press, 1953, pp. 9, 16, 18.
9 H. Kohn, *American Nationalism: An Interpretive Essay*, New York: Macmillan, 1957, p. 8.
10 See E.S. Corwin, 'The "higher law" background of American constitutional law', *Harvard Law Review*, vol. 42, no. 2 (1928), pp. 149–85; *Harvard Law Review*, vol. 42, no. 3 (1929), pp. 365–409; Corwin, 'The natural law and constitutional law', in R. Loss (ed.) *Presidential Power and the Constitution: Essays by Edward S. Corwin*, Ithaca: Cornell University Press, 1976, pp. 1–22; Commager, 'Constitutional history and the higher law', in C. Read (ed.) *The Constitution Reconsidered*, New York: Columbia University Press, 1938, pp. 225–45; B.F. Wright, *American Interpretations of Natural Law: A Study in the History of Political Thought*, Cambridge: Harvard University Press, 1931, pp. 124–48, 280–306.
11 Commager, *The American Mind*, p. 319.
12 L. Hartz, *The Liberal Tradition in America: An Interpretation of American Political Thought*, New York: Harcourt Brace Jovanovich, 1955, p. 103.
13 J.H. Ely, 'Constitutional interpretivism: its allure and impossibility', *Indiana Law Journal*, vol. 53 (1978), pp. 399.
14 The accounts of the 'imperial presidency' episode used in this study were drawn from the following sources: A.M. Schlesinger, Jr., *The Imperial Presidency*, London: Andre Deutsch, 1974; Schlesinger, *The Crisis of Confidence: Ideas, Power and Violence in America*, London: Andre Deutsch, 1969; Commager, *The Defeat of America: Presidential Power and the National Character*, New York: Simon & Schuster, 1974; R.E. Pynn (ed.) *Watergate and the American Political Process*, New York: Praeger, 1975; G.E. Reedy, *The Twilight of the Presidency*, New York: New American Library, 1971; F.G. Hutchins, 'Presidential autocracy in America', in R.G. Tugwell and T.E. Cronin (eds) *The Presidency Reappraised*, New York: Praeger, 1974, pp. 35–55; T.H. White, *Breach of Faith: The Fall of Richard Nixon*, London: Jonathan Cape, 1975; J. Dean, *Blind Ambition: The White House Years*, London: Star Books, 1976; L. Chester, C. McCrystal, S. Aris and W. Shawcross, *Watergate: The Full Inside Story*, New York: Ballantine, 1973; A.J. Lucas, *Nightmare: The Underside of the Nixon Years, 1969–1974*, New York: Viking, 1976; D. Rather and G.P. Gates, *The Palace Guard*, New York: Harper & Row, 1974; B. Woodward and C. Bernstein, *The Final Days*, New York: Simon & Schuster, 1976; P.J. Halpern (ed.) *Why Watergate?*, Pacific Palisades: Palisades, 1975; T.E. Cronin, *The State of the Presidency*, 2nd edn, Boston: Little, Brown & Co., 1980, pp. 187–222; Cronin, 'Making the

presidency safe for democracy', in J.F. Manley (ed.) *American Government and Public Policy*, New York: Macmillan, 1976, pp. 363-72; R.N. Goodwin, 'Advise, consent, and restraint: dismantling the presidency', in Manley (ed.) *American Government and Public Policy*, pp. 352-63; J. Nathan, 'The roots of the imperial presidency: public opinion, domestic institutions and global interests', *Presidential Studies Quarterly*, vol. 5 (1975), pp. 63-74; I. Horowitz, 'The rise of presidential militarism', in Horowitz (ed.) *Ideology and Utopia in the United States*, New York: Oxford University Press, 1977, pp. 26-35; E.C. Hargrove, *The Power of the Modern Presidency*, New York: Alfred A. Knopf, 1974, pp. 3-32.

15 Schlesinger, *The Imperial Presidency*, p. 252.

16 See J.M. Burns, *Presidential Government: The Crucible of Leadership*, Boston: Houghton Mifflin, 1973, pp. 249-60; D.B. James, *The Contemporary Presidency*, New York: Pegasus, 1969, pp. ix-xv; L. Koenig, *The Chief Executive*, 3rd edn, New York: Harcourt Brace Jovanovich, 1975, pp. 294-325; J.L. Sundquist, *Politics and Power: The Eisenhower, Kennedy and Johnson Years*, Washington DC: Brookings Institute, 1968.

17 J. Lehman, *The Executive, Congress and Foreign Policy: Studies of the Nixon Administration*, New York: Praeger, 1976, pp. 1-18; C.V. Crabb and P.M. Holt, *Invitation to Struggle: Congress, the President and Foreign Policy*, Washington DC: Congressional Quarterly Press, 1980, pp. 5-32; J. Spanier, 'Introduction — Congress and the presidency: the weakest link in the policy process', in J. Spanier and J.L. Nogee (eds) *Congress, the Presidency and American Foreign Policy*, New York: Pergamon, 1981, pp. ix-xxxii; D.M. Abshire, 'Foreign policy makers: president v. Congress', in D.M. Abshire and R.N. Nurnberger (eds) *The Growing Power of Congress*, Beverly Hills: Sage, 1981, pp. 43-81; J. Spanier and E.M. Ulsaner, *Foreign Policy and the Democratic Dilemmas*, 3rd edn, New York: Holt, Rinehart & Winston, 1982, pp. 25-78; A. Wildavsky, 'The two presidencies', in A. Wildavsky and N.W. Polsby (eds) *American Governmental Institutions: A Reader in the Policy Process*, Chicago: Rand McNally, 1968, pp. 93-102; R.M. Pious, *The American Presidency* New York: Basic, 1979, pp. 36-8, 47-51, 83-5, 392-6; C.H. Pyle and R.M. Pious, *The President, Congress and the Constitution: Power and Legitimacy in American Politics*, New York: Free Press, 1984, pp. 233-43; K.R. Tulsky, 'Judicial review of presidential initiatives', *University of Pittsburgh Law Review*, vol. 46, no. 2 (1985), pp. 425-31.

18 W.F. Mullen, *Presidential Power and Politics*, New York: St Martin's Press, 1976, p. 1.

19 T.J. Lowi, 'Presidential power: restoring the balance', *Political Science Quarterly*, vol. 100, no. 2 (1985), p. 189.

20 See T.E. Cronin, 'The textbook presidency and political science', in S. Bach and G.T. Sulzner (eds) *Perspectives on the Presidency: A Collection*, Lexington: D.C. Heath, 1974, pp. 54-74; Cronin, *The*

State of the Presidency, pp. 75–118; R.E. Neustadt, *Presidential Power: The Politics of Leadership*, New York: John Wiley, 1960; H. Finer, *The Presidency: Crisis and Regeneration*, Chicago: University of Chicago Press, 1960; R.G. Tugwell, *The Enlargement of the Presidency*, New York: Doubleday, 1960; Koenig, *The Chief Executive*; C. Rossiter, *The American Presidency*, rev. edn, New York: Mentor, 1960; F.I. Greenstein, 'What the president means to Americans: presidential "choice" between elections', in J.D. Barber (ed.) *Choosing the President*, Englewood Cliffs: Prentice-Hall, 1974, pp. 121–47; R.S. Sigel, 'Image of the American presidency — part II of an exploration into popular views of presidential power', *Midwest Journal of Political Science*, vol. 10, no. 1 (1966), pp. 123–37.

21 Cronin, *The State of the Presidency*, p. 188.
22 Neustadt, *The Power of the President*, p. 185.
23 Burns, *Presidential Government*, p. 81.
24 G.E. Reedy, 'The presidency in 1976: focal point of political unity', in W.C. Havard and J.L. Bernd (eds) *200 Years of the Republic in Retrospect*, Charlottesville: University Press of Virginia, 1976, p. 229.
25 Reedy, *The Twilight of the Presidency*, p. 28.
26 In his seminal article ('The power of the contemporary president', in Wildavsky and Polsby (eds) *American Governmental Institutions: A Reader in the Policy Process*, pp. 133–46), R.S. Hirschfield insisted that the modern presidency should be recognized as possessing an extra-constitutional dimension of power despite the best efforts of constitutional theorists and lawyers to obscure the fact.

> Extraconstitutional presidential prerogative is the most difficult to assay . . . because it is acknowledged in our political theory and unrecognised in our jurisprudence. Unwilling to face the dilemma created by exercises of power which transcend the established bounds of legitimate authority, our public law has refused to distinguish between necessity and constitutionality in judging presidential actions. Jurists and political scientists have, instead, equated these two very different bases of action (p. 136).

Hirschfield strongly objected to this traditional sleight of hand. A president may

> suspend the basic law in order to assure its ultimate survival, and the only standard by which the validity of his actions can be measured is necessity, not constitutionality. Regardless of what American political theory and jurisprudence may hold, history demonstrates clearly that the executive does possess extraconstitutional power, and its existence as an essential part of the office must be acknowledged if we are to understand the presidency of our time (p. 137).

27 See A.M. Bickel, *The Least Dangerous Branch: The Supreme Court at the Bar of Politics*, Indianapolis: Bobbs-Merrill, 1962, pp. 183–98; C. Black, *Perspectives in Constitutional Law*, Englewood Cliffs: Prentice-Hall, 1963, pp. 14–18.

28 See L. Henkin, *Foreign Affairs and the Constitution*, Mineola: Foundation Press, 1972, pp. 37-66; R. Funston, *A Vital National Seminar: The Supreme Court in American Political Life*, Palo Alto: Mayfield, 1978, pp. 63-95; E.S. Corwin, *The President: Office and Powers, 1787-1948*, 3rd edn, New York: New York University Press, 1948, pp. 207-317; C. Rossiter, *The Supreme Court and the Commander in Chief*, Ithaca: Cornell University Press, 1951.
29 *The Prize Cases*, 67 U.S. 635, 669 (1863).
30 T. Roosevelt, 'The "stewardship theory" ', in R.S. Hirschfield (ed.) *The Power of the Presidency: Concepts and Controversy*, New York: Alfred A. Knopf, 1968, p. 82.
31 *In re. Neagle* 135 U.S. 1 (1890).
32 *United States v. Curtiss-Wright Export Corp.* 299 U.S. 304, 320 (1936).
33 *Youngstown Sheet and Tube Co. v. Sawyer* 343 U.S. 579 (1952).
34 *Youngstown Sheet and Tube Co. v. Sawyer* 343 U.S. 579, 645 (1952).
35 Funston, *A Vital National Seminar*, p. 64.
36 Funston, *A Vital National Seminiar*, p. 91.
37 See G.S. Wood, *The Creation of the American Republic, 1776-1787*, Chapel Hill: University of North Carolina Press, 1969, pp. 471-564; W.H. Riker, *Democracy in the United States*, 2nd edn, New York: Macmillan, 1965, pp. 121-49.
38 H.S. Truman, 'Speech on presidential power', in Hirschfield (ed.) *The Power of the Presidency*, p. 112.
39 H.S. Truman quoted in L. Fisher, *President and Congress: Power and Policy*, New York: Free Press, 1972, p. 40.
40 *Youngstown Sheet and Tube Co. v. Sawyer* 343 U.S. 579, 610-11. (1952).
41 E.S. Corwin, *The President: Office and Powers*, 2nd edn, New York: New York University Press, 1941, pp. 114-15.
42 Rossiter, *The American Presidency*, p. 228.
43 Schlesinger, *The Imperial Presidency, passim*.
44 Hutchins, 'Presidential autocracy in America', in Tugwell and Cronin (eds) *The Presidency Reappraised*, p. 51.
45 A.S. Miller, 'Separation of powers: an ancient doctrine under modern challenge', *Administrative Law Review*, vol. 28, no. 3 (1976), pp. 304, 313.
46 W.J. Fulbright, 'The decline — and possible fall — of constitutional democracy in America', in Bach and Sulzner (eds) *Perspectives on the Presidency*, pp. 359, 355.
47 Schlesinger, *The Imperial Presidency*, p. ix.
48 Commager, *The Defeat of America*, p. 15.
49 Information for the case study on impoundment was drawn from the following sources: L. Fisher, *Presidential Spending Power*, Princeton: Princeton University Press, 1975, pp. 147-201; Fisher, *President and Congress: Power and Policy*, pp. 106-10, 122-7; Fisher, *Constitutional Conflict between Congress and the President*, Princeton: Princeton University Press, 1985, pp. 236-39; Fisher, 'The politics of

impounded funds', *Administrative Science Quarterly*, vol. 15, no. 3 (1970), pp. 361–77; Fisher, 'Funds impounded by the president: the constitutional issues', *George Washington Law Review*, vol. 38, no. 1 (1969), pp. 124–37; J.P. Pfiffner, *The President, the Budget, and Congress: Impoundment and the 1974 Budget Act*, Boulder: Westview, 1979, pp. 49–76; R.M. Pious, *The American Presidency*, pp. 278–88; Schlesinger, *The Imperial Presidency*, pp. 235–40, 307–400; A. Glass, 'Impoundment policy fuels political struggle with Congress', *National Journal*, 15 April 1971, pp. 1027–39; US Congress, Senate, Committee on the Judiciary, *Impoundment of Appropriated Funds by the President*, joint hearings before the ad hoc subcommittee on impoundment of funds of the Committee on Government Operations and the subcommittee on separation of powers of the Committee on the Judiciary, 93rd Cong., 1st Sess., Washington DC: Government Printing Office, 1973, hereinafter cited as *1973 Senate Hearings*; F. Church, 'Impoundment of appropriated funds: the decline of congressional control over executive discretion', *Stanford Law Review*, vol. 22, no. 6 (1970), pp. 1240–53; 'Impoundment of funds', *Harvard Law Review*, vol. 86, no. 8 (1973), pp. 1505–35; Pyle and Pious, *The President, Congress and the Constitution*, pp. 224–32.

50 Quoted in Pious, *The American Presidency*, p. 279.
51 See Fisher, *Presidential Spending Power*, pp. 148–70; Fisher, 'The politics of impounded funds', *Administrative Science Quarterly*, vol. 15, no. 3 (1970), pp. 361–72; Pfiffner, *The President, the Budget, and Congress*, pp. 31–40; 'Impoundment of funds', *Harvard Law Review*, vol. 86, no. 8 (1973), pp. 1507–12; A.S. Miller, 'Presidential power to impound appropriated funds — an exercise in constitutional decision-making', *North Carolina Law Review*, vol. 43 (1965), pp. 502–47.
52 See P. Woll, *American Bureaucracy*, New York: Norton, 1963, pp. 124–9; Fisher, *Presidential Spending Power*, pp. 163–5; Fisher, 'The politics of impounded funds', pp. 361–9.
53 Fisher, 'Funds impounded by the president: the constitutional issues', p. 137.
54 Fisher, 'The politics of impounded funds', p. 361.
55 Cronin, *The State of the Presidency*, p. 195.
56 Fisher, *Constitutional Conflicts between Congress and the President*, p. 236.
57 The point-by-point criticisms listed above were drawn from Pfiffner, *The President, the Budget, and Congress*, pp. 41–4.
58 P.B. Edelman, 'The battle with Congress: checks and balances', in A. Gartner, C. Greer and F. Riessman (eds) *What Nixon Is Doing to Us,*, New York: Harper & Row, 1973, p. 197.
59 *1973 Senate Hearings*, p. 7.
60 Schlesinger, *The Imperial Presidency*, p. 239.
61 Quoted in Glass, 'Impoundment policy fuels political struggle with Congress', *National Journal*, 15 April 1971, p. 1034.
62 Quoted in 'The president's news conference', 31 January 1973, in

> *Public Papers of Presidents of the United States: Richard Nixon, January 2 to December 31, 1973*, Washington DC: Government Printing Office, 1975, p. 62.
63. *1973 Senate Hearings*, p. 359.
64. *1973 Senate Hearings*, p. 361.
65. *1973 Senate Hearings*, p. 369.
66. R.M. Nixon, *The Memoirs of Richard Nixon*, New York: Grosset & Dunlap, 1978, p. 772.
67. Fisher, *Presidential Spending Power*, p. 201.
68. As L. Fisher notes, 'What the Impoundment Control Act (1974) intended is impossible to say . . . . There is enough ambiguity in the act to allow the executive ample room for interpretation', *Constitutional Conflicts between Congress and the President*, pp. 237–38. See also 'Impoundment Act: a time for testing', *Congressional Quarterly Guide to Current American Government*, Fall 1975, pp. 56–60; 'Impoundment creates new headaches for Congress, *Congressional Quarterly Guide to Current American Government*, Spring 1976, p. 11; 'Congress limits presidential impoundment authority', *National Journal*, 15 June 1974; 'Impoundment: key budget issue', *National Journal*, 18 May 1974; Fisher, *Presidential Spending Power*, p. 198–201; A Schick, 'The battle of the budget', in H.C. Mansfield (ed.) *Congress Against the President*, Montpelier, Vt.: Capitol City Press, 1975, pp. 61–4.
69. See *National Council of Community Health Centers v. Weinberger*, 361 F. Supp 897 (D.D.C. L973); *State Highway Commission of Missouri v. Volpe* 479 F 2d 1099 (8th Cir. 1973); *Train v. City of New York*, 420 U.S. 35 (1975).
70. Even the much vaunted War Powers Resolution (1973), which supposedly epitomized Congress's resurgence as an institution and its intention to stipulate and thereby control the limits of executive discretion, in fact only 'reveals congressional ambivalence with respect to staking down the executive' (p. 117). Robert Scigliano concludes that the 'constitutional issues raised by the War Powers remain. They are not resolved by the resolution or by practice since its enactment' (p. 124), 'The war powers resolution and the war powers', in J.M. Bessette and J. Tulis (eds) *The Presidency in the Constitutional Order*, Baton Rouge: Louisiana State University Press, 1981, pp. 115–53. James L. Sundquist agrees. The most important issue at stake, he writes, was whether Congress was prepared to codify the war power and, therefore, to assert that the president's only discretion was within the stipulated limits laid down by Congress. But, by a device of legal draftsmanship, this 'crucial constitutional issue was evaded' (p. 258), *The Decline and Resurgence of Congress*, Washington DC.: Brookings Institute, 1981, pp. 252–65. See also T.M. Franck and E. Weisband, *Foreign Policy by Congress*, New York: Oxford University Press, 1979, pp. 68–76, 141–54; Fisher, *Constitutional Conflicts between Congress and the President*, pp. 272–80, 307–25; Cronin, *The State of the Presidency*, pp. 196–202; T.F. Eagleton, *War and Presidential*

Power: A Chronicle of Congressional Surrender, New York: Liveright, 1974; Miller, 'Separation of powers: an ancient doctrine under modern challenge', pp. 313–18; F.E. Rourke, 'Executive secrecy: change and continuity', in F.E. Rourke (ed.) *Bureaucratic Power in National Politics*, Boston: Little, Brown & Co., 1978, pp. 355–70; P.B. Kurland, *Watergate and the Constitution*, Chicago: University of Chicago Press, 1978, pp. 47–50; W. Taylor Reveley III, 'The power to make war', in F.O. Wilcox (ed.) *The Constitution and the Conduct of Foreign Policy*, New York: Praeger, 1976, pp. 83–125; C.H. Pyle and R.M. Pious, *The President, Congress and the Constitution: Power and Legitimacy in American Politics*, New York: Free Press, 1984, pp. 341, 361–90; J.C. Daly (ed.) *War Powers and the Constitution*, Washington DC: American Enterprise Institute, 1983; W. Hardy, 'A tug of war: the war powers resolution and the meaning of hostilities', *Pacific Law Journal*, vol. 15 (1984), pp. 306–40; M. Rubner, 'The Reagan administration, the 1973 war powers resolution and the invasion of Grenada', *Political Science Quarterly*, vol. 100, no. 4 (1985–1986), pp. 627–47; D.G. Alder, 'The constitution and presidential warmaking', *Political Science Quarterly*, vol. 103, no. 1 (1988), pp. 1–36; J.A. Nathan and J.K. Oliver, *Foreign Policy Making and the American Political System*, 2nd edn, Boston: Little, Brown & Co., 1987, pp. 168–90.

Chapter 4: Constitutional gaps and the arts of prerogative

1 H. Trevor-Roper, 'Nixon — America's Charles I?', *The Spectator*, 11 August 1973, p. 176.
2 R. Ashton, *The English Civil War: Conservatism and Revolution, 1603–1649*, London: Weidenfeld & Nicolson, 1978, p. 91.
3 'King's speech (17 March, 1628)', in J.P. Kenyon, *The Stuart Constitution: Documents and Commentary*, Cambridge: Cambridge University Press, 1966, p. 81.
4 Quoted in 'Appendix 2. meeting: the President and Dean, Oval Office, February 28, 1973', in G. Gold (ed.) *The White House Transcripts: The Full Text of the Submission of Recorded Presidential Conversations to the Committee on the Judiciary of the House of Representatives by President Richard Nixon*, intro. by R.W. Apple, New York: Bantam, 1974, p. 80.
5 R.M. Nixon, *The Memoirs of Richard Nixon*, New York: Grosset & Dunlap, 1978, p. 770.
6 Nixon, *The Memoirs of Richard Nixon*, p. 771.
7 L. Stone, *The Causes of the English Revolution, 1529–1642*, London: Routledge & Kegan Paul, 1972, p. 92.
8 See W.U. Solberg (ed.) *The Federal Convention and the Formation of the Union*, Indianapolis: Bobbs-Merrill, 1958, pp. xxxiii–xxxv; C. Robbins, *The Eighteenth-Century Commonwealthman: Studies in the Transmission, Development and Circumstance of English Liberal Thought from the Restoration of Charles II until the War with the*

Thirteen Colonies, Cambridge: Harvard University Press, 1959, pp. 22–55, 320–88; W.B. Gwyn, *The Meaning of the Separation of Powers: An Analysis of the Doctrine from its Origin to the Adoption of the United States Constitution*, Tulane: Tulane University Press, 1965, pp. 37–65, 100–30; C.M. Walsh, *The Political Science of John Adams: A Study in the Theory of Mixed Government and the Bicameral System*, New York: Knickerbocker Press, 1915, pp. 227–61.

9 E.S. Corwin, *The President: Office and Powers, 1787–1948*, 3rd edn, New York: New York University Press, 1948, p. 48.
10 G. McConnell, *The Modern Presidency*, New York: St Martin's Press, 1967, pp. 1, 14.
11 A.M. Schlesinger, Jr., *The Imperial Presidency*, London: Andre Deutsch, 1974, p. ix.
12 Schlesinger, 'American political institutions after Watergate: a discussion', in D. Caraley (ed.) *Political Science Quarterly*, vol. 89, no. 4 (1974–5), p. 746.
13 C. Rossiter, *The American Presidency*, rev. edn, New York: New American Library, 1960, p. 103.
14 A. de Grazia, *Republic in Crisis*, New York: Federal Legal, 1965, p. 70.
15 E.J. Hughes, *The Living Presidency: The Resources and Dilemmas of the American Presidential Office*, Baltimore: Penguin, 1973, p. 56.
16 T.H. White, *Breach of Faith: The Fall of Richard Nixon*, London: Jonathan Cape, 1975, p. 232.
17 C. Hill, *The Century of Revolution, 1630–1714*, London: Abacus, 1978, pp. 62–4.
18 R.S. Hirschfield, 'The power of the contemporary president', in A. Wildavsky and N.W. Polsby (eds) *American Governmental Institutions: A Reader in the Policy Process*, Chicago: Rand McNally, 1968, p. 137.
19 *New York Times*, 20 May 1977.
20 See J.R. Hurtgen, 'The case for presidential prerogative', *Toledo Law Review*, vol. 7 (1975), p. 59.
21 Quoted in L. Koenig, *The Chief Executive*, 3rd edn, New York: Harcourt Brace Jovanovich, 1975, p. 18.
22 Corwin, *The President: Offices and Powers, 1787–1948*, p. 16.
23 G.E. Reedy, *The Twilight of the Presidency*, New York: New American Library, 1970, pp. 18–19.
24 J. Locke, *Two Treatises of Government*, intro. P.J. Laslett, Cambridge: Cambridge University Press, 1960, pp. 392–3.
25 Schlesinger, *The Imperial Presidency*, p. 9.
26 J.M. Bessette and J. Tulis, 'The constitution, politics, and the presidency' in J.M. Bessette and J. Tulis (eds) *The Presidency in the Constitutional Order* Baton Rouge: Louisiana State University Press, 1981, p. 25.
27 H.C. Mansfield alludes to the nature of executive power in the following terms: 'the Machiavellian prince was regularized as an office, named the executive, and juxtaposed to the legislative power, in

the ambivalence we recognize: now subordinate, now independent. In the deliberate construction of this ambivalence may be found the modern doctrine of executive power', Mansfield, 'The ambivalence of executive power', in Bessette and Tulis (eds) *The Presidency in the Constitutional Order*, p. 331. Deliberate or not, Richard Pious recognizes that 'constitutional ambiguity is at the heart of the problem of Presidential power', Pious, *The American Presidency*, New York: Basic, 1979, p. 50. See also Hurtgen, 'The case for presidential prerogative', pp. 59–85.

28 See Koenig, *The Chief Executive*, pp. 3–5; Reedy, *The Twilight of the Presidency*, pp. 1–17; Pious, *The American Presidency*, pp. 3–5; W.F. Mullen, *Presidential Power and Politics*, New York: St Martin's Press, 1976, pp. 158–72; C.W. Dunn, 'The president — servant to sun king?', in C.W. Dunn (ed.) *The Future of the American Presidency*, Morristown: General Learning Press, 1975, pp. 1–25; R. Sherrill, *Why They Call It Politics: A Guide to America's Government*, 2nd edn, New York: Harcourt Brace Jovanovich, 1974, pp. 2–18.

29 See L. Heren, *The New American Commonwealth*, London: Weidenfeld & Nicolson, 1968, pp. 3–35; H. Brogan, *The Pelican History of the United States of America*, Harmondsworth: Penguin, 1985, pp. 216–17; H. Fairlie, *The Kennedy Promise: The Politics of Expectations*, New York: Dell, 1974, passim.

30 Brogan, *The Pelican History of the United States of America*, p. 216.

31 D.W. Brogan quoted in Sherrill, *Why They Call It Politics*, p. 9.

32 L. Heren, 'Power to the populists?', *The Times*, 10 June 1972.

33 C.H. McIlwain, *Constitutionalism: Ancient and Modern*, rev. edn. Ithaca: Cornell University Press, 1947, p. 127.

34 'The King's reasons for declining the jurisdiction of the high court justice, 21 January, 1649' in S.R. Gardiner (ed.) *The Constitutional Documents of the Puritan Revolution, 1625–1660*, Oxford: Clarendon, 1906, pp. 374–6.

35 B. Woodward and C. Bernstein, *The Final Days*, New York: Simon & Schuster, 1976, p. 275.

36 T.M. Franck (ed.) *The Tethered Presidency: Congressional Restraints on Executive Power*, New York: New York University Press, 1981; G.R. Ford, 'Imperiled, not imperial', *Time*, 10 November 1980; T.E. Cronin, 'An imperiled presidency?', in V. Davis (ed) *The Post-imperial Presidency*, New Brunswick: Transaction, 1980, pp. 137–51.

37 For example, see Chapter 3, footnote 70.

38 R.G. McCloskey, *The American Supreme Court*, Chicago: University of Chicago Press, 1960, p. 14.

39 McCloskey, *The American Supreme Court*, pp. 12–13.

40 A.M. Bickel, *The Supreme Court and the Idea of Progress*, New York: Harper & Row, 1970, p. 112.

41 McCloskey, *The American Supreme Court*, p. 15.

42 McCloskey, *The American Supreme Court*, p. 5.

43 In 1642, Charles I himself resorted to just such a defence. In his 'Answer to the Nineteen Propositions', Charles formally espoused the

principle of a mixed and balanced government. See C.C. Weston, 'The theory of mixed monarchy under Charles I and after', *The English Historical Review*, no. 296 (1960), pp. 426–43; Weston, *English Constitutional Theory and the House of Lords, 1556–1832*, London: Routledge & Kegan Paul, 1965, pp. 23–43; F.D. Wormuth, *The Origins of Modern Constitutionalism*, New York: Harper & Row, 1949, pp. 50–8.

44 Members of Congress and executive officers preserve their working practices within a context of constitutional ambiguity and evasion — even in the face of an unusually sweeping Supreme Court intervention geared to clarifying the constitutional status of the legislative veto convention *Immigration and Naturalization Service v. Chadha* 462 U.S. 919 (1983). For an illustrative case study, see 'Court bans legislative veto, but Congress finds alternatives', *Congressional Quarterly Guide to Current American Government*, Spring 1986, pp. 80–2; see also L. Fisher, 'Judicial mismanagement about law-making process: the legislative veto case', *Public Administration Review*, vol. 45 (1985), pp. 705–11; 'Legislative vetoes enacted after Chadha', Congressional Research Service, Library of Congress, 1985.

45 *Colegrove v. Green* 328 U.S. 549, 556 (1946).
46 *Coleman v. Miller* 307 U.S. 433, 454–5 (1938).
47 *Colegrove v. Green* 328 U.S. 549, 556 (1946).
48 *Ashwander v. T.V.A.* 297 U.S. 288, 347 (1936).
49 McCloskey, *The American Supreme Court*, p. 20. See also P. Strum, *The Supreme Court and 'Political Questions': A Study in Judicial Evasion*, University: University of Alabama Press, 1974; L.H. Tribe, *The Constitutional Structure of American Government: Separation and Division of Powers*, New York: Foundation Press, 1978, pp. 71–9; A.M. Bickel, 'The Supreme Court, 1960 term — foreword: the passive virtues', *Harvard Law Review*, vol. 75, no. 1 (1961), pp. 40–79; Bickel, *The Least Dangerous Branch: The Supreme Court at the Bar of Politics*, Indianapolis: Bobbs-Merrill, 1962, pp. 23–8, 69–71; L. Henkin, 'Is there a "political question" doctrine', *Yale Law Journal*, vol. 85, no. 5 (1971), pp. 597–625.
50 *Youngstown Sheet and Tube Co. v. Sawyer* 343 U.S. 579, 593, 595 (1952).
51 *Springer v. Government of the Philippine Islands* 277 U.S. 189, 209 (1928).
52 E.S. Corwin, *The President: Office and Powers*, New York: New York University Press, 1940, p. 200.
53 P. Gregg, *King Charles I*, London: J.M. Dent, 1981, p. 448.
54 As Gillian Peele succinctly puts it, 'because conventions and practices, customs and usages are subject to the specific political circumstances which they are meant to govern (rather than vice versa) it is often when they are most needed that they will be most elusive', 'Comparing constitutions', in D. Kavanagh and G. Peele (eds) *Comparative Government and Politics: Essays in Honour of S.E. Finer*, London: Heinemann, 1984, p. 199.

55 I. Jennings, *The Law and the Constitution*, 5th edn, London: University of London, 1967, p. 111.
56 Jennings, *The Law and the Constitution*, p. 113.

Chapter 5: The theory of abeyances and modern constitutional unsettlement in Britain and the US

1 O. Hood Phillips, *Constitutional and Administrative Law*, 6th edn, London: Sweet & Maxwell, 1978, p. 46.
2 Ivor Jennings, *Parliament*, 2nd edn, Cambridge: Cambridge University Press, 1969, p. 520.
3 W.D.B. Mitchell, 'The causes and effects of the absence of a system of public law in the United Kingdom', in W.J. Stankiewicz (ed.) *British Government in an Era of Reform*, London: Collier Macmillan, 1976, p. 27.
4 Mitchell, 'Public law', p. 29.
5 J.P. Mackintosh, *The Government and Politics of Britain*, London: 2nd edn, Hutchinson, 1971, pp. 12, 14.
6 J. Harvey and L. Bather, *The British Constitution and Politics*, 5th edn, London: Macmillan, 1982, p. 15.
7 See Walter Bagehot, *The English Constitution*, London: Fontana 1963; Albert V. Dicey, *Introduction to the Study of the Law of the Constitution*, 10th edn, London: Macmillan, 1960; I. Jennings, *The Law and the Constitution*, 5th edn, London: University of London Press, 1967; L.S. Amery, *Thoughts on the Constitution*, 2nd edn, Oxford: Oxford University Press, 1953; David Lidderdale (ed.) *Erskine May's Treatise on the Law, Privileges, Proceedings and Usage of Parliament*, 19th edn, London: Butterworths, 1976; Hood Phillips, *Constitutional and Administrative Law*.
8 F.F. Ridley, 'There is no British constitution: a dangerous case of the emperor's clothes', *Parliamentary Affairs*, vol. 41, no. 3 (1988), pp. 340–61.
9 Quoted in A.H. Hanson and Malcom Walles, *Governing Britain: A Guidebook to Political Institutions*, London: Fontana/Collins, 1970, p. 19.
10 Jennings, *The Law and the Constitution*, p. 117.
11 See Note 7.
12 Dicey, *Law of the Constitution*, p. 195.
13 John F. McEldowney, 'Dicey in historical perspective — a review essay', in Patrick McAuslan and John F. McEldowney (eds) *Law, Legitimacy and the Constitution*, London: Sweet & Maxwell, 1985, p. 59.
14 Ronald Butt, *The Power of Parliament*, 2nd edn, London: Constable, 1969, p. 2.
15 Jennings, *The Law and the Constitution*, p. 8.
16 David G. Smith, 'British civil liberties and the law', *Political Science Quarterly*, vol. 101, no. 4 (1986), p. 643.
17 Geoffrey Marshall and Graeme C. Moodie, *Some Problems of the*

Constitution, 3rd edn, London: Hutchinson, 1964, p. 15.
18 Dicey, *Law of the Constitution*, p. 39.
19 Ridley, 'There is no British constitution: a dangerous case of the emperor's clothes', pp. 345–50.
20 Graeme C. Moodie, *The Government of Great Britain*, London: Methuen, 1964, p. 106.
21 See Harry Street and Rodney Brazier, *Constitutional and Administrative Law*, 5th edn, Harmondsworth: Penguin, 1985, pp. 123–63; Colin R. Munro, *Studies in Constitutional Law*, London: Butterworths, 1987, pp. 159–84; E.C.S. Wade and A.W. Bradley, *Constitutional and Administrative Law*, 10th edn, London: Longman, 1985, pp. 229–55.
22 *Burmah Oil Co v. Lord Advocate* (1965) AC 75 at 99.
23 L.L. Blake, *Sovereignty: Power beyond Politics*, London: Shepheard-Walwyn, 1988, p. 50.
24 Gillian Peele, 'Comparing constitutions', in Gillian Peele and Dennis Kavanagh (eds) *Comparative Government and Politics: Essays in Honour of S.E. Finer*, London: Heinemann, 1984, pp. 206–7.
25 Smith, 'British civil liberties and the law', p. 644.
26 See Samuel H. Beer, *Modern British Politics: A Study of Parties and Pressure Groups*, 2nd edn, London: Faber & Faber, 1969.
27 J.A.G. Griffith, 'The political constitution', *The Modern Law Review*, vol. 42, no. 1 (1979), p. 6.
28 Amery, *Thoughts on the Constitution*, p. 15.
29 See, for example, David Kogan and Maurice Kogan, *The Battle for the Labour Party*, 2nd edn, London: Kogan Page, 1983, pp. 133–5.
30 Philip Norton, *The Constitution in Flux*, Oxford: Martin Robertson, 1982, p. 1.
31 Peele, 'Comparing constitutions', in Peele and Kavanagh (eds) *Comparative Government and Politics: Essays in Honour of S.E. Finer*, p. 204.
32 M.J.C. Vile, 'The rise and fall of Parliamentary government', in W.J. Stankiewicz (ed.) *British Government in an Era of Reform*, p. 23.
33 Anthony Lester, 'The constitution: decline and renewal', in Jeffrey Jowell and Dawn Oliver (eds) *The Changing Constitution*, Oxford: Clarendon, 1985, p. 274.
34 Hanson and Walles, *Governing Britain*, p. 19.
35 Hugh Berrington, 'British government: the paradox of strength', in Peele and Kavanagh (eds) *Comparative Government: Essays in Honour of S.E. Finer*, pp. 21–2.
36 Berrington, 'British government', p. 22.
37 Gabriele Ganz, *Understanding Public Law*, London: Fontana, 1987, p. 9.
38 Ganz, *Public Law*, p. 9.
39 Bernard Crick, 'Pandora's box, sovereignty and the referendum', *Political Quarterly*, vol. 46, no. 2 (1975), p. 123.
40 Nevil Johnson, *In Search of the Constitution: Reflections on State and Society in Britain*, Oxford: Pergamon 1977, pp. 1, 135.

41 See Norton, *Constitution in Flux*; Geoffrey Smith and Nelson W. Polsby, *British Government and Its Discontents*, New York: Basic, 1981; W.B. Gwyn and Richard Rose (eds) *Britain: Progress and Decline*, London: Macmillan, 1980; William L. Miller, *The End of British Politics?*, Oxford: Oxford University Press, 1981; Vernon Bogdanor, *Devolution*, Oxford: Oxford University Press, 1979; Tam Dalyell, *Devolution: The End of Britain*, London: Jonathan Cape, 1977; Anthony H. Birch, *Political Integration and Disintegration in the British Isles*, London: George Allen & Unwin, 1977; Samuel H. Beer, *Britain Against Itself: The Political Contradictions of Collectivism*, London: Faber & Faber, 1982; David Butler and Uwe Kitzinger, *The 1975 Referendum*, London: Macmillan, 1976; Andrew Gamble, *Britain in Decline*, London: Macmillan, 1981.

42 See H.M. Drucker, *Multi-party Britain*, London: Macmillan, 1979; Bogdanor, *Multi-party Politics and the Constitution*, Cambridge: Cambridge University Press, 1983; S.E. Finer (ed.) *Adversary Politics and Electoral Reform*, Anthony Wigram, 1975; S.E. Finer, *The Changing British Party System, 1945-1979*, Washington DC: American Enterprise Institute, 1980; Ian Bradley, *Breaking the Mould?: The Birth and Prospects of the Social Democratic Party*, Oxford: Martin Robertson, 1981; Bo Sarlvik and Ivor Crewe, *Decade of Dealignment: The Conservative Victory of 1979 and Electoral Trends in the 1970s*, Cambridge: Cambridge University Press, 1983.

43 David Marquand, 'Britain as a corporate state', *Guardian Weekly*, 18 April 1976.

44 Anthony King, 'Foreword' and 'The problem of overload', in Anthony King (ed.) *Why is Britain Becoming Harder to Govern?*, London: British Broadcasting Corporation, 1976, pp. 6, 26.

45 See Samuel Brittan, 'The economic contradictions of democracy', *The British Journal of Political Science*, vol. 6, no. 2 (1975), pp. 129-60; King, 'The problem of overload', in King (ed.) *Why is Britain Becoming Harder to Govern?*, pp. 8-30; Wayne Parsons, 'Politics without promises: the crisis of "overload" and governability', *Parliamentary Affairs*, vol. 35, no. 4 (1982), pp. 421-35.

46 Mackintosh, *Government . . . of Britain*, p. 29.

47 Mackintosh, *Government . . . of Britain*, p. 30.

48 David Marquand, 'What's wrong with Britain', *London Review of Books*, 6 March 1980.

49 King, 'Foreword', in King (ed.) *Why is Britain Becoming Harder to Govern?*, p. 6.

50 David Butler, 'Politics: the vanishing certainties', *Sunday Times*, 17 April 1977.

51 John Dearlove and Peter Saunders, *Introduction to British Politics: Analysing a Capitalist Democracy*, London: Polity, 1984, p. 81.

52 Lord Hailsham, 'Elective dictatorship', *The Listener*, October 21 1976.

53 Hailsham, 'Elective dictatorship'.

54 Leslie Scarman, *English Law — The New Dimension*, London: Stevens, 1974, p. 19.

55 Scarman, *The New Dimension*, p. 20. See also Michael Zander, *A Bill of Rights?*, London: Barry Rose, 1975; Peter Wallington and Jeremy McBride, *Civil Liberties and a Bill of Rights*, London: Cobden Trust, 1976; Frank Stacey, *A New Bill of Rights for Britain*, London: David & Charles, 1973; O. Hood Phillips, *Reform of the Constitution*, London: Chatto & Windus, 1970, pp. 144-62; C.M. Campbell (ed.) *Do We Need a Bill of Rights?*, London: Temple Smith, 1980.
56 Lord Denning, 'Coke's law', *The Listener*, November 27 1980.
57 Alistair Buchan, 'The cure cannot begin until the sickness is identified', *The Times*, January 2 1976.
58 Dearlove and Saunders, *Introduction to British Politics*, p. 81.
59 Patrick McAuslan and John E. McEldowney, 'Legitimacy and the constitution: the dissonance between theory and practice', in McAuslan and McEldowney (eds) *Law, Legitimacy and the Constitution*, pp. 7, 13. See also Dawn Oliver, 'Politicians and the courts', *Parliamentary Affairs*, vol. 41, no. 1 (1988), pp. 13-33; Graham Zellick, 'Government beyond the law', *Public Law* (Summer 1985), pp. 283-308; Clive Ponting, *The Right to Know: The Inside Story of the Belgrano Affair*, London: Sphere, 1985.
60 'Time to break the spell', *The Times*, 15 August 1988.
61 Alan Watkins, 'When Margaret's eyes glaze over', *The Observer*, 31 May 1981.
62 McAuslan and McEldowney, 'Legitimacy and the constitution', in McAuslan and McEldowney (eds) *Law, Legitimacy and the Constitution*, p. 32.
63 James Cornford, 'The constitutional dimension', *Public Administration*, vol. 64, no. 3 (1986), p. 278.
64 Ian Harden and Norman Lewis, *The Noble Lie: The British Constitution and the Rule of Law*, London: Hutchinson, 1986, p. 11.
65 Tam Dayell, *Misrule*, London: New English Library, 1988, p. 192.
66 Dalyell, *Misrule*, p. 36.
67 Dalyell, *Misrule*, p. 195.
68 J.A.G. Griffith, *The Politics of the Judiciary*, London: Fontana/Collins, 1977, pp. 24-31, 187-216.
69 Watkins, 'When Margaret's eyes glaze over', *The Observer*, 31 May 1981.
70 Oliver, 'Politicians and the courts', p. 22.
71 Oliver, 'Politicians and the courts', p. 32.
72 Tony Manwaring and Nick Singler (eds) *Breaking the Nation: A Guide to Thatcher's Britain*, London: Pluto Press/New Socialist, 1985, pp. 160, 170-1.
73 See H.F. Rawlings, 'Judicial review and the "control of government"', *Public Administration*, vol. 64, Summer (1986), pp. 135-45; Sir Michael Kerry, 'Administrative law and judicial review — the practical effects of developments over the last 25 years on administration in central government', *Public Administration*, vol. 64 (Summer 1986), pp. 163-72; David Feldman, 'Judicial review: a way of controlling government', *Public Administration*, vol. 66 (Spring 1988), pp. 21-34.

74 See James Michael, *The Politics of Secrecy*, Harmondsworth: Penguin, 1982, pp. 9-78; Christopher Andrew, 'Whitehall's dangerous obsession with the cult of secrecy', *The Observer*, 24 July 1977; Andrew, 'The last taboo in British politics', *The Listener*, 12 August 1982; Adam Raphael, 'Whitehall clings to our secrets', *The Observer*, 23 July 1978; Raphael, 'Whitehall — where nanny knows best', *The Observer*, 18 June 1978; David Hooper, *Official Secrets: The Use and Abuse of the Act*, London: Secker & Warburg, 1987; David Leigh, *The Frontiers of Secrecy: Closed Government in Britain*, London: Junction, 1980.
75 'Quis Custodiet', *The Times*, 23 July 1984.
76 Harold Wilson, *The Governance of Britain*, London: Sphere, 1977, p. 205.
77 Edward Shils quoted in James Cornford, 'The right to know secrets', *The Listener*, 31 August 1978.
78 'Whitehall unbuttons', *The Economist*, 2 July 1988.
79 See Simon Lee, 'GCHQ: prerogative and public law principles', *Public Law* (Summer 1985), pp. 186-93; Gavin Drewry, 'The GCHQ case — a failure of government communications', *Parliamentary Affairs*, vol. 38, no. 4 (1985), pp. 371-86.
80 *Council for Civil Service Unions v. Minister for the Civil Service* (1984) 3 All E.R. 935.
81 Graham Paterson, 'Conservatives could pay dear for their own town hall contempt', *Sunday Telegraph*, 8 May 1988.
82 Analysis and figures drawn from *The Times*, 24 May 1988, and from the BBC Newsnight programme broadcast on 23 May 1988.
83 Marquand, 'What's wrong with Britain'.
84 Mackintosh, *Government . . . of Britain*, p. 94.
85 Vernon Bogdanor, 'The Social Democrats and the constitution', *Political Quarterly*, vol. 52, no. 3 (1981), p. 293.
86 Keith Middlemas, *Politics in Industrial Society*, London: Andre Deutsch, 1979.
87 S.E. Finer, 'Ending Britain's "archaic lottery" ', *The Observer*, 12 October 1975.
88 Peter Hain, *Political Strikes: The State and Trade Unionism in Britain*, Harmondsworth: Penguin, 1986, p. 202.
89 Lord Crowther-Hunt, 'We could have months and perhaps years of constitutional fireworks', *The Listener*, 4 December 1980.
90 Harden and Lewis, *The Noble Lie*, p. 9.
91 Moodie, *The Government of Great Britain*, p. 16.
92 M. Kammen, *A Machine that Would Go of Itself*, New York: Alfred A. Knopf, 1986, p. 70.
93 Louis Hartz, *The Liberal Tradition in America*, New York: Harcourt Brace Jovanovich, 1955, p. 9.
94 Alexis de Tocqueville, *Democracy in America*, Oxford: Oxford University Press, 1946, p. 207.
95 Quoted in William C. Havard, *The Government and Politics of the United States*, London: Hutchinson, 1965, p. 44.

96 Philip Allott, 'Making sense of the law: lawyers and legal philosophy', *The Cambridge Review*, vol. 108, no. 2297 (1987), p. 66.
97 Robert A. Dahl, 'Decision-making in a democracy: the Supreme Court as a national policy-maker', *Journal of Public Law*, vol. 6 (1957), pp. 279-95.
98 See Laurence H. Tribe, *The Constitutional Structure of American Government: Separation and Division of Powers*, New York: Foundation Press, 1978, pp. 52-80; C. Herman Pritchett, *Constitutional Law of the Federal System*, Englewood Cliffs: Prentice-Hall, 1984, pp. 156-68.
99 *Ashwander v. TVA* 297 U.S. 288, 347, 348 (1936).
100 See Chapter 5, note 40.
101 *Marbury v. Madison* 1 Cranch 137, 173 (1803).
102 Jesse H. Choper, *Judicial Review and the National Political Process*, Chicago: University of Chicago Press, 1980, p. 139.
103 Choper, *Judicial Review*, p. 162.
104 Alexander M. Bickel, *The Supreme Court and the Idea of Progress*, New York: Harper & Row, 1970, p. 112.
105 Henry J. Abraham, *The Judiciary: The Supreme Court in the Governmental Process*, Boston: Allyn & Bacon, 1965, p. 116.
106 See Leonard W. Levy (ed.) *The Supreme Court under Earl Warren*, New York: Quadrangle, 1972; Philip B. Kurland, *Politics, the Constitution and the Warren Court*, Chicago: University of Chicago Press, 1970.
107 See Bickel, *The Idea of Progress*.
108 M.J.C. Vile, *Politics in the USA*, 3rd edn, London: Hutchinson, 1983, p. 241.
109 See Stephen L. Wasby, *Continuity and Change: From the Warren Court to the Burger Court*, Santa Monica: Goodyear, 1976; Richard Y. Funston, *Constitutional Counter-revolution? The Warren Court and the Burger Court* New York: John Wiley, 1977; Richard Hodder-Williams, 'Is there a Burger court?', *The British Journal of Political Science*, vol. 9, no. 2 (1979), pp. 173-200.
110 *Roe v. Wade* 410 U.S. 113.
111 See Herbert Weschler, 'Toward neutral principles of constitutional law', *Harvard Law Review*, vol. 73, no. 1 (1959), pp. 1-35; Robert H. Bork, 'Neutral principles and some first amendment problems', *Indiana Law Journal*, vol. 47, no. 2 (1971); William H. Rehnquist, 'The notion of a living constitution', *Texas Law Review*, vol. 54 (1976), pp. 693-707; Walter Berns, 'Government by lawyers and judges', *Commentary*, June 1987, pp. 17-24.
112 See Abram Chayes, 'The role of the judge in public law litigation', *Harvard Law Review*, vol. 89, no. 7 (1976), pp. 1281-1316; Arthur S. Miller, *Toward Increased Judicial Activism: The Political Role of the Supreme Court*, Westport: Greenwood, 1982; Richard Neely, *How the Courts Govern America*, New Haven: Yale University Press, 1981; Choper, *Judicial Review and the National Political Process*. For a discussion of both sides of the debate, see Stephen C. Halpern and

Charles M. Lamb (eds) *Supreme Court Activism and Restraint*, Lexington: Lexington, 1982.
113 Bickel, *The Supreme Court and the Idea of Progress*, p. 94. See also Kurland, *Politics, the Constitution and the Warren Court*; Kurland, 'Toward a political Supreme Court', *University of Chicago Law Review*, vol. 37, no. 1 (1969), pp. 19–46.
114 Miller, *Toward Increased Judicial Activism*, p. 9.
115 Ronald Dworkin, *Law's Empire*, Cambridge: Harvard University Press, 1986.
116 Christopher Wolfe, *The Rise of Modern Judicial Review: From Constitutional Interpretation to Judge-made Law*, New York: Basic, 1986, p. 205.
117 Berns, 'Government by lawyers and judges', p. 18.
118 Berns, 'Government by lawyers and judges', p. 19.
119 Quoted in 'Constitutional debate renewed', *Congressional Quarterly Guide to Current American Government* (Fall 1986), p. 74.
120 See 'The attorney general's view of the Supreme Court: toward a jurisprudence of original intent', *Public Administration Review*, vol. 45 (November 1985), pp. 701–4; Thomas C. Grey, 'Do we have an unwritten constitution?', in Malcom M. Feely and Samuel Krislov, *Constitutional Law*, Boston: Little, Brown & Co., 1985, pp. 42–6; Bork, *Tradition and Morality in Constitutional Law*, Washington DC: American Enterprise Institute, 1985; Wolfe, *The Rise of Modern Judicial Review*; Bork and Tribe, 'Interpreting the constitution', *Dialogue*, no. 75 (January 1987), pp. 29–32; 'The battle for the constitution', *Policy Review*, vol. 35, (Winter 1986), pp. 32–5; David Fellman, 'Original intent — a footnote', *The Review of Politics*, vol. 49, no. 4 (1987), pp. 574–9; H. Jefferson Powell, 'The original understanding of original intent', *Harvard Law Review*, vol. 98, no. 5 (1985), pp. 885–948; Jefferson-Powell, 'The modern misunderstanding of original intent', *The University of Chicago Law Review*, vol. 54, no. 4 (1987), pp. 1513–44.
121 Dworkin, 'The Bork nomination', *New York Review of Books*, 13 August 1987, p. 3.
122 See *Congressional Quarterly Guide to Current American Government* (Spring 1988), pp. 104–113; 'Advice and dissent', *Time*, 21 September 1987; 'A Bork without a bite', *Time*, 28 September 1987; 'Gone with the wind', *Time*, 12 October 1987; David P. Bryden, 'How to select a Supreme Court justice: the case of Robert Bork', *The American Scholar* (Spring 1988), pp. 201–17; Simon Lee, 'Bicentennial Bork, tercentennial spycatcher: do the British need a bill of rights', *University of Pittsburgh Law Review*, vol. 49, no. 1 (1988), pp. 795–804.
123 Henry J. Abraham, *Justices and Presidents: A Political History of Appointments to the Supreme Court*, Oxford: Oxford University Press, 1974.
124 Quoted in 'Gone with the wind', *Time*, 12 October 1987.
125 Tribe, *The Constitutional Structure of American Government*, p. 13.

126 Walter F. Murphy, James E. Fleming and William F. Harris II, *American Constitutional Interpretation*, New York: Mineola, 1986, p. 55.
127 Norton, *The Constitution in Flux*, p. 1.
128 Cornford, 'The constitutional dimension', p. 278.
129 Quoted in Ponting, *The Right to Know*, p. 190.
130 Richard Norton-Taylor, 'Judge who alienated jury', *Guardian Weekly*, 24 February 1985.

Bibliography

Abraham, H.J. (1965) *The Judiciary: The Supreme Court in the Governmental Process*, Boston: Allyn & Bacon.
—— (1974) *Justices and Presidents: A Political History of Appointments to the Supreme Court*, Oxford: Oxford University Press.
Abshire, D.M. and Nurnberger, R.N. (1981) *The Growing Power of Congress*, Beverly Hills: Sage.
Adair, D. (1957) ' "That politics may be reduced to a science": David Hume, James Madison and the Tenth Federalist', *The Huntingdon Library Quarterly*, vol. 20, no. 4, pp. 343–60.
Adams, E.M. (ed.) (1977) *The Idea of America: A Reassessment of the American Experience*, Cambridge, Mass.: Ballinger.
Aiken, W.A. and Henning, B.D. (eds) (1960) *Conflict in Stuart England*, London; Jonathan Cape.
Alder, D.G. (1988) 'The constitution and presidential war-making', *Political Science Quarterly*, vol. 103, no. 1, pp. 1–36.
Allott, P. (1987) 'Making sense of the law: lawyers and legal philosophy', *The Cambridge Review*, vol. 108, no. 2297, pp. 65–9.
Amery, L.S. (1953) *Thoughts on the Constitution*, 2nd edn, Oxford: Oxford University Press.
Aron, R. (1968) *Main Currents in Sociological Thought: 1*, trans. R. Howard and H. Weaver, Harmondsworth: Penguin.
Ashley, M. (1961) *England in the Seventeenth Century*, Harmondsworth: Penguin.
Ashton, R. (1978) *The English Civil War: Conservatism and Revolution, 1603–1649*, London: Weidenfeld & Nicolson.
Aylmer, G.E. (1975) *The Struggle for the Constitution: England in the Seventeenth Century*, 4th edn, London: Blandford.
Bach, S. and Sulzner, G.T. (eds) (1974) *Perspectives on the Presidency: A Collection*, Lexington: D.C. Heath.
Bagehot, W. (1963) *The English Constitution*, London: Fontana.
Barber, J.D. (ed.) (1974) *Choosing the President*, Englewood Cliffs: Prentice-Hall.
Beer, S.H. (1969) *Modern British Politics: A Study of Parties and Pressure Groups*, 2nd edn, London: Faber & Faber.
—— (1982) *Britain Against Itself: The Political Contradictions of*

Collectivism, London: Faber & Faber.
Beitzinger, A.J. (1972) *A History of American Political Thought*, New York: Dodd, Mead & Co.
Berns, W. (1987) 'Government by lawyers and judges', *Commentary*, June, pp. 17–24.
Bessette, J.M. and Tulis, J. (eds) (1981) *The Presidency in the Constitutional Order*, Baton Rouge: Louisiana State University Press.
Bickel, A.M. (1961) 'The Supreme Court, 1960 term — forward: the passive virtues', *Harvard Law Review*, vol. 75, no. 1, pp. 40–79.
—— (1962) *The Least Dangerous Branch: The Supreme Court at the Bar of Politics*, Indianapolis: Bobbs-Merrill.
—— (1970) *The Supreme Court and the Idea of Progress*, New York: Harper & Row.
Birch, A.H. (1967) *The British System of Government*, London: George Allen & Unwin.
—— (1977) *Political Integration and Disintegration in the British Isles*, London: George Allen & Unwin.
Black, C. (1963) *Perspectives in Constitutional Law*, Englewood Cliffs: Prentice-Hall.
Blake, L.L. (1988) *Sovereignty: Power beyond Politics*, London: Shepheard-Walwyn.
Blondel, J. (1969) *An Introduction to Comparative Government*, London: Weidenfeld & Nicolson.
Bogdanor, V. (1979) *Devolution*, Oxford: Oxford University Press.
—— (1981) 'The Social Democrats and the constitution', *Political Quarterly*, vol. 52, no. 3, pp. 285–94.
—— (1983) *Multi-party Politics and the Constitution*, Cambridge: Cambridge University Press.
Boorstin, D.J. (1953) *The Genius of American Politics*, Chicago: University of Chicago Press.
Bork, R.H. (1971) 'Neutral principles and some first amendment problems', *Indiana Law Journal*, vol. 47, no. 2.
—— (1985) *Tradition and Morality in Constitutional Law*, Washington DC: American Enterprise Institute.
—— and Tribe, L.H. (1987) 'Interpreting the constitution', *Dialogue*, no. 75.
Bradley, I. (1981) *Breaking the Mould?: The Birth and Prospects of the Social Democratic Party*, Oxford: Martin Robertson.
Brittan, S. (1975) 'The economic contradictions of democracy, *The British Journal of Political Science*, vol. 6, no. 2.
Brogan, H. (1985) *The Pelican History of the United States*, Harmondsworth: Penguin.
Bromhead, P. (1974) *Britain's Developing Constitution*, London: George Allen & Unwin.
Bryden, D.P. (1988) 'How to select a Supreme Court justice: the case of Robert Bork', *The American Scholar*, Spring, pp. 201–17.
Burns, J.M. (1963) *The Deadlock of Democracy: Four Party Politics in America*, London: John Calder.

—— (1973) *Presidential Government: The Crucible of Leadership*, Boston: Houghton Mifflin.
Butler, D. and Kitzinger, U. (1976) *The 1975 Referendum*, London: Macmillan.
Butt, R. (1969) *The Power of Parliament*, 2nd edn, London: Constable.
Campbell, C.M. (ed.) (1980) *Do We Need a Bill of Rights?*, London: Temple Smith.
Chester, L., McCrystal, C., Aris, S. and Shawcross, W. (1973) *Watergate: The Full Inside Story*, New York: Ballantine.
Choper, J.H. (1980) *Judicial Review and the National Political Process*, Chicago: University of Chicago Press.
Chrimes, S.B. (1967) *English Constitution History*, 4th edn, London: Oxford University Press.
Chayes, A. (1976) 'The role of the judge in public law litigation', *Harvard Law Review*, vol. 89, no. 7, pp. 1281-316.
Church, F. (1970) 'Impoundment of appropriated funds: the decline of Congressional control over executive discretion, *Stanford Law Review*, vol. 22, no. 6, pp. 1240-53.
Commager, H.S. (1970) *The American Mind: An Interpretation of American Thought and Character since the 1880s*, New York: Bantam.
—— (1974) *The Defeat of America: Presidential Power and the National Character*, New York: Simon & Schuster.
—— (1978) *The Empire of Reason: How Europe Imagined and America Realized the Enlightenment*, London: Weidenfeld & Nicolson.
Cornford, J. (1986) 'The constitutional dimension', *Public Administration*, vol. 64, no. 3, pp. 277-84.
Corwin, E.S. (1928) ' "The higher law" background of American constitutional law, part 1', *Harvard Law Review*, vol. 42, no. 2, pp. 149-85.
—— (1929) ' "The higher law" background of American constitutional law, part 2', *Harvard Law Review*, vol. 42, no. 3, pp. 365-409.
—— (1940) *The President: Office and Powers*, New York: New York University Press.
—— (1941) *The President: Office and Power*, 2nd edn, New York: New York University Press.
—— (1948) *The President: Office and Powers*, 3rd edn, New York: New York University Press.
Crabb, C.V. and Holt, P.M. (1980) *Invitation to Struggle: Congress, the President and Foreign Policy*, Washington DC: Congressional Quarterly Press.
Crick, B. (1975) 'Pandora's box, sovereignty and the referendum, *Political Quarterly*, vol. 46, no. 2, pp. 123-6.
Cronin, T.E. (1980) *The State of the Presidency*, 2nd edn, Boston: Little, Brown & Co.
Curtis, M. (1968) *Comparative Government and Politics: An Introductory Essay in Political Science*, New York: Harper & Row.
Dahl, R.A. (1957) 'Decision-making in a democracy: the Supreme Court as a national policy-maker', *Journal of Public Law*, vol. 6, pp. 279-95.

Daly, J.C. (ed.) (1983) *War Powers and the Constitution*, Washington DC: American Enterprise Institute.
Dalyell, T. (1977) *Devolution: The End of Britain*, London: Jonathan Cape.
—— (1988) *Misrule*, London: New English Library.
Davis, V. (ed.) (1980) *The Post-Imperial Presidency*, New Brunswick: Transaction.
Dean, J. (1976) *Blind Ambition: The White House Years*, London: Star Books.
Dearlove, J. and Saunders, P. (1984) *Introduction to British Politics: Analysing a Capitalist Democracy*, London: Polity.
De Grazia, A. (1965) *Republic in Crisis*, New York: Federal Legal.
De Tocqueville, A. (1946) *Democracy in America*, Oxford: Oxford University Press.
Dicey, A.V. (1960) *Introduction to the Study of the Law of the Constitution*, 10th edn, New York: Macmillan.
Drewry, G. (1985) 'The GCHQ case — a failure of government communications', *Parliamentary Affairs*, vol. 38, no. 4, pp. 371–86.
Drucker, H.M. (1979) *Multiparty Britain*, New York: Macmillan.
Dunn, C.W. (ed.) (1975) *The Future of the American Presidency*, Morristown: General Learning Press.
Dworkin, R. (1986) *Law's Empire*, Cambridge: Harvard University Press.
Eagleton, T.F. (1974) *War and Presidential Power: A Chronicle of Congress Surrender*, New York: Liveright.
Eckstein, H. and Apter D.E. (eds) (1963) *Comparative Politics: A Reader*, New York: Free Press.
Ely, J.H. (1978) 'Constitutional interpretivism: its allure and impossibility', *Indiana Law Journal*, vol. 53, pp. 399–448.
Fairlie, H. (1974) *The Kennedy Promise: The Politics of Expectation*, New York: Dell.
Feely, M.M. and Krislov, S. (1985) *Constitutional Law*, Boston: Little, Brown & Co.
Feldman, D. (1988) 'Judicial review: a way of controlling government', *Public Administration*, vol. 66, Spring, pp. 21–34.
Fellman, D. (1987) 'Original intent — a footnote', *The Review of Politics*, vol. 49, no. 14, pp. 574–9.
Finer, H. (1949) *Theory and Practice of Modern Government*, rev. edn, London: Methuen.
—— (1960) *The Presidency: Crisis and Regeneration*, Chicago: University of Chicago Press.
Finer, S.E. (1974) *Comparative government*, Harmondsworth: Penguin.
—— (ed.) (1975) *Adversary Politics and Electoral Reform*, Anthony Wigram.
—— (1980) *The Changing British Party System, 1945–1979*, Washington DC: American Enterprise Institute.
Fisher, L. (1969) 'Funds impounded by the President: The constitutional issues', *George Washington Law Review*, vol. 38, no. 1, pp. 124–37.
—— (1970) 'The politics of impounded funds', *Administrative Science Quarterly*, vol. 15, no. 3, pp. 361–77.

—— (1972) *President and Congress: Power and Policy*, New York: Free Press.
—— (1975) *Presidential Spending Power*, Princeton: Princeton University Press.
—— (1985) *Constitutional Conflicts between Congress and the President*, Princeton: Princeton University Press.
—— (1985) 'Judicial mismanagement about law-making process: the legislative veto case', *Public Administration Review*, vol. 45, pp. 705–11.
Fletcher, A. (1981) *The Outbreak of the Civil War*, London: Edward Arnold.
Franck, T.M. (ed.) (1981) *The Tethered Presidency: Congressional Restraints on Executive Power*, New York: New York University Press.
Franck, T.M. and Weisband, E. (1979) *Foreign Policy by Congress*, Oxford: Oxford University Press.
Funston, R.Y. (1977) *Constitutional Counter-Revolution? The Warren Court and the Burger Court*, New York: John Wiley.
—— (1978) *A Vital National Seminar : The Supreme Court in American Political Life*, Palo Alto: Mayfield.
Ganz, G. (1987) *Understanding Public Law*, London: Fontana.
Gamble, A. (1981) *Britain in Decline*, London: Macmillan.
Gardiner, S.G. (1906) *The Constitutional Documents of the Puritan Revolution, 1625–1660*, 3rd edn, Oxford: Clarendon.
Gartner, A., Greer, C. and Riessman, F. (eds) (1973) *What Nixon is Doing to Us*, New York: Harper & Row.
Gay, P. (1970) The Enlightenment, an Interpretation, Vol. II: The Science of Freedom, London: Weidenfeld & Nicolson.
Gilmour, I. (1978) *Inside Right: Conservatism, Policies and the People*, London: Quartet Books.
Glass, A. (1970) 'Impoundment policy fuels political struggle with Congress', *National Journal*, 15 April, pp. 1027–39.
Gold, G. (ed.) (1974) *The White House Transcripts: The Full Text of the Submission of Recorded Presidential Conversations to the Committee on the Judiciary of the House of Representatives by President Richard Nixon*, New York: Bantam.
Greenstein, F.I. and Polsby, N.W. (eds) (1975) *Handbook of Political Science, Volume 5: Governmental Institutions and Processes*, Reading: Addison-Wesley.
Gregg, P. (1981) *King Charles I*, London: J.M. Dent.
Griffith, J.A.G. (1977) *The Politics of the Judiciary*, London: Fontana/Collins.
—— (1979) 'The political constitution', *The Modern Law Review*, vol. 42, no. 1, pp. 1–21.
Gwyn, W.B. (1965) *The Meaning of the Separation of Powers: An Analysis of the Doctrine from its Origins to the Adoption of the United States Constitution*, Tulane: Tulane University Press.
—— and Rose, R. (eds) (1980) *Britain: Progress and Decline*, London: Macmillan.

Hain, P. (1986) *Political Strikes: The State and Trade Unionism in Britain*, Harmondsworth: Penguin.

Halpern, P.J. (ed.) (1975) *Why Watergate?*, Pacific Palisades: Palisade.

Halpern, S.C. and Lamb, C.M. (eds) (1982) *Supreme Court Activism and Restraint*, Lexington: Lexington.

Hanson, A.H. and Walles, M. (1970) *Governing Britain: A guidebook to Political Institutions*, London: Fontana.

Harden, I. and Lewis, N. (1986) *The Noble Lie: The British Constitution and the Rule of Law*, London: Hutchinson.

Hardy, W. (1984) 'A tug of war: the war powers resolution and the meaning of hostilities', *Pacific Law Journal*, vol. 15, pp. 306–40.

Hargrove, E.C. (1974) *The Power of the Modern Presidency*, New York: Alfred A. Knopf.

Hartz, L. (1955) *The Liberal Tradition in America: An Interpretation of American Political Thought*, New York: Harcourt Brace Jovanovich.

Harvey, J. and Bather, L. (1964) *The British Constitution*, London: Macmillan.

—— (1982) *The British Constitution and Politics*, 5th edn, London: Macmillan.

Harvard, W.C. (1965) *The Government and Politics of the United States*, London: Hutchinson.

Henkin, L. (1971) 'Is there a "political question" doctrine? *Yale Law Journal*, vol. 85, no. 5, pp. 597–625.

—— (1972) *Foreign Affairs and the Constitution*, Mineola: Foundation Press.

Heren, L. (1968) *The New American Commonwealth*, London: Weidenfeld & Nicolson.

Hill, C. (1965) *Intellectual Origins of the English Revolution*, Oxford: Clarendon.

—— (1968) *Puritanism and Revolution: Studies in Interpretation of the English Revolution of the 17th Century*, London: Panther.

—— (1978) *The Century of Revolution, 1603–1714*, London: Abacus.

Hinton, R.W.K. (1957) 'The decline of Parliamentary government under Elizabeth I and the early Stuarts', *Cambridge Historical Review*, vol. 37, pp. 116–32.

—— (1960) 'English constitutional theories from Sir John Fortescue to Sir John Eliot', *English Historical Review*, no. 296, pp. 410–25.

Hirschfield, R.S. (ed.) (1968) *The Power of the Presidency: Concepts and Controversy*, New York: Alfred A. Knopf.

Hodder-Williams, R. (1979) 'Is there a Burger court?' *The British Journal of Political Science*, vol. 9, no. 2, pp. 173–200.

Hofstadter, R. (1967) *The American Political Tradition*, London: Jonathan Cape.

Hood Phillips, O. (1970) *Reform of the Constitution*, London: Chatto & Windus.

—— and Jackson, P. (1978) *Constitutional and Administrative Law*, 6th edn, London: Sweet & Maxwell.

Hooper, D. (1987) *Official Secrets: The Use and Abuse of the Act*,

London: Secker and Warburg.
Horowitz, I. (ed.) (1977) *Ideology and Utopia in the United States*, Oxford: Oxford University Press.
Hughes, E.J. (1973) *The Living Presidency: The Resources and Dilemmas of the American Presidential Office*, Baltimore: Penguin.
Hurtgen, J.R. (1975) 'The case for Presidential prerogative', *Toledo Law Review*, vol. 7, pp. 59–85.
—— (1973) 'Impoundment of funds', *Harvard Law Review*, vol. 86, no. 8, pp. 1505–35.
James, D.B. (1969) *The Contemporary Presidency*, New York: Pegasus.
Jefferson-Powell, H. 'The original understanding of original intent', *Harvard Law Review*, vol. 98, no. 5, pp. 885–945.
—— (1987) 'The modern misunderstanding of original intent', *University of Chicago Law Review*, vol. 54, no. 4, pp. 1513–44.
Jennings, I. (1967) *The Law and the Constitution*, 5th edn, London: University of London Press.
—— (1969) *Parliament*, 2nd edn, Cambridge: Cambridge University Press.
Johnson, N. (1977) *In Search of the Constitution: Reflections on State and Society in Britain*, London: Pergamon.
Jones, W.J. (1971) *Politics and the Bench: The Judges and the Origins of the English Civil War*, London: George Allen & Unwin.
Jowell, J. and Oliver, D. (eds) (1985) *The Changing Constitution*, Oxford: Clarendon.
Judson, M.A. (1949) *The Crisis of the Constitution: An Essay in Constitutional and Political Thought in England, 1603–1645*, New Brunswick: Rutgers University Press.
Kammen, M.(1986) *A Machine That Would Go of Itself*, New York: Alfred A. Knopf.
Kavanagh, D. and Peele, G.(1984) *Comparative Government and Politics: Essays in Honour of S.E. Finer*, London: Heinemann.
Keir, D.L. (1964) *The Constitutional History of Modern Britain Since 1485*, London: Adam & Charles Black.
Kenyon, J.P. (1966) *The Stuart Constitution: Documents and Commentary*, Cambridge: Cambridge University Press.
Kerry, M. (1986) 'Administrative law and judicial review — the practical effect of development over the last 25 years on administration in central government', *Public Administration*, vol. 64, Summer, pp. 163–72.
King, A. (ed.) (1976) *Why is Britain Becoming Harder to Govern?*, London: British Broadcasting Corporation.
Koenig, L. (1975) *The Chief Executive*, 3rd edn, New York: Harcourt Brace Jovanovich.
Kogan, D. and Kogan, M. (1983) *The Battle for the Labour Party*, 2nd edn, London: Kogan page.
Kohn, H. (1957) *American Nationalism: An Interpretive Essay*, New York: Macmillan.
Kurland, P.B. (1969) 'Toward a political Supreme Court', *University of Chicago Law Review*, vol. 37, no. 1, pp. 19–46.
—— (1970) *Politics, the Constitution and the Warren Court*, Chicago:

University of Chicago Press.
—— (1978) *Watergate and the Constitution*, Chicago: University of Chicago Press.
Landau, M. (ed.) (1979) *Political Theory and Political Science: Studies in the Methodology of Political Inquiry*, Hassocks: Harvester.
Lee, S. (1985) 'GCHQ: Prerogative and public law principles', *Public Law*, Summer, pp. 186-93.
—— (1988) 'Bicentennial Bork, tercentennial spycatcher: do the British need a "bill of rights"', *University of Pittsburgh Law Review*, vol. 49, no. 1, pp. 777-822.
Lehman, J. (1976) *The Executive, Congress and Foreign Policy: Studies of the Nixon Administration*, New York: Praeger.
Levy, L.W. (ed.) (1972) *The Supreme Court under Earl Warren*, New York: Quadrangle.
Lidderdale, D. (ed.) (1976) *Erskine May's Treatise on the Law, Privileges, Proceedings and Usage of Parliament*, 19th edn, London: Butterworth.
Lippmann, W. (1962) *A Preface to Politics*, Ann Arbor: University of Michigan Press.
Locke, J. (1960) *Two Treatises of Government*, intro. P.J. Laslett, Cambridge: Cambridge University Press.
Loss, R. (ed.) (1976) *Presidential Power and the Constitution: Essays by Edward S. Corwin*, Ithaca: Cornell University Press.
Lovell, C.R. (1962) *English Constitutional and Legal History: A Survey*, Oxford: Oxford University Press.
Lowi, T.J. (1985) 'Presidential power: restoring the balance', *Political Science Quarterly*, vol. 100, no. 2, pp. 185-213.
Lucas, A.J. (1976) *Nightmare: The Underside of the Nixon Years, 1969-1974*, New York: Viking.
McAuslan, P. and McEldowney, J.F. (eds) (1985) *Law, Legitimacy and the Constitution*, London: Sweet & Maxwell.
McCloskey, R.G. (1960) *The American Supreme Court*, Chicago: University of Chicago Press.
McConnell, G. (1967) *The Modern Presidency*, New York: St Martin's Press.
McIlwain, C.H. (1947) *Constitutionalism: Ancient and Modern*, rev. edn, Ithaca: Cornell University Press.
Mackintosh, J.P. (1971) *The Government and Politics of Britain*, 2nd edn, London: Hutchinson.
Maitland, F.W. (1931) *The Constitutional History of England*, Cambridge: Cambridge University Press.
Manley, J.F. (ed.) (1976) *American Government and Public Policy*, New York: Macmillan.
Manning, B. (1956) 'The nobles, the people and the constitution', *Past and Present*, vol. 9, pp. 42-64.
—— (1976) *The English People and the English Revolution, 1640-1649*, London: Heinemann.
—— (1984) 'What was the English revolution?', *History Today*, March, pp. 18-21.
Mansfield, H.C. (ed.) (1975) *Congress against the President*, Montpelier,

Vermont: Capital City Press.
Manwaring, T. and Singler, N. (eds) (1985) *Breaking the Nation: A Guide to Thatcher's Britain*, London: Pluto Press/New Socialist.
Marshall, G. (1985) 'What are constitutional conventions?', *Parliamentary Affairs*, vol. 38, no. 1, pp. 33-9.
—— and Moodie, G.C. (1964) *Some Problems of the Constitution*, 3rd edn, London: Hutchinson.
Michael, J. (1982) *The Politics of Secrecy*, Harmondsworth: Penguin.
Middlemas, K. (1979) *Politics in Industrial Society*, London: Andre Deutsch.
Miller, A.S. (1965) 'Presidential power to impound appropriated funds — an exercise in constitutional decision-making', *North Carolina Law Review*, vol. 43, pp. 502-47.
—— (1976) 'Separation of powers: an ancient doctrine under modern challenge, *Administrative Law Review*, vol. 28, no. 3, pp. 299-325.
—— (1982) *Toward Increased Judicial Activism: The Political Role of the Supreme Court*, Westport: Greenwood.
Miller, W.L. (1981) *The End of British Politics?* Oxford: Oxford University Press.
Montesquieu, Baron de (1940) *The Spirit of the Laws*, trans. T. Nugent, New York: Hafner.
Moodie G.C. (1964) *The Government of Great Britain*, London: Methuen.
Morgan, K.O. (ed.) (1985) *The Sphere Illustrated History of Britain, 1485-1789*, London: Sphere.
Morrill, J. (1984) 'What was the English revolution?', *History Today*, March, pp. 11-16.
Mosier, R.D. (1952) *The American Temper: Patterns of Our Intellectual Heritage*, Berkeley: University of California Press.
Mullen, W.F. (1976) *Presidential Power and Politics*, New York: St Martin's Press.
Munro, C.R. (1987) *Studies in Constitutional Law*, London: Butterworths.
Munro, W.B. (1930) *Makers of the Unwritten Constitution*, New York: Macmillan.
Murphy, W.F., Fleming, J.E. and Harris II, W.F. (1986) *American Constitutional Interpretation*, New York: Mineola.
Nathan, J. (1975) 'The roots of the imperial presidency: public opinion, domestic institutions and global interests', *Presidential Studies Quarterly*, vol. 5, pp. 63-74.
Nathan, J. and Oliver, J.K. (1987) *Foreign Policymaking and the American Political System*, 2nd edn, Boston: Little, Brown & Co.
Neely, R. (1981) *How the Courts Govern America*, New Haven: Yale University Press.
Neustadt, R.E. (1960) *Presidential Power: The Politics of Leadership*, New York: John Wiley.
Nixon, R.M. (1978) *The Memoirs of Richard Nixon*, New York: Grosset & Dunlap.
Norton, P. (1982) *The Constitution in Flux*, Oxford: Martin Robertson.
Oliver, D. (1988) 'Politicians and the courts', *Parliamentary Affairs*, vol. 41, no. 1, pp. 13-33.

Parsons, W. (1982) 'Politics without promises: the crisis of "overload" and governability', *Parliamentary Affairs*, vol. 35, no. 4, pp. 421-35.
Pfiffner, J.P. (1979) *The President, the Budget and Congress: Impoundment and the 1974 Budget Act*, Boulder: Westview.
Pious, R.M. (1979) *The American Presidency*, New York: Basic.
Pocock, J.G.A. (1967) *The Ancient Constitution and the Feudal Law: A Study of English Historical Thought in the Seventeenth Century*, New York: Norton.
—— (ed.) (1980) *Three British Revolutions, 1641, 1688, 1776*, Princeton: Princeton University Press.
Ponting, C. (1985) *The Right to Know: The Inside Story of the Belgrano Affair*, London: Sphere.
Price, D.K. (1985) *America's Unwritten Constitution: Science, Religion and Political Responsibility*, Cambridge: Harvard University Press.
Pritchett, C.H. (1984) *Constitutional Law of the Federal System*, Englewood Cliffs: Prentice-Hall.
—— (1975) *Public Papers of Presidents of the United States: Richard Nixon, January 2 to December 31, 1973*, Washington DC: Government Printing Office.
Punnett, R.M. (1976) *British Government and Politics*, 3rd edn, London: Heinemann.
Pyle, C.H. and Pious, R.M. (1984) *The President, Congress and the Constitution: Power and Legitimacy in American Politics*, New York: Free Press.
Pynn, R.E. (ed.) (1975) *Watergate and the American Political Process*, New York: Praeger.
Ranney, A. (1976) ' "The divine science": political engineering in American culture', *The American Political Science Review*, vol. 70, no. 1, pp. 140-8.
Rather, D. and Grates, G.P. (1974) *The Palace Guard*, New York: Harper & Row.
Rawlings, H.F. (1986) 'Judicial review and the "control of government" ', *Public Administration*, vol. 64, Summer, pp. 135-45.
Read, C. (ed.) (1938) *The Constitution Reconsidered*, New York: Columbia University Press.
Reagan, M.D. (1972) *The New Federalism*, Oxford: Oxford University Press.
Reedy, G.E. (1971) *The Twilight of the Presidency*, New Yale: New American Library.
Rehnquist, W.H. (1976) 'The notion of a living constitution', *Texas Law Review*, vol. 54, pp. 693-707.
Ridley, F.F. (1988) 'There is no British constitution: a dangerous case of the emperor's clothes', *Parliamentary Affairs*, vol. 41, no. 3, pp. 340-61.
Riker, W.H. (1965) *Democracy in the United States*, 2nd edn, New York: Macmillan.
Robbins, C. (1959) *The Eighteenth Century Commonwealthman: Studies in the Transmission, Development and Circumstance of English Liberal*

Thought from the Restoration of Charles II until the War with the Thirteen Colonies, Cambridge: Harvard University Press.

Rose, R. (1974) *Politics in England Today: An Interpretation*, London: Faber & Faber.

Rossiter, C. (1951) *The Supreme Court and the Commander in Chief*, Ithaca: Cornell University Press.

—— (1960) *The American Presidency*, rev. edn, New York: Mentor.

Rourke, F.E. (ed.) (1978) *Bureaucratic Power in National Politics*, Boston: Little, Brown & Co.

Rubner, M. (1985–86) 'The Reagan administration, the 1973 war powers resolution and the invasion of Grenada, *Political Science Quarterly*, vol. 103, no. 4, pp. 627–47.

Russell, C. (1976) 'Parliamentary history in perspective, 1604–1629', *History*, vol. 61, pp. 12–27.

Russell, C. (ed.) (1973) *The Origins of the English Civil War*, London: Macmillan.

Sabine, G.H. and Thorson, T.L. (1973) *A History of Political Theory*, 4th edn, Hinsdale: Dryden.

Sarlvik, B. and Crewe, I. (1983) *Decade of Dealignment: The Conservative Victory of 1979 and Electoral Trends in the 1970s*, Cambridge: Cambridge University Press.

Scarman, L. (1974) *English Law — The New Dimension*, London: Stevens.

Schlesinger, Jr., A.M. (1969) *The Crisis of Confidence: Ideas, Power and Violence in America*, London: Andre Deutsch.

—— (1974) *The Imperial Presidency*, London: Andre Deutsch.

Sharp, A. (1983) *Political Ideas of the English Civil Wars, 1641–1649*, London: Longman.

Shaw, M. (1968) *Anglo-American Democracy*, London: Routledge & Kegan Paul.

Sherrill, R. (1974) *Why They Call It Politics: A Guide to America's Government*, 2nd edn, New York: Harcourt Brace Jovanovich.

Sigel, R.S. (1966) 'Image of the American presidency — part II of an exploration into popular views of presidential power', *Midwest Journal of Political Science*, vol. 10, no. 1, pp. 127–37.

Sils, D.L. (ed.) (1968) *The International Encyclopaedia of Social Science, Volume 3*, New York: Crowell, Collier & Macmillan.

Smith, A.G.R. (ed.) (1973) *The Reign of James VI and I*, London: Macmillan.

Smith, D.G. (1986) 'British civil liberties and the law', *Political Science Quarterly*, vol. 101, no. 4, pp. 637–60.

Smith, G. and Polsby, N.W. (1981) *British Government and its Discontents*, New York: Basic.

Solberg, W.U. (ed.) (1958) *The Federal Convention and the Formation of the Union*, Indianapolis: Bobbs-Merrill.

Sommerville, J.P. (1986) *Politics and Ideology in England, 1603–1640*, London: Longman.

Spanier, J. and Nogee, J.L. (eds) (1981) *Congress, the Presidency and American Foreign Policy*, London: Pergamon.

—— and Ulsaner, E.M. (1982) *Foreign Policy and the Democratic Dilemmas*, 3rd edn, New York: Holt, Rinehart & Winston.
Stacey, F. (1973) *A New Bill of Rights for Britain*, London: David & Charles.
Stankiewicz, W.J. (ed.) (1976) *British Government in an Era of Reform*, London: Collier-Macmillan.
Stone, L. (1972) *The Causes of the English Revolution, 1529–1642*, London: Routledge & Kegan Paul.
Street, H. and Brazier, R. (eds) (1985) *Constitutional and Administrative Law*, 5th edn, Harmondsworth: Penguin.
Strum, P. (1974) *The Supreme Court and 'Political Questions': A Study in Judicial Evasion*, University of Alabama Press.
Sundquist, J.L. (1968) *Politics and Power: The Eisenhower, Kennedy and Johnson Years*, Washington DC: Brookings Institute.
—— (1981) *The Decline and Resurgence of Congress*, Washington DC: Brookings Institute.
Taswell-Langmead, T.P. (1946) *English Constitutional History: From the Teutonic Conquest to the Present Time*, 10th edn, rev. and enlarged by T.F.T. Plucknett, London: Sweet & Maxwell.
—— (1985) 'The attorney general's view of the Supreme Court: toward a jurisprudence of original intent', *Public Administration Review*, vol. 45, November, pp. 701–4.
—— (1986) 'The battle for the constitution', *Policy Review*, vol. 35, Winter, pp. 32–5.
Tomlinson, H. (eds) (1983) *Before the English Civil War: Essays on Early Stuart Politics and Government*, London: Macmillan.
Tribe, L.H. (1978) *The Constitutional Structure of American Government: Separation and Division of Powers*, New York: Foundation.
Tugwell, R.G. (1960) *The Enlargement of the Presidency*, New York: Doubleday.
—— and Cronin, T.E. (1974) *The Presidency Reappraised*, New York: Praeger.
Tulsky, K.R. (1985) 'Judicial review of presidential initiatives', *University of Pittsburgh Law Review*, vol. 46, no. 2, pp. 425–31.
Underdown, D. (1984) 'What was the English revolution?', *History Today*, March, pp. 22–5.
US Senate (1973) Committee on the Judiciary, *Impoundment of Appropriated Funds by the President*, joint hearings before the ad hoc subcommittee on impoundment of funds of the Committee on Government Operations and the subcommittee on separation of powers of the Committee on the Judiciary, 93rd Congress, 1st Session, DC: Government Printing Office.,
Vile, M.J.C. (1967) *Constitutionalism and the Separation of Powers*, Oxford: Clarendon.
—— (1983) *Politics in the USA*, 3rd edn, London: Hutchinson.
Wade, E.C.S. and Phillips, C.G. (1977) *Constitutional and Administrative Law*, 9th edn, London: Longman.
—— and Bradley, A.W. (1985) *Constitutional and Administrative Law*,

Bibliography

10th edn, London: Longman.

Wallington, P. and McBride, J. (1976) *Civil Liberties and a Bill of Rights*, London: Cobden Trust.

Walsh, C.M. (1915) *The Political Science of John Adams: A Study in the Theory of Mixed Government and the Bicameral System*, New York: Knickerbocker Press.

Wasby, S.L. (1976) *Continuity and Change: From the Warren Court to the Burger Court*, Santa Monica: Goodyear.

Wedgwood, C.V. (1983) *The King's Peace, 1637–1641*, Harmondsworth, Penguin.

Weschler, H. (1959) 'Toward neutral principles of constitutional law', *Harvard Law Review*, vol. 73, no. 1, pp. 1–35.

Weston, C.C. (1960) 'The theory of mixed monarchy under Charles I and after', *The English Historical Review*, no. 296, pp. 426–43.

—— (1965) *English Constitutional Theory and the House of Lords, 1556–1832*, London: Routledge & Kegan Paul.

Wheare, K.C. (1966) *Modern Constitutions*, 2nd edn, London: Oxford University Press.

White, T.H. (1975) *Breach of Faith: The Fall of Richard Nixon*, London: Jonathan Cape.

Wilcox, F.O. (ed.) (1976) *The Constitution and the Conduct of Foreign Policy*, New York: Praeger.

Wildavsky, A. and Polsby, N.W. (eds) (1968) *American Governmental Institution: A Reader in the Policy Process*, Chicago: Rand McNally.

Wilson, H. (1972) *The Governance of Britain*, London: Sphere.

Wilson, W. (1908) *Constitutional Government in the United States*, New York: Columbia University Press.

Wolfe, C. (1986) *The Rise of Modern Judicial Review from Constitutional Interpretation to Judge-made Law*, New York: Basic.

Wolf-Phillips, L. (ed.) (1968) *Constitutions of Modern States: Selected Texts*, London: Pall Mall.

Woll, P. (1963) *American Bureaucracy*, New York: Norton.

Wood, G.S. (1969) *The Creation of the American Republic, 1776–1787*, Chapel Hill: University of North Carolina.

Woodward, B. and Bernstein, C. (1976) *The Final Years*, New York: Simon & Schuster.

Wormuth, F.D. (1939) *The Royal Prerogative, 1603–1649*, Ithaca: Cornell University Press.

—— (1949) *The Origins of Modern Constitutionalism*, New York: Harper & Row.

Wright, B.F. (1931) *American Interpretations of Natural Law: A Study in the History of Political Thought*, Cambridge: Harvard University Press.

Zander, M. (1975) *A Bill of Rights?*, London: Barry Rose.

Zellick, G. (1985) 'Government beyond the law', *Public Law*, Summer, pp. 283–308.

Index

abeyances: definitions ix–xi, 9–11, 81–2,, 98, 128–30; and the American Constitution x, 40, 48–9, 56, 58, 63, 66, 68–9, 73–6, 78–80, 126–8; and the British Constitution 80–1, 92, 97–9, 109, 112–15, 119–20, 126–8; and crises x–xi, 10–11, 30–1, 33–4, 39–41, 48–9, 56–7, 59–60, 62–3, 67–9, 72–3, 99–103, 114–15; and the Stuart Constitution x, 16, 20–2, 29–31, 34, 61–2, 73–4, 79–82, 130; and the Supreme Court 75, 77–9, 117–20, 125
Act of Settlement (1701) 15, 86
Act of Union (1707) 15, 86
Allott, P. 116
Anti-Deficiency Act (1950) 50
Ashley, M. 23
Ashton, R, 59
Ashwander v. TVA 117
Aylmer, G.E. 17, 27

Bacon, Francis 19
Balfour, A. 89, 114
Berns, W. 123
Bessette, J.M. 70
Bickel, A. 75
Bill of Rights (1689) 15, 86
Birch, A. 4
Boorstin, D. 37
Bork, R. Judge 121, 124–5
Brandeis, L. 122
Brennan, W. Justice 123

British judiciary 90, 94, 107–9, 127
Brogan, H. 71
Bromhead, P. 4
Buckingham, Duke of 25
Buchan, A. 104
Budget and Accounting Act (1974) 57
Burns, J.M. 37, 43
Butler, D. 103
Butt, R. 91

Cardozo, B. 122
Charles I, 15, 18–20, 24–30, 33, 59–60, 62–3, 68, 72, 80
checks and balances 36–7, 39, 44–5, 65, 73
Chelwood, Lord 110–11
Coke, E. 19
Colegrove v. Green 77
Coleman v. Miller 77
Coleridge, S.T. 8
Commager, H.S. 38, 48
Common Law 18–9, 39, 86, 90–2
Commons, House of 98, 106, 110, 112
Community charge 110
Corwin, E.S. 47, 64, 69, 79–80
crises of the 1970s 99–100, 103–4, 111–2, 114
Cronin T.E. 42, 52
Crowther-Hunt, Lord 113

Dalyell, T. 106
De Grazia, A. 65
Denning, Lord 104

Index

De Tocqueville, A. 4, 115, 125
Devlin, Lord 104
Dicey, A.V. 6, 90-1, 93
divine right 23-4, 39
Dworkin, R. 122, 124

Economic Stabilisation Act (1971) 53
Edelman, P.B. 53
Ehrlichman, J. 68
Eliot, Sir J. 30
Elizabeth I 32, 59, 61-2
Ellsberg, D. 68
Elton, G.R. 28
Ely, J.H. 39
Employment Act (1946) 33
Enlightenment, the 36
Ervin, S. 54
European Economic Community membership 101, 111

Federal Impoundment and Information Act (1972) 54
federalism 74
Finer, H. 6-7
Finer, S.E. 5
Fisher, L. 51-2, 56
Flannery, M. 112
Founding Fathers 36-38, 69-71, 79, 123
Fourteenth Amendment 121, 123
Frankfurter, F. Justice 47, 78
Franklin, B. 36
Friedrich, C. 7
Fulbright, W.J. 48
Funston, R. 46

Gardiner, S.R. 26
Glorious Revolution, the 15, 21, 80, 93-4, 114
Government Communications Headquarters (GCHQ) 105, 110
Grant, U.S. 50
Gregg, P. 80
Griffith, J.A.G. 107

Hailsham, Lord 103-4, 107-8
Hamilton, A. 36
Hanson, A.H. 98
Hartz, L. 39

Harvey, J. and Bather, L. 88
Hawkins, M. 22
Heath, Edward 100
Heren, L. 71
Hill, C. 28-9, 66
Holmes, O.W. 122
Hood Phillips, O. 86
Hoover, H. 50
Hughes, C.E. 116
Hughes, E.J. 65
Hulme, H. 26, 28
Hutchins, F.G. 48

'imperial presidency' x, 40-1, 48, 60, 70,73
impoundment: Congress's response to, 54-5, 57; Nixon's use of 52-4, 55-6; origins 49-52
impositions 25, 27, 135n 26
intelligence services 109

Jackson, R. Justice 46
James I 15, 18, 20, 24, 32-3, 61-2
Jay, J. 69
Jefferson, Thomas 50-1, 55
Jennings, I, 4, 6, 80, 86, 90, 92
Johnson, Lyndon B. 50-1, 54, 60
Johnston, J.B. 125
Jones, W.J. 19, 27, 29
Judicial review 75, 77-8, 115-21, 126
Judiciary Committee, House of Representatives 72
Judson, M. 16, 17, 20, 28, 31, 33

Kennedy, John Fitzgerald 50-51
Kenyon, J. 17, 21, 24, 31
King, A. 101, 103
Koestler, A. 82
Kohn, H. 37

Labour government (1974-79) 100-1, 102
Lester, A. 98
Lincoln, Abraham 67
Lippmann, W. 36
Locke, John 69-70
Lords, House of 26, 93, 110-11, 113

171

Index

Lowi, T.J. 42

McAuslan, P. 105
McCloskey, R.G. 75, 77
McConnell, G. 64
McCowan, Justice 127
McEldowney, J.F. 91, 105
McIlwain, C. 30-1, 72
Mackintosh, J.P. 88, 103
Madison, J. 36
Manning, B. 32
Marquand, D. 103
Marshall, G. 93
Mates, M. 110
mechanistic view of the United States Constitution 38-9, 79
Meese, E. 123
Middlemas, K. 111
Miller, A.S. 48, 122
miners' strike (1984-5) 108, 112
Mitchell, W.D.B. 86-7
modern crown prerogative 86, 95, 110
modern presidency, the 41-3, 64
Montesquieu, Baron de 8
Moodie, G.C. 4, 93-4, 113
Mullen, W.F. 42

Neustadt, R.E. 42
Nixon, Richard Milhouse 40-1, 48-9, 51-9, 60, 66-8, 72
Norton, P. 96

Oakeshott, M. xi
Office of Management and Budget 52
Official Secrets Act (1911) 105, 109
Oliver, D. 108

Parliamentary Acts (1911 and 1949) 86
Parliamentary rights 17-8, 26-9, 30-1, 33, 39
Parliamentary sovereignty 90-4
Peele, G. 95-97
Pentagon Papers, the 68
Petition of Right (1628) 25-6, 28-30, 33, 63
Phillips, K. 37

Pious, R.M. 50
Police and Criminal Evidence Act (1984) 105
'political questions' 44, 77-8, 117-8
Ponting, C. 127
Powell, L. 124
presidential mystique 64-5, 69
presidential prerogative 44-7, 55, 58, 64-8, 70-1
Prize Cases, the 44
Punnett, R.M. 4
Pym, J. 29

Ranney, A. 36
Reagan, Ronald 121, 124
Reedy, G. 69
Representation of the People Acts 86
Restoration Settlement, the 80
Revenue and Expenditure Control Act (1968) 51
Roe v. Wade 121
Roosevelt, F.D. 50, 60
Rose, R. 4
Rossiter, C. 47, 64

Sabine, G.H. and Thorson, T.L. 31
Scarman, Lord 104
Schlesinger, Jr. A.M. 40, 48, 64, 70
separation of powers 36, 76
Separation of Powers Sub-committee, Senate Judiciary Committee 54-55
Shaw, M. 4
Shils, E. 109
Smith, D. 93, 95
Sneed, J.T. 55
Sommerville, J.P. 31
Springer v. Government of the Phillipine Islands 79
Stone, L. 30, 33, 61
Stuart judiciary, the 18-9
Stuart Parliament, 17-8, 25, 72
Stuart royal prerogative 23-4, 26, 28, 30-2, 39
Supreme Court, the 44-6, 72, 74, 77-8, 115, 117-20

172

Thatcher, M. 104–6, 109–10, 111
tonnage and poundage 25–7, 30
Trevor-Roper, H. 59
Tribe, L.H. 126
Truman, H.S. 46–7, 50
Tulis, J. 70

U.S. v. Curtiss-Wright Export Corporation 45
U.S. v. Nixon 72

Vile, M.J.C. 36
Vinson, C. 51

Walles, M. 98
Watergate 40–1

Watkins, A. 107
Wentworth, T. 34
Wheare K.C. 4, 6–7
White, T. 65
Whitelocke, J. 17–8
Wilson, H. 109
Wolfe, C. 123
Wolf-Phillips, L. 6
Woodward, B. 72
Wormuth, F. 22
'written–unwritten' distinction in constitutions ix, 3–9, 11, 35–6, 81–2

Youngstown Sheet and Tube Company v. Sawyer 46, 78